CHANDIGARH
IN SEARCH OF AN IDENTITY

Ravi Kalia

SOUTHERN ILLINOIS UNIVERSITY PRESS
Carbondale and Edwardsville

Copyright © 1987 by the Board of Trustees
Southern Illinois University
All rights reserved
Printed in the United States of America
Designed by Loretta Vincent
Production supervised by Natalia Nadraga
90 89 88 87   4 3 2 1

Library of Congress Cataloging-in-Publication Data

Kalia, Ravi.
Chandigarh : in search of an identity.
Bibliography: p.
Includes index.
1. City planning—India—Chandīgarh. 2. Urban policy—India. 3. Chandīgarh (India)—Social conditions. I. Title.
HT169.57.I42C485 1987   307.1'2'0954552 86-13947
ISBN 0-8093-1310-3

The paper used in this publication meets the minimum requirements of American National Standard for Information Sciences—Permanence of Paper for Printed Library Materials, ANSI Z39.48–1984.

To Barkat Ram Kalia and Sheela Kalia,
my parents and oldest teachers

CONTENTS

Illustrations vii

Preface ix

1. Genesis 1

2. Architects 21

3. The Mayer Plan 45

4. The Le Corbusier Plan 70

5. A Planned City 121

6. Conclusions 144

Notes 159

Bibliography 177

Index 191

ILLUSTRATIONS

pages 91–102

PLANS

Mayer plan
Le Corbusier plan
Chandigarh Urban Complex
Inter State Chandigarh Region

PHOTOGRAPHS

High Court Building
Secretariat
Assembly
City Center
Jan Marg (People's Avenue)
Chowk, or piazza, at the heart of the City Center
Madhya Marg (Middle Avenue)
Bicycle track, or V-8 road, in Sector 11
Gandhi Bhavan (House)
Sukhna Lake
Low-cost housing in Sector 27
Low-cost housing in Sector 7
Chandigarh Railway Station
Railway colony for employees
Unauthorized *rehri* (hawker) market colony
Unauthorized *jhuggi* (squatter) colony

PREFACE

The development of Chandigarh represents a fascinating study of practical politics, personal ambitions of politicians and planners, and the high ideals of Prime Minister Jawaharlal Nehru and the planner Le Corbusier. The new capital city of Punjab also represents India's pride and best urban hopes for the future. Chandigarh was to serve as a training school for Indian planners, who could then duplicate their experience in other cities to improve communication systems, raise economic standards, and permit light and air to penetrate tightly knit unauthorized neighborhoods. It was to rehabilitate refugees and the displaced Punjab government, to restore the dignity of the Indian Punjabi damaged by partition and the loss of Lahore. It was also hoped that Chandigarh would bring law and order to a state torn by communal frenzy, promote economic activities in the region, and improve the lot of those who had suffered losses during the partition of the subcontinent. But above everything else it was to serve as a symbol of India's break with the past.

The speed with which the decision was made to build Chandigarh and with which technical help was acquired from the West demonstrates the failure of the newly independent state to meet its technological needs and its continued dependence on Western know-how for modernization. India, which inherited from the British a large and sophisticated bureaucracy but no technical tradition, was forced to look to the West for the construction of the city. The American Albert Mayer provided the initial master plan for Chandigarh, which was finally put in place, with modifications, by the Swiss-born French architect Charles-Edouard Jeanneret, popularly known as Le Corbusier, his cousin Pierre Jeanneret, and the English husband-and-wife team of Edwin Maxwell Fry and Jane Beverly Drew.

Equally important has been the role of communal relations in the development of Chandigarh. In postpartition Punjab, the two dominant communities were Hindus and Sikhs. The tragic loss by Sikhs and Hindus of their homes and land in Pakistan accentuated and strained relations between the two communities. The Sikhs, accustomed to a privileged position under British rule, failed to adjust fully to their changed political status under a dominant Hindu culture. Punjab was affected also by the process of absorption of the princely states of British India, which brought many problems, including the integration of administrative and legal systems into a common and secular national structure. The subsequent division of Punjab in 1966 along linguistic lines accentuated already existing differences between the Hindus and Sikhs—differences that have come to bear strongly on the fate of Chandigarh.

The story of Chandigarh is not one of success or failure or even of comparative satisfaction with the quality of life in a new city. It is, rather, a chronicle of a period during which India made a bold attempt to make a break with her past within the confines of a sociourban experiment that included, along with an innovative master plan, exaggerated capitol buildings, new land use patterns, provisions for education, recreation, medical and social services, the careful and deliberate inclusion of ideas that had their origin in a culture far removed from her own. Between the ideas of the planners and hopes of the government officials there lies a narrative of a planned city and the people who inhabit it.

The development of Chandigarh has wider implications for communal relations, the fiscal and social wisdom of building new cities, the urban-political tradition, architectural developments, and the conflict between traditional and colonial influences far beyond a new city environment. Chandigarh has shown that new designs and construction do not by themselves make the dream of planning and building a modern urban environment come true. Instead, Chandigarh demonstrates that it is not the personal narrative of a deified ruler nor an exaggerated account of a mythic planner, but rather the individual and collective account of its citizens, striving for self-determination, self-knowledge, and self-actualization. That these elements must be embodied in the city is what makes the story of Chandigarh interesting and one worth telling. After all, a new town cannot be any better (or worse) than the people who live in it, the planners who design it, or those who manage it.

Of course, this story could not have been written without the help of many people. I am most grateful to Mrs. Manmohini Sahgal and Mr. Inder Gujral for their help in securing the literature on Chandigarh. My special thanks are due the late *Shrimati* Indira Gandhi for letting me consult the files on the early development of Chandigarh. Mr. H. Y. Sharada Prasad, the information adviser to the prime minister, was most accommodating in letting me consult the Jawaharlal Nehru files on Chandigarh in his office; and Mr. Wajahat Habibullah, the director of communications, Prime Minister's Office, generously assisted me in photocopying the material. Dr. Rakesh Mohan, the senior consultant in the Planning Commission, Government of India, and his fine staff were most cooperative in opening the full resources of their library.

I thank the staff of the National Archives in New Delhi for their generous assistance in my research. To Mr. S. S. Shafi, the chief planner at the Town and Country Planning Organization, New Delhi, my sincere thanks for sharing many valuable insights on Indian planning and for letting me read the "Report on the Inter State Chandigarh Region" (1982). To M. S. Randhawa, the former chief commissioner of Chandigarh, I am indebted for historic insights into the development of Chandigarh and for sharing his personal papers at the Chandigarh Museum. To Sardar Surjeet Singh, the chief architect, Union Territory Administration, and to Jeet Malhotra, the chief architect, Punjab, I give my thanks for their many courtesies and assistance in collecting the data on Chandigarh.

I am also indebted to several individuals, who either had worked with Le Corbusier or have been connected with Chandigarh, for granting me interviews on very short notice. These include, in India, Professor S. S. Bhati, Mrs. U. E. Chowdhury, J. K. Chowdhury, R. N. Dogra, Professor Victor D'Souza, Professor P. C. Khanna, M. N. Sharma, S. D. Sharma, P. L. Varma, and B. B. Vohra; and in England, Maxwell Fry, Jane Drew, and Professor Otto Koenigsberger. I incurred an additional debt to Max and Jane, who were gracious hosts on my visit to England in 1982 on a research scholarship from the Chancellor's Office, University of California, Los Angeles, and later for reading the early chapters of the manuscript. I deeply regret, however, that I was unable to take advantage of the personal recollections of P. N. Thapar, who served as the first officer on special duty for Chandigarh. We have since permanently lost this valuable resource on Chandigarh.

My gratitude and appreciation is extended to Charlotte Spence of the University Research Library, University of California, Los Angeles, for assistance in procuring books on short notice. My special thanks are due the staffs of the Fondation Le Corbusier, Paris, and the Southern Asia Reference Center, University of Chicago, for promptly furnishing material on Le Corbusier and Albert Mayer, respectively. I thank Manmohan Dayal, Shyam Kala, and Madhu Sarin for letting me read their unpublished reports on Chandigarh.

Warmest thanks are extended to my mentor, Professor Stanley Wolpert, for his skillful guidance throughout my research and for his many acts of kindness that sustained me in many a moment of doubt that a doctoral candidate must typically experience. I thank Professors Eric Monkkonen, Timothy Vreeland, D. R. SarDesai, Richard Sisson, Frank Mittelbach, and Richard Spiese for many valuable suggestions. A special word of mention must be made of my late friend Professor George Crane, who on many occasions patiently listened to my ideas late into the night, even though his own interest in English literature was far removed from my involvement with cities.

I am grateful to Vice President for Academic Affairs David J. Danelski for allowing me to use freely the resources at Occidental College, and to my colleagues in the history department for their encouragement during the final shaping of the book. To Luisa Reyes and Grace Allen, who typed the manuscript, heartfelt thanks.

I thank Robert S. Phillips for having become so excited about the idea of this book, and Stephen W. Smith for his help in bringing it to press.

I thank Mr. Justice Jagjit Singh and his gracious wife for providing me with home and comfort in Chandigarh during my visits in 1982 and 1983. Warmest thanks are extended to Yashwani Varma, Shakti Patel, Virender Varma, Bhupinder Kalia, Jitender Tuli, and Prem Kumar, for attending to my many needs in Delhi and Chandigarh during my visits in 1982, 1983, and 1984. I am truly indebted to my father, Barkat, for introducing me to Chandigarh as a young boy, and to my mother, Sheela, for instilling in me faith and forbearance. I can never thank my wife, Annette, enough for coming to my rescue on many occasions, and especially when I was reading the Le Corbusier papers in Paris, but I hope by now that she knows how much I appreciate her labors of love.

CHANDIGARH

.I.
GENESIS

Since independence in 1947, India has erected three new capital cities—Bhubaneswar, Chandigarh, and Gandhinagar—besides several refugee, lesser administrative, and other industrial towns. While New Delhi, the national capital, has itself gone through a considerable modification and expansion in the past three decades, new state capitals for Assam, Arunachal, Nagaland, and Haryana, a twin capital at Bombay, and the redevelopment of the capital for Himachal Pradesh at Simla are at the drawing-board stages. In fact, the Town Planning Institute at New Delhi, in order to generate economic activity and provide for balanced regional urbanization and settlement patterns for India, has postulated building at least three hundred new cities by the end of this century.[1]

Among all the new cities of India, Chandigarh, located 241 miles (388 kms) north of New Delhi, is the most visible example of a planned city. Conceived amid the crises and political confusion accompanying independence, Chandigarh was designed to fulfill deep-rooted psychological needs and meet pressing political exigencies then facing India. Independence had divided British India into two nations: India and Pakistan. In the north, West Punjab became West Pakistan; in the east, East Bengal became East Pakistan, since 1971 the present-day Bangladesh. Because of the bifurcation of India, between 1947 and 1951 about 6.2 million Muslims left India for Pakistan, and 7.5 million Hindus and Sikhs came to India from across the border.[2]

The Second World War and the refugee influx caused by the partition of India accelerated the growth of urban population during the decade 1941–51, accounting for 6.2 percent of the urban growth.[3] Even excluding the impact of refugee migration to and from Pakistan, the growth rate of the urban population for the 1941–51 decade was 34.5 percent, most of it taking place in big cities.[4] The influx of refugees was also heavy in big cities. Punjab was worst hit, because displaced persons from West Pakistan had left behind 6.7 million acres compared to the 4.7 million acres abandoned by Muslim evacuees in East Punjab and PEPSU (Patiala and East Punjab State Union) or, in terms of "standard acres" into which differences in quality of land and differences in rights were reduced, 3.9 and 2.4 million acres respectively.[5]

The problem of rehabilitating the refugees acquired a sense of urgency, both for the government of East Punjab and for the government of India, since in the 1940s India was already experiencing a surge in urban population. The 1941 census reported that it "is the fact that city life has begun really to appeal to the ordinary middle class or lower middle class Indians."[6] During the forty years, from 1901 to 1941, the net increase in the Indian urban population was 18.3 million compared to 18.3 in a single decade, 1941–51.[7] In a broadcast to the nation from New Delhi in August 1947, the Indian prime minister Pundit Jawaharlal Nehru noted, "We have had to face a refugee problem of such magnitude that I doubt whether any other country in the world has had to face anything similar."[8] On another occasion he added, "One of the first tasks of our government was to think of the Punjab. . . . In both Amritsar and Lahore we heard a ghastly tale and we saw thousands of refugees, Hindus, Muslims, and Sikhs."[9]

Moreover, by the Radcliff Award Indian Punjab had lost its capital, Lahore,[10] the ancient and beloved city of the Punjabis, to Pakistan, rendering the East Punjab government itself homeless and forcing the government of India to find an "instant" alternative to administer the strife-stricken state and rehabilitate the refugees. It was among such confusing and compelling circumstances that representatives of the government of India and East Punjab state, meeting in the Himalayan summer capital of British India, Simla, decided to plan a new capital for East Punjab.

The logic of building a new city was that the addition of capital functions to one of the existing cities—all of which were lacking in essential amenities, with inadequate infrastructures, reeling under burgeoning populations—would be as costly as building a new city. Recognizing the inadequacy of existing cities, the government of India between 1947 and 1951 had undertaken the construction of fourteen new townships, scattered over eight states of the union, accommodating nearly 470,000 refugees from East and West Pakistan.[11] Situated in carefully chosen areas, with industry and other means of sustaining their economy, these townships, beside accommodating refugees from Sind, Northwest Frontier Province, and Bahawalpur (who—unlike the refugees from West Punjab—had completely lost their provinces of origin to West Pakistan) were also expected to bring prosperity to neighboring areas. The government felt that none of the existing cities possessed sufficient magnificence and glamor to make up for the psychological loss of Lahore suffered by the strife-stricken but proud Punjabis.[12] Although East Bengal (Pakistan), too, had been dispossessed of its historic capital, Calcutta, which had remained in West Bengal on the Indian side, it retained Dacca, which had been the headquarters of that partitioned province between 1905 and 1912 and therefore could relatively quickly replace Calcutta.

East Punjab did include Simla, which had been summer headquarters of the Punjab government and also the summer capital of British India; but its severe winters, its disagreeable location almost on the edge of the new state, its limited accessibility, lack of adequate floor space for government operations, and absence of good communications made it impossible to convert this small town into the permanent headquarters of the government of East Punjab. The frivolous suggestion that a couple of Swiss mountain-road engineers could open Simla to good communications, that a few extra diesel engines could solve the problems of water and electricity, and that the city could expand downward toward Kalka, with the industrial unit later to be built at Chandigarh,[13] never seriously engaged anyone's attention.

Because Simla had proved inadequate to accommodate fully the government machinery, the East Punjab government was forced to scatter its different offices all over the state at Jullundar, Ambala, Kalka, Kasauli, Dagshai, and several other places.[14] This arrangement not only made it difficult for the public to reach the seat of government but also imposed unnecessary travel expense on the government itself. Three major considerations played on the minds of the decision makers: 1) strategic and military security against the neighboring hostile state of Pakistan, 2) adequate space for new government machinery, for refugees, and for future expansion, and 3) the potential to replace the material and psychological loss of Lahore, which had been the hub of commercial and cultural activities of the Punjabis.[15] Moreover, it was hoped that the new capital would have a sufficiently large industrial complex to accommodate uprooted businesses from West Pakistan, that it would be connected with other important cities and commercial centers in India by air, road, and rail links, that it would be able to accommodate some government of India offices, and that it would help ease the population pressure in existing cities of Punjab by attracting people from other parts of the state.[16] Conspicuously missing from this litany of projected aims, however, was the need for integrating physical planning with economic planning and, at the same time, linking this integration to the hierarchy of towns in the hinterland and to the region—an omission which would later hinder the administration in preserving the planned character of the city.

Without any scientific survey or feasibility study, government officials held no unanimous or informed opinion as to the size of the new capital. After partition, East Punjab was left with approximately a total population of 11,548,000 inhabiting an area of roughly 29,120 square miles. The center of gravity of the province was located in the central districts of Doaba, Ludhiana, and Ambala, which together contained 60 percent of the province's population, with a density of population of about 678 persons per square mile—as against 200 to 300 persons per square mile in the other districts of the province.

It was felt, therefore, that for the sake of administrative convenience, as well as for the sake of economic and social considerations, the choice of the new capital should preferably fall upon these three central districts. Furthermore, considering the general trend of urbanization in India, the failure of the land to sustain the entire rural population, the need for industrial development consequent upon the attainment of independence, and the most important problem of the rehabilitation of the refugees, the East Punjab government had estimated the total population of the new capital to be near a half million.

To ascertain the population of the new capital, the government of East Punjab had invited applications from the public as early as 1948; by 1949 the government had received 32,000 applications, of which 3,000 belonged to industrialists, 9,000 to businessmen and 20,000 to prospective residents of the city. Calculating twenty industrial workers to each industrial unit and two families for each business premise (insurance companies, banking concerns, and large stores employing greater numbers of workers), and providing five members per family on the average, P. L. Varma, chief engineer, development, East Punjab, estimated as follows the population demands of the new capital: industries, 300,000; business, 90,000; and residents, 100,000.[17] To these figures were added another 50,000 government employees who would migrate to the city with the administration and another 50,000 who would come with the university.

Assuming that the rate of growth of the capital would likely require the total demand of a population of a half million to be met evenly in the first ten years, Varma estimated that 50 percent of the plots under various categories would be sold within the first five years and 10 percent each year in the succeeding years. The total cost for the scheme was calculated at rupees 49.58 crores (excluding water and electricity costs), of which rupees 27.50 crores was considered recoverable through sale of plots. (One crore equals 10,000,000.) To encourage applicants to invest and build in the new capital, it was proposed that for the first five years only the rent on land (i.e., interest on the application price of undeveloped land) would be charged; thereafter, the total value of developed land was recoverable in fifteen years in equal yearly installments, there being no encumbrance on the purchaser in the twenty-first year when the land would be transferred to him as his property.

Not everyone within the East Punjab administration agreed with this optimistic proposal. The opposing view was articulated by A. L. Fletcher, officer on special duty (capital), East Punjab, who observed, "It will be wrong [to assume] that our capital will grow to a population of 500,000 at the end of 10 or even 20 years."[18] Citing the examples of Washington, D.C., New Delhi, Ottawa, and other new towns, he emphasized that new towns do not grow as rapidly as visualized by the chief engineer. History has proved Varma wrong in his optimism. Fletcher, a conservative-pragmatist from the cadre of the Indian Civil Service, was more in favor of a modest plan that would accommodate 100,000 people. He rightly argued that Lahore was the growth of centuries and that "any government that attempts to replace Lahore in 18 years is, to say the least, as optimistic as unrealistic."[19] He was equally skeptical of the cost estimates and observed, "We are unhappily aware of the fact that the first rough and ready estimates put out by an engineering authority have seldom proved accurate when actual construction work has been taken in hand, and more often than not, Government find themselves faced with a much bigger liability than they had bargained for."[20]

Proving equally elusive was the decision on where to build the new capital. With Simla ruled out, Amritsar, Jullundar, Ludhiana, and Ambala were the other four cities considered as possible alternative sites for the new capital. Amritsar, like Simla (almost at the edge of the new state), was too close to the Indo-Pakistan border to serve as the capital of East Punjab. The argument circulating in some government circles that if Lahore, next door to India, could serve as the capital for West Punjab, then Amritsar could serve the same task for East Punjab never gained currency because, it was argued, Lahore was restricted by its historic role as the capital of undivided Punjab while East Punjab could develop a new city on a new site. Also rejected was Indian Defense Minister Baldev Singh's plea to place the new capital at Amritsar to restore confidence in the border areas and also help retain important industry and trade there.[21]

The concern for security for the new capital, in view of the outbreak of hostilities in Kashmir between India and Pakistan immediately following independence, was sincere and legitimate, and it dominated the thinking of Indian officials. Superintendent Engineer D. C. Khanna of the Public Health Circle, East Punjab, and Executive Engineer R. N. Dogra, East Punjab, in a preliminary note on the selection of a site for the new capital, made the following observation (obviously referring to Pakistan) to the committee set up in response to a government of India directive of September 18, 1947:[22] "The province [of East Punjab] being on the frontier of India, it is necessary in view of the apparently hostile attitude of the community occupying the neighbouring state, to have the capital at a considerable distance from the border."[23]

In fact, in the early years of independence an all-out war with Pakistan was considered imminent, and the concern for security was so consuming in certain circles that Constituent Assembly members Tajamul Husain and K. Hanumanthaiya proposed in the Assembly to shift the capital of India from Delhi to some central part of India and name it Gandhipura.[24] Such a move, it was also argued, would spare the legislators from the harsh climate of Delhi and prevent overcrowding of government offices in a city that was already overcrowded.²⁵ The idea was not entirely novel. In 1327 Muhammad Tughluk (1325–51), with a view to having a capital in the center of India, had moved his capital from Delhi to Devagiri, 700 miles south. The move created a series of problems, including economic drain from the Tughluk treasury, forcing Muhammad Tughluk seventeen years later to move back to Delhi. Conscious of India's history and recognizing the impracticability of moving the capital city, both Pundit Nehru and Sardar Patel ignored the proposal.

In the case of Amritsar serving as the new capital of East Punjab, however, there were additional problems: it was situated in a natural basin or depression and there had been a steady rise in the water table for the past two decades; it had a poor drainage system, which was unfit to cope with the increase in population inevitable with the status of a capital; and it was already struggling to service a population of four lakhs.²⁶ (One lakh equals 100,000.)

The same security reasons ruled out the selection of Jullundar as a site for the new capital, notwithstanding its good climate, good communication facilities, and a strong infrastructure.²⁷ Ludhiana was ruled out because of its poor communication facilities. Of particular concern was the absence of a system to disperse traffic in all directions. There was only one bridge across the Sutlej River, which, if put out of action during an emergency, would leave no alternative routes for the traffic except by a long detour. There was additional concern over the overwhelmingly Muslim population of the city, which could cause tensions with predominantly Hindu refugees. Moreover, the city lacked a sound infrastructure; it was already overcrowded; it lacked a military cantonment; and its essentially industrial character was considered, from the town planning viewpoint, unsuitable for an administrative center.²⁸ Likewise, Ambala was ruled out because of its predominantly military character, poor water facilities, absence of electricity, and its vulnerability to epidemics of plague.²⁹ Karnal and Phillaur, the two other alternatives, were also rejected for similar reasons.³⁰

If inadequate facilities and poor infrastructure precluded the conversion of an existing city to be the new capital of East Punjab, the lobbying by strong political pressure groups to support claims of different cities made the selection impossible. Considering the economic and political benefits which accrue from a capital city, each political leader of the state wanted his constituency either to be an integral part of the new capital or to be close to it. In a country where urbanization has not necessarily been stimulated by industrialization,[31] the Indian political system continues to draw its strength from the agricultural-rural sector in which the capital cities play a significant role.

There is a distinct political advantage in moving to a capital city: it is there that the laws of the land are conceived and legislated; it is there that the chief executive of the state is located; and it is to capital cities that people of the land look for inspiration, for economic development, and for political favors. Moreover, any political, cultural, or social movement seeking national attention, like that of the Sikhs in Punjab since independence, directs its efforts to the capital city. The polarization of the Hindus and the Sikhs in Punjab and the subsequent bifurcation of the state explains why the new capital has become the object of discord between Punjab and Haryana states.

Expressing his exasperation with the prevailing mood of indecision among the officials on the selection of the site and the obvious economic and technical limitations of the state, the governor of East Punjab wrote to Prime Minister Nehru that "in the existing circumstances it is out of the question to start planning a new capital for East Punjab." He added: "A capital must grow spontaneously and not be planned on a gigantic scale as was done in the case of New Delhi. And, in any case, the project of building a new capital need not be taken in hand in these days of inflation and should await a period of disinflation."[32] If the new capital were to meet the aspirations of the Punjabis and if it were to be protected against vested political interests, it was best to postpone its construction to a time when a more agreeable mood prevailed in Punjab. If the new capital were to replace the psychological and material loss of Lahore, it would require more than economic and technical support; it would require political consensus.

Such a consensus was absent in East Punjab. It would be a waste of economic resources and would be politically inexpedient to construct the capital at a site that did not enjoy a political consensus and therefore had to be shifted later. The governor of East Punjab explained the situation to the governor general of India in his letter of July 13, 1949: "It cannot be said that the building of an administrative capital for East Punjab is an urgent one or, at any rate, a compelling necessity. An administrative capital would cost [something] like rupees 15 crores, if not more. There will be no financial returns from such a capital. If, on the other hand, we build only a temporary capital for administrative purposes, the cost would, no doubt, be less, but the money would be wasted if we had to shift the capital." In the governor's view, Punjab needed "not purely an administrative capital, but a capital which will be a cultural, commercial and industrial centre." Such a conception of the capital postulated, the governor felt, "rehabilitation of displaced persons like industrialists, commercial firms, government servants, etc." The new capital "would be the nerve centre of the Province, and from it would flow life and activity throughout the Province."[33]

Because the new capital, in addition to serving as an administrative center, was also expected to serve as the bastion of business and economic activity, the stakes of the project naturally rose. Clearly no existing town could meet the expectations outlined in the governor of East Punjab's letter to the governor general of India. Clearly, too, the construction of a small town would not meet the bill. Regardless of what site was selected, either one close to an existing town or away from it, the new capital called for a major construction effort. What further vexed the decision makers in East Punjab was their economic limitation. The central government was already financially overcommitted and, in view of other pressing political and economic issues facing the nation, unable to commit itself financially to the Capital Project of East Punjab. The prime minister made this abundantly clear to the government of East Punjab when he said, "You refer in [your letter] to your demand for money for your capital project. I am afraid I cannot help you at all in this matter. . . . We are at the present moment cutting expenditure to the bone. . . . The financial position [of the country] is a very serious one."[34]

Although the government of East Punjab felt that, in light of the controversy over the selection of the site for the new capital, it might be expedient to defer the decision to a more propitious moment when political consensus could be obtained from all concerned parties, it also realized that indefinite delay might result in the relocation of business from West Pakistan to some other city, outside Punjab. Such a development would mean a permanent loss of a source for economic revenue for the state. Thus the governor of East Punjab advised the government of India that "big business and industry uprooted from West Punjab are already leaving East Punjab, and if the Capital Project is not proceeded with immediately or shelved for the time being, all business and industrial talent and enterprise, which has come to us from West Punjab, would be lost permanently to our province."[35]

If paucity of resources made the government of East Punjab dependent on the central government, the failure of the provincial government to reach a decision on the selection of the site and the construction of the new capital further assured the central government's role in the Capital Project. The failure of the East Punjab government to reach a decision on the selection of the site can be explained by the strong ties of India's regional and local bureaucracy to its colonial origin. Because of these ties, the Indian bureaucracy is highly centralized and not open to adequate supervision. Accountability is not defined in terms that determine specific responsibilities of the various echelons. There is a pronounced tendency to evade responsibility by multiple reviews and cross-references in such a fashion that in the end "everybody is responsible for everything before anything is done."[36] The results of this excessive bureaucratization are administrative delays that at almost every step interfere with the implementation of general economic and development programs.

The debate over the new capital might have continued indefinitely if Prime Minister Nehru had not personally intervened. Admonishing the government of East Punjab for postponing the decision on the construction of the new capital, Nehru wrote to the premier of East Punjab that "right from September 1947 the Government of India have been laying great stress on the urgency of this matter from every point of view, practical as well as psychological. In a sense the rehabilitation of East Punjab centres round it and yet because of doubt and uncertainty and repeated changes of policy and decision, nothing so far has been finalized." He added, "I think this is very bad for your government and for East Punjab. To go on waiting for large grants from the Centre is not a worthwhile policy. . . . I would strongly suggest to you to go ahead with this matter even though you do not get any financial support from the Centre."[37]

After considerable indecision, in early 1948 the choice for the new capital was finally narrowed down to three sites, which came to be known, in order of preference, as 1) the Ambala site, 2) the Chandigarh site, and 3) the Ludhiana site. Reporting the results of the search to Prime Minister Nehru, the governor of East Punjab noted that the Ambala site was better than the Chandigarh site from several points of view. It was better served by railway communication. A large cantonment and a well-equipped "aerodrome" already existed there, and canalization of chos (hill torrents) and terracing of the site would not have to be undertaken. The cost of acquisition, however, was estimated at rupees 3 crores for the Ambala site and rupees 2.13 crores for the Chandigarh site. "The difference is," the governor reasoned, "likely to be more than outweighed by the cost of canalising of chos, the terracing of the site and new railway construction, if the latter is undertaken. It is also better than the Ludhiana site because a) the cost of land acquisition is much smaller; and b) it is more central and farther away from the frontier."[38]

However, the Ambala site was disqualified because out of its total 50 square miles of area only 4.5 square miles was in East Punjab territory and the remainder of about 45.5 square miles was in Patiala state. Selection of this site would require, it was argued, negotiations with Patiala state for the transfer of a large area to East Punjab. The governor of East Punjab perceptively noted, "We are not in a position to assess the expediency of starting these negotiations or the difficulties likely to be encountered." He anticipated a demand for some kind of quid pro quo from Patiala state, for example, transfer to Patiala state of some East Punjab territory forming an enclave within the state, or some other concession or consideration. The future shape of things so far as East Punjab and Patiala were concerned, was uncertain. "There are at present two movements," the governor observed, "one for the formation of a union of Sikh states in East Punjab and another for the merger of East Punjab states with East Punjab, though the latter movement has not gathered momentum, it may be that the Government of India will not wish to be under the obligation of the Patiala state in order that they may be able to retain a free hand in their dealings with the state in future. . . . We are not inclined to press for this site."[39] Ironically, however, twenty years later the new capital of Punjab, Chandigarh, was to become a center of territorial dispute between Haryana and Punjab—a dispute which has continued to rankle the government of India and the two state governments to this day.

Considering the differential in acquisition costs for Chandigarh, rupees 2.13 crores, and for Ludhiana, rupees 7 crores, Chandigarh's safe distance from the Pakistan border and the prospect of building a new town on modern lines, the government of East Punjab, in consultation with the government of India, in late March 1948, selected the site at Chandigarh, in the Kharar tehsil of the Ambala district, for the new capital of East Punjab.[40] The decision received the enthusiastic support of Prime Minister Nehru, who said on his first visit to Chandigarh: "The site chosen is free from the existing encumbrances of old towns and old traditions. Let it be the first large expression of our creative genius flowering on our newly earned freedom."[41]

Moving quickly, the government of East Punjab issued a notification on March 23, 1948, placing the whole of the area in the Kharar tehsil under prohibition for purposes of building and the sale of land. The total area proposed to be acquired for the two phases of the development of the new capital consisted approximately of 28,000 acres of land in fifty-eight villages with a population of 21,000 people or 6,228 families.[42] Of the total land proposed to be acquired, 22,000 acres was cultivated land and 6,000 acres uncultivated land, out of which 500 acres belonged to Muslims. The number of landholders affected by the decision was 6,807, out of which 91 percent, or 6,215, possessed less than 10 acres of land. Only 16 landholders possessed more than 50 acres.[43] Considering that land acquisition costs rise with development, it was proposed that the whole of this land be acquired at once under the Land Acquisition Act of 1894, but that the people inhabiting the area be allowed to remain in possession of their land and cultivate it as tenants of the government until the land was needed for building purposes.

It was thought that as the construction of the capital got under way, some of these people who had lost their land could be employed in the construction work, which they might find better paying than their existing vocation of agriculture. For others, it was recommended that land for land be given either in the Ambala district, where 277,876 acres of Muslim evacuee land existed, or in the Kharar tehsil itself, where 33,897 acres of Muslim evacuee land existed, so that they might continue in their traditional vocation of agriculture. It was further proposed that in its first phase the city should be developed to accommodate 150,000 people and by the end of phase two the total population of the city should reach 500,000.

While the question of the site for the new capital was being considered, the breakdown of constitutional machinery in Punjab demanded the autonomous rule of the president of India. It was the Indian Parliament, therefore, which first passed the Capital of Punjab (Development and Regulation) Act early in 1952, once again reassuring the place of the central government in the Capital Project. After the first general elections in 1951–52, the Punjab legislature passed the Capital of the Punjab (Development and Regulation) Act in 1952, and the Punjab New Capital (Periphery Control) Act followed soon after in the same year. Under the Development and Regulation Act, Building Rules and Chandigarh (Sale and Site) Rules were made in the same year and the Chandigarh (Tree Preservation) Order issued.

The Chandigarh site, located at the bottom of the picturesque Shivalik Range of the towering Himalayas, was selected from airplane reconnaissance. Bounded on east and west by two seasonal rivers, Sukhna Cho and Patiala Rao, respectively, the area is flat, but with a gentle slope ideal for drainage. The 8,500 acres of fertile land, dotted with groves of mango trees, spread over seventeen villages or hamlets, was to cover the first phase of ten square miles of the capital. Abundant in a natural supply of underground water, the site was also close to sources of building material like sand, cement, and stone, and derived its name from a temple of the goddess Chandi (Power) located in one of the acquired villages. Later, twenty-four villages toward the southwest were acquired and similarly added to the capital.

Lying on longitude of 76 degrees 48 minutes and latitude 30 degrees 50 minutes, the altitude of Chandigarh varies from 304.8 to 365.76 meters above sea level. It has an extreme climate, temperatures rising to an unbearably hot 45 degrees Celsius in summer and falling to almost freezing in winter. The total rainfall is about 1.01 meters, distributed mostly from June to August in the summer and January to February in the winter. Prevalent winds are from the southeast in the summer and the northwest in the winter. Reflecting on Chandigarh's climate, Maxwell Fry, one of the architects connected with the Capital Project, observed, "Now which of these seasons dominated it was hard to tell, but looking at Mughal architecture and traditional village building and taking the facts for themselves, we came down in favour of the hot season; protection from the sun and from the dust-laden winds of the hot season was the architectural imperative, the rest was secondary."[44]

The early development of the city was guided by two men, P. N.

Thapar, a member of the Indian Civil Service, who became administrative head of the Capital Project in 1949, and P. L. Varma, the chief engineer of Punjab, who had been recalled from the United States, where he headed an Indian delegation studying road construction. While in the United States, Varma was instructed by the Punjab government to consult American town planners with a view toward building the new capital.

From the beginning, however, the Chandigarh site was fraught with controversy—a controversy that kept the construction work tentative for a long time. Writing to Nehru, the premier of East Punjab said, "There is a good deal of agitation against the building of our new provincial capital on a site near Chandigarh, and which in my view is not without justification." Agitating against the site were displaced farmers, who were unwilling to give up their fertile land. "Sometime ago I met the Prime Minister of PEPSU [Patiala and East Punjab State Union]," the premier added, "and asked him whether we could get some land near Ambala City for building our capital and he has now written to say that there should be no difficulty in getting land for land and that PEPSU land near Ambala City would be available if we part with our Sidhowal area which is a small 'island' in the PEPSU territory. We are collecting the necessary information and if the negotiations between the two governments reach a satisfactory conclusion, we may have to change the site of our proposed capital."[45]

The idea of situating the new capital at Ambala indeed made sense if, as contemplated by the central government, there was to be at a later date a merger of PEPSU with East Punjab.[46] Such a decision would spare the rich and fertile agricultural land at Chandigarh from unwelcome urban tyranny. To the farmers of the seventeen villages, on which the first phase of the new capital was to begin, the government decision was unacceptable. Rallying to defend their land, they staged widespread demonstrations against the government throughout the state. The initial response by the government was to arrest the demonstrators, take them out to the valley, and release them to walk home. Still fresh from the Gandhian experience of satyagraha against the British Raj, the farmers set up a courier system. They hoped to marshal popular support for their cause through these demonstrations. To embarrass the police, women were placed in the front ranks.

In an effort to appease the agitators, the premier of East Punjab, Gopichand Bhargava, in a statement published in the *Tribune* on April 25, 1948, declared that the government's policy was to use the least fertile tract of the land and dislodge the least number of persons. Three months later, however, the East Punjab government published the scheme for the new capital under which fifty square miles (32,000 acres) between Sukhna Cho and Patiala Rao, comprising fifty-eight villages, with a population of 21,000 was requisitioned. (According to the Anti-Capital Committee, called the Anti-Rajdhani Committee, the figure was 36,000.) Blaming the government for creating another refugee problem, the Anti-Rajdhani Committee—comprising the Socialist party, District Congress Committee (Ambala), Akali Dal, the Hind Kisan Panchayat, and the affected villagers—issued a press statement in which it pointed out that the requisitioned area had a density of 611 persons per square mile and that it yielded forty maunds (3,291.20 pounds) of rice, ninety maunds (7,405.20 pounds) of sugar, and thirty-two maunds (2,632.96 pounds) of wheat per acre.[47] The press statement further declared that in the event all legitimate and constitutional means failed to bring around the government to revise its policy, the Anti-Rajdhani Committee would immediately start a peaceful and nonviolent satyagraha against the government.

Of special concern to the government of East Punjab was the Socialists' support for these agitations. Reporting these incidents to the Indian prime minister, the premier of East Punjab wrote: "In order to prevent the Socialists from instigating tenants not to give batai [rent] to their landowners in Ferozpore district, a ban had to be placed on public meetings. It is reported that about 6,000 volunteers have been enlisted by them for launching satyagraha against location of the capital at Chandigarh and they intend to raise the figure to 20,000 volunteers in the near future." He ominously concluded, "An anti-Rajdhani Committee was recently formed at Ambala where they held a meeting under the presidentship of Lala Duni Chand of Ambala for doing propaganda for the acceptance of Ambala as capital."[48]

To the greater political discomfort of the government of East Punjab, the anti-Capital, Socialist-sponsored agitation was also aided by the Akalis.[49] Although the agitation was originally directed against a capital at Chandigarh, sometimes it seemed that the agitation was against the very idea of a new capital city. Duni Chand, a prominent lawyer from Ambala, warned the Indian prime minister that the agitation against locating the capital at Chandigarh was genuine and that the 30,000 people affected by such a step did not wish the capital to be at Chandigarh.[50] Worse, with the advent of the Bhim Sain Sachar's government in East Punjab in April 1949, the choice of the Chandigarh site once again became uncertain.[51] Sachar was not at all keen on having the capital at Chandigarh; he was more in favor of having the capital at or near Ambala.[52] Likewise, there were other leaders within the Congress party, both at provincial and national levels, who did not favor the Chandigarh site for the capital. In the Indian Parliament, Sardar Hukum Singh criticized the construction of the capital at Chandigarh and strongly recommended the consideration of Amritsar and Jullundar,[53] both predominantly Sikh cities. Such a move could have assured a more dominant role for the Sikh community in Punjab politics and would, possibly, have made the demand for a separate Sikh state by the Akalis[54] more threatening. Besides it would have spared Baldev Singh's constituents at Chandigarh, which area Singh had represented for twelve years. Rajkumari Amrit Kaur, another member of the Parliament and a close associate of Nehru, was equally opposed to the Chandigarh site and "constantly complained about it" to Nehru.[55] Nehru good-naturedly always brushed aside such criticisms.

In Punjab, however, the objection to the Chandigarh site took a more serious expression. Lala Jagat Narain, general secretary of the Provincial Congress Committee, publicly charged the additional district commissioner, capital project, Sardar Jaswant Singh Uppal, and his tehsildar (land assessor) for allotting preferred plots to friends and government officials and neglecting the needy refugees "for whose rehabilitation this capital is being built."[56] This sent a wave of consternation throughout the Punjabi community and discouraged its members from investing "in a project which may never materialize."[57] The government of East Punjab had already issued a press statement specifying the order of preference to be followed in allotting plots to applicants at Chandigarh: the first preference was to be given to groups of displaced persons, the second preference was to be given to groups of displaced and nondisplaced persons of whom displaced persons numbered more than 50 percent, the third preference was to be given to individually displaced applicants, the fourth preference was to be given to mixed groups in which displaced persons numbered less than 50 percent, the fifth preference was to be given to groups of nondisplaced persons, and the last preference was to be given to nondisplaced individual applicants.[58] The unsatisfied applicants were to be kept on a waiting list until other plots opened up after planning.

Jagat Narain's charges were serious enough to bring prompt response from the central government, and Nehru instructed the governor of East Punjab to investigate the allegations, so that the public would not get the impression "that there is a partiality."[59] Nehru was equally concerned about the agitation by the agriculturists who were to be dispossessed at Chandigarh and ordered an investigation into the matter. Reassuring Nehru, the chief minister of Punjab wrote: "I quite understand the reluctance of agriculturalists to see their land acquired by government, but in this particular case we are offering them alternative land. So, apart from sentiment, there is no reason for this agitation."[60] What the chief minister failed to mention was whether the "alternative land" was qualitatively comparable to the land at Chandigarh.

Meanwhile, the work of surveying and acquiring land for the proposed capital site had started soon after the decision of March 1948. In their report of June 30, 1949, the surveyors M. R. Sahni and B. R. C. Iyengar endorsed the Chandigarh site unequivocally on six grounds: 1) the stability of the site area, 2) the exceptionally favorable water supply conditions, 3) the favorable ground slope for a drainage system, 4) the close proximity of large-scale limestone deposits for setting up a cement factory of considerable dimensions, 5) the possibility of setting up subsidiary industries, and 6) the occurrence of inexhaustible supplies of building stone in the neighborhood.[61] As early as August 28, 1948, the Cabinet Sub-Committee (New Capital) had decided to construct in advance a self-contained neighborhood unit at a cost of rupees 4.42 crores for accommodating 20,000 to 30,000 people so that government headquarters might shift to it at the earliest.[62] In addition, the Sub-Committee noted that the capital would be built on a unit system, according to which each neighborhood unit in the township was to be devoted to a particular usage, for example, commercial, residential, and so forth, and that it was to be a complete and self-contained unit in itself as far as its character, shopping facilities, educational system, recreational system, and so forth, were concerned. The most important unit of the capital was to be the administrative center with an approximate population of 100,000. The second unit of the capital was to be the university township with a fifty square mile radius, possibly ten to fifteen miles away from the capital so as not to put heavy population pressure on the capital. And the third unit was envisaged as a satellite industrial town, constructed on the principles of a garden city, with "no heavy and obnoxious industries."[63] It was also decided that the administrative capital would not have any industry, except service industries like laundries, bakeries, and so forth; that the airport for the new capital would be placed at least five miles from the periphery of the capital to prevent noise pollution; and that a cement factory would be constructed at Chandigarh with an output of 750 to 1,500 tons per day.[64] To provide communication and transport facilities for the new capital, the government of East Punjab negotiated with the Railway Board and the Ministry of Transport, government of India, and instructions were issued to the Northern Railway to divert the main line, between Ambala and Kalka, through the new capital at Chandigarh.[65]

The water supply for the new capital, which has always proved inadequate for the population of Chandigarh, was envisaged as coming from two sources: 1) from the reservoir formed as a result of the damming of the Ghaggar River at Chandigarh, and 2) from the subterranean water supply at the site of the capital. Although there were widespread doubts concerning the reliability of subterranean water supplies at the site, government reports argued that there was sufficient water available through this source and that this source was cheaper at rupees 6 crores as against rupees 12 crores for the Ghaggar project. It was also rumored that the waters of the Ghaggar were dangerously deficient in iodine and other minerals, because of which lack there was a high incidence of mental illness in the area.[66] However, there was no basis to these rumors and it was decided that, in order to prevent water shortages in the future as the population of the capital increased, the Ghaggar River waters should be diverted to Chandigarh "by paying compensation to the zamindars who are at present entitled to its use"[67]—a proposal which never materialized to the disappointment of the people of Chandigarh because of the later-day interstate dispute between Haryana and Punjab. The primary water supply of the city, therefore, came to be obtained from tube wells at a rate of thirty gallons per inhabitant per day.⁶⁸ Presently, there are 141 tube wells catering to a population of 450,000 (1981 census) at the rate of seventy gallons per inhabitant per day.⁶⁹

During World War II, the 1941 census records were either lost or damaged, no provincial reports published, no age figures tabulated, no occupational distribution of the population included, and no actuarial figures noted.⁷⁰ The government of India, therefore, decided to take a census of displaced persons, issuing notification on May 16, 1949, and taking a census in all territories affected by partition.⁷¹ Under the notification, a displaced person was defined as one "who entered India, having left or been compelled to leave his home in Western Pakistan, on or after the 1st March, 1947, or his home in Eastern Pakistan on or after the 15th October, 1946, on account of civil disturbances or the fear of such disturbances or on account of the setting up of the two Dominions of India and Pakistan."⁷²

There were legitimate doubts, however, about the success of such an exercise, particularly in the partition-affected territories of Assam, West Bengal, and East Punjab where a proper ground organization for such a census survey was conspicuously missing.⁷³ Forced to rely on applications it had been receiving since the middle of 1948, the government of East Punjab by April 1952 had sold nearly 2,500 residential plots at Chandigarh for a total amount of rupees 120 lakhs, with an even larger number of applications still remaining on file to be processed.⁷⁴ Although not an overwhelming vote of confidence for the capital project, it was nevertheless a modest endorsement for the development of the new capital.

Somewhat encouraged by this modest response from the people, and galvanized into action by Nehru's admonishments and the central government's growing impatience, the governor of East Punjab reported to the governor general of India in January 1950: "We have now reached what appears to be a final decision about the site of our capital. It is to be at Chandigarh. Planning is to be entrusted to Mr. Albert Mayer (an American planner working in India)."⁷⁵ It was hoped that by providing alternative land to agriculturalists who were losing their land at Chandigarh, the government will be able to further take the wind out of the anti-Rajdhani agitation. As if to spite the government decision in a last ditch effort, the ousted agriculturalists cut fruit trees and timber from their land and had to be restrained by government intervention. By October 1950, however, an agreement had been effected with the villagers concerned and a committee of local representatives set up to advise the government in rehabilitating the oustees from Chandigarh; and, to the relief of the East Punjab government, the Socialist-Akali sponsored anti-Capital agitation had temporarily faded.[76]

In its revised phase of the construction plan, the new capital was to accommodate a modest population of 150,000 covering an area of 8,000 acres,[77] at a cost of rupees 10 crores as against 50 crores for a population of 500,000 originally envisaged. And a decision had been taken as early as 1949 to send one of the chief engineers from East Punjab to England for consultation there, and to bring an expert architect back to assist in the preparation and the execution of a master plan for the new capital.[78] Whatever public doubts remained on the question of the site for the new capital were finally put to rest in the spring of 1952, four years after the decision had been taken, when the *Hindustan Times* reported, "The decision to build a new capital of Punjab at Chandigarh is final and irrevocable and anyone who has any doubt about it is sadly mistaken."[79] Privately, however, the doubts were to remain until the reorganization of the state along linguistic lines in 1966 would once again stimulate public discussion as to the uncertain fate of the capital.

.2.
ARCHITECTS

If Indian leaders lacked unanimity as to the location of the new capital, they nonetheless shared a common vision concerning the nature of that city. Prime Minister Nehru best articulated this common vision: "Let this be a new town symbolic of the freedom of India, unfettered by the traditions of the past . . . an expression of the nation's faith in the future."[1] Even his minister of health, Rajkumari Amrit Kaur, who was most vocal in her opposition to the Chandigarh site, endorsed Nehru's sentiment, noting: "As a Punjabi I want the new capital of the Punjab to be the last word in beauty, in simplicity and in standards of such comfort as it is our duty to provide to every human-being."[2] Punjab's chief minister, Gopichand Bhargava, hoped that Chandigarh would be "the world's most charming capital."[3]

Because of the centralized control inherent in a new city's development, many national governments in the twentieth century have looked to its creation as a solution for urban congestion, inhibiting rural depopulation, and restoring regional balance. The Indian government recognized the effectiveness of urban planning as a policy tool for providing jobs and homes for refugees, absorbing excess population from older urban areas, encouraging economic growth, and providing population stability in economically depressed regions. The experience of England, where the modern new towns movement was first started by Sir Ebenezer Howard (1850–1928), was not lost on Cambridge-educated Pundit Nehru. In his book *To-morrow: A Peaceful Path to Real Reform*[4] (1898), Howard had described the parts of a city in organic relationship to each other, and had accordingly placed a functional limit on the growth of any one element. Reaffirming Aristotle's conception that there was a right size for the city—big enough to encompass all its functions but not too big to interfere with them—Howard had sought to relieve the pressure of congested London by colonizing its excess population in new centers limited in area and population.

To Indian leaders, who had themselves witnessed the character of their cities modified under colonial rule to conform to the needs of an alien government, new towns provided "a way of starting afresh, so as to overcome the hatreds, tensions or gross inequities of existing cities."[5] New towns frequently conjure up images of fresh approaches to urban development and departures from past or current modes of city building, providing potential laboratories for applying new ideas, theories, and designs. Because of this belief, to people like Nehru big dams represented "temples of new faith," while to others steel mills represented the crux of economic development, national power, and autonomy.[6] Psychological symbols and national power may legitimately compete with national economic goals. In the creation of Chandigarh, Indian leaders saw the potential for accommodating the Bhakra-Nangal project, which was to become the core energy source for northern India, and of meeting their commitment to the establishment of a welfare state, vis-à-vis the rehabilitation of refugees. For Indian leaders Chandigarh would ideally fulfill both these legitimate needs and would also provide much needed town-planning experience.

Noteworthy here is the counterforce of Gandhian sarvodaya, which, like Nyerere's "African Socialism," Mao Tse-tung's mobilization of the communes, and Israel's kibbutz movement, sought to recreate the rural community as a means of rediscovering the spirit of the nation.[7] Nehru's association with Gandhi had brought him face to face with India's past rooted in Vedantic philosophy. Gandhi's influence only reinforced the duality inherent in Nehru's nature. On the one hand, Nehru could romanticize: "I should like to take [children] with me not so much to the great cities of India but to the mountains and the forests and the great rivers and the old monuments, all of which tell us something of India's story."[8] On the other hand, he fervently hoped to break the fetters of the past and get into the mainstream of modern life. For him, only science, technology, and industrialization could usher India into the modern age and preserve her independence.[9] In the end the state that made Chandigarh possible was not the pan-Indian community based on agriculture and cloth-weaving that Gandhi had anticipated; it was the new nation, eager to become an adult member of the family of industrial powers to which it had been attached for so long as a mere appendage—"a nation whose leaders were waiting for the occasion to create a monument to the new national self-awareness."[10]

The American town planner Albert Mayer, with whom the East Punjab government first contracted, promised to deliver the Indian dream. Five months after his appointment in late December 1949, he wrote to Prime Minister Nehru: "I feel in all solemnity that this [Chandigarh] will be a source of great stimulation to city building and re-planning in India. But I also feel that it will be the most complete synthesis and integration in the world to date of all that has been learned and talked of in planning over the last thirty years, but which no one has yet had the great luck to be allowed actually to create. Yet I feel we have been able to make it strongly Indian in feeling and function as well as modern."[11] The city that finally emerged, however, was not the result of the efforts of one man but of several men. Mayer and his associates provided the basic master plan and a detailed architectural scheme for one superblock, which was finally put in place, with modifications, by the Swiss-born French architect Charles-Edouard Jeanneret, popularly known as Le Corbusier, his cousin Pierre Jeanneret, and the English husband-and-wife team of Edwin Maxwell Fry and Jane Beverly Drew. The half-experienced but enthusiastic Indians, who held these wise men from the West in divine awe, provided the manpower. To the disappointment of Indians, however, neither Mayer nor Corbusier would agree to live in India for any appreciable length of time.

Although eager to build the new capital that would compensate for the loss of Lahore, the Indians were nevertheless poorly equipped to carry out their intention. Administered by a large and sophisticated bureaucracy trained in the impersonal idiom of colonial rule, India was still woefully inexperienced in technical areas. Architectural schools were virtually nonexistent, indigenous architectural tradition had practically faded, and local craft skills were visibly on the decline.

In the eighteenth and nineteenth centuries, the British in their building programs had consciously ignored the older traditional areas, known as "native" towns or, in the French-influenced Pondicherry, *villes noires* or black towns. On the other hand, military cantonments and civil lines planned as exclusive residential areas and serviced by the native population of the native town for the British were laid out and built on an elaborate scale. Consequently, most of the district towns—and there are more than 360 in India—were really towns within towns. There were the elegant towns of parks, open spaces, and playgrounds meant for a handful of British officials, the *bara sahibs*, employed by the imperial government; and there were the native towns, congested, walled-in, and badly neglected. As Nehru discovered to his dismay when he was chairman of the Allahabad Municipality in the 1920s, it was the native town that was made responsible for the welfare and maintenance of the newly laid out civil lines and cantonments.

The lapse of effective local government during two centuries of British rule had further reduced once large and thriving Indian cities to mere shantytowns, leaving them congested and deprived of basic civic amenities. The resulting decline in the local building professions, which had been largely in the hands of master craftsmen, eventually alarmed some Indophiles in the British administration, and during the latter part of the nineteenth century attempts were made to revive local tradition and form what was disparagingly called an "Anglo-Indian" style. *Types of Modern Indian Buildings*,[12] written in 1913 by Gordon Sanderson, was one direct result of such efforts, followed by other publications by E. B. Havell[13] and Percy Brown.[14]

The first Indian town planning law, passed by the Bombay government in 1915, coincided with the arrival of Patrick Geddes in India, who subsequently produced reports on eighteen Indian cities. The resulting efforts from Geddes' reports, however, were directed not toward comprehensive planning but toward exercising control on population, clearing slums, and generally improving hygienic conditions through restoring authority to the local government. Soon, other town planning acts followed on the lines of the British Housing and Town Planning Act of 1909.

Throughout the British period, however, the involvement of Indians in town planning remained lamentably poor. The industrial city of Jamshedpur was planned by Fred Temple, a British sanitary engineer. The construction of other industrial towns, built as a result of the impetus provided to industrialization by the First World War, was also the work of British personnel. Even the imperial capital at New Delhi, built in 1912 in the beaux arts tradition and disliked strongly by Nehru, was planned and designed by Sir Edwin Lutyens, assisted by his friend Herbert Baker. Indian architects on municipal bodies of most cities were largely confined to drawing elevations for beautification of building facades. The paltry number of Indian town planners can be ascertained from the fact that in 1948, when an Indian Board of Town Planners was constituted, it had only eight members, mostly architects who had also taken on town planning responsibilities.[15]

This poor preparedness in matters of town planning notwithstanding, the Indians had already taken a lead in building rehabilitation towns after independence. Unlike the new towns around London, which were started for the deployment of the population and for attracting new industry, Indian refugee towns—such as Nilokheri and Faridabad—were started to train newcomers for productive work, which would enable them to design better cities.[16]

The Chandigarh project, however, demanded greater experience. Committed to achieving in Chandigarh an architectural form "without specific national connotations which could grow from the exigencies of the project itself and the unique conditions of its creation,"[17] the founders of Chandigarh remained ambivalent about where to procure the talent for the city. Although the Punjabi officials were inclined to visit Europe to find a suitable architect-planner for Chandigarh, Prime Minister Nehru disagreed with them.

Already present in India were some Western town planners, prominent among them being Albert Mayer and Otto Koenigsberger. A native of America, Albert Mayer had served as a lieutenant colonel in India during World War II, was acquainted with Nehru, and had gained through his experimental rural development program in the Etawah district of the Western United Provinces a familiarity with India and her problems. Otto Koenigsberger was a German Jew who had fled Nazi Germany and had arrived in India at the invitation of the diwan (minister) of Mysore. Koenigsberger was also known to Nehru, having been engaged in several developmental projects in India, including the planning of Orissa's new capital, Bhubaneshwar, and serving as a consultant for Faridabad, near Delhi. The blueprint for the other major postindependence urban settlement, Gandhidham in Gujarat, had also been prepared by Koenigsberger in consultation with the Americans Frederick Adams and Roland Greeley, who were in India under President Truman's Point Four agricultural program, and the Italian architect Mario Bachiocci. In West Bengal, Kalyani had been planned by the Swiss architect-planner Werner Moser.

Speaking before the third meeting of the National Development Council of the Planning Commission, Prime Minister Nehru acknowledged that "the major difficulty is trained personnel and every underdeveloped country has to face that grave difficulty. . . . We want trained personnel in hundreds of thousands. . . . Apart from the apparatus of training, institutions, etc., that have to be built up, the training itself takes time."[18] The Punjab government officials, on the other hand, unimpressed by any of the Western planners already present in India, proposed to hold an international competition for selecting the planner for Chandigarh. The man responsible for the idea of international competition was Chief Engineer P. L. Varma. As before, he was opposed by Officer on Special Duty (Capital Project) A. L. Fletcher, who pointedly observed, "The idea . . . is intrinsically unsound and will involve our Government in expenditure which . . . will not be justified by the results."[19] Agreeing with Fletcher, the Punjab government decided to send one of its officials to Europe and England and, after interviewing several planners, to select the most suitable person for building Chandigarh. Communicating the decision to Prime Minister Nehru, the premier of Punjab wrote: "It has now been decided that one of our Chief Engineers will fly to England and after consultations bring an expert Town Planner for preparation of a master plan of the new Capital. This will be done as quickly as possible to enable us to take further steps for the early execution of this scheme."[20]

A romantic at heart, Nehru also had a practical side to him. Considering the expense and delay involved in hiring a planner from the West, he immediately replied: "I do not wish to come in your way in this matter. But I wonder if you have explored the possibilities of getting the master plan made in India." Assuring that he was not opposed to "getting the best possible advice, even though [it] might cost a lot," Nehru added that "there is too great a tendency for our people to rush up to England and America for advice. The average American or English town-planner," he continued, "will probably not know the social background of India. He will therefore be inclined to plan something which might suit England or America, but not so much India." Pointing to New Delhi as an example, he concluded, "This is attractive in a way, but most inconvenient and most un-Indian."[21] As an alternative to the Punjab government's proposal, he strongly recommended the choice of Koenigsberger or Mayer.

Just as history has shown Nehru to be the chief architect of independent India, he was in the very nature of things also the architect-planner of Chandigarh. As in so many other things, so too in the case of Chandigarh, Nehru provided the inspiration and impetus. If the senseless communal frenzy, the alarming decline in political rationalism, and the growing bureaucratic inertia had tarnished independent India's singular triumph, they had also assured a more prominent role for Nehru in India's several developmental projects, of which Chandigarh was one. Committed to individual freedom, social justice, popular participation, planned development, a posture of nonalignment in international affairs and, above all, national self-reliance, Nehru was poised to shape a new path of economic growth for India away from the prescriptions of either Adam Smith or Karl Marx. To Nehru, communism and democracy represented two antagonistic alternatives in the form of an authoritiarian leviathan and an egalitarian weltanschauung, respectively. Democratic socialism achieved by planning, secularism, or, more correctly, equal rights for all communities in the Indian family, rising standards of living for the masses, and the preservation of individual rights—these were Nehru's fixed objectives.[22] Articulating his convictions later in a speech on the draft outline of the First Five Year Plan, Nehru said, "I doubt if any other plan has been worked out in such close collaboration with various organizations, parties, states, opinions and viewpoints, in fact, with all the elements that go to make up a nation's life. . . . We are dealing with India and not any other country. We should not try to reproduce conditions which obtain elsewhere."[23]

If Nehru's passion for a rational approach and for scientific skepticism, a result of his upbringing and Western education, gave him a distinctive and modernistic character, his close association with Gandhi provided the humanistic and Indian side to his personality. Stalin could justify to Churchill the sufferings experienced by the Russian peasantry in the pursuit of collectivization by proudly proclaiming, "What is one generation?" The Chinese Foreign Minister Chen Yi could declare without remorse, "China will have an atomic bomb even if all Chinese have to go without pants." It was not in Nehru's nature to disregard an individual. "Our plan for future progress," he would say, "must cope with the amalgam and variety we have in India." He stressed, "We are, all of us, working together to make a new India—not abstractly for a nation but for the 360 million people who are wanting to progress as individuals and as groups."[24]

Nehru's ideas about architecture dovetailed into his ideas about India's economic and social planning and deserve to be fully quoted. Speaking at the Seminar and Exhibition of Architecture on March 17, 1959, in New Delhi, almost six years after the official inauguration of Chandigarh, he observed:

> Architecture to a large extent is a product of the age. It cannot isolate itself from the social conditions, the thinking and the objectives and the ideals of the age to which it belongs. . . . [T]he static condition in regard to architecture in India in the last 200 or 300 years . . . really was a reflection of the static condition of the Indian mind or Indian conditions. In fact, India has been static, architecturally considered, for the last few hundred years. The great buildings which we admire date back to an earlier period. We were static even before the British came. In fact, the British came because we were static. A society which ceases to go ahead necessarily becomes weak. This weakness shows itself in all forms of creative activity.
>
> Apart from these basic considerations, the nature of architecture depends on many factors. It depends on climate, obviously. It depends on the type of functions which the people living in the buildings have to perform. It depends on the state of technological growth, and on the material used.
>
> The purpose which a building serves depends to a large extent on the functions which a society performs. There is often a lag between architectural designs, or indeed, the social framework and the changes taking place in the technological field. Gothic cathedrals . . . in many ways were representative of the age in which they grew up. But in the early years of the industrial revolution when the steam engine and the railways came and when railway stations had to be built, the architect tried to make some of the big railway stations look as if they were Gothic cathedrals. They were not able to get out of the clutches of the past. The past was good— but only when it was the present. We cannot bring it forward and put up a Gothic cathedral and call it a railway terminus. I give this

example because there is a tendency to do this kind of thing, more so in a country like India where we hold fast to traditions. No tradition which makes one a prisoner of one's mind or body is ever good.

The architect is obviously limited by his material. If technology gives us more materials and more power to mould those materials, new avenues open up for using them. Today I believe very good work is being done all over the world by creative architects. It is a delight to see plans and designs and pictures of this new work being done. We should not be afraid of innovations.

I have welcomed very greatly one experiment in India, Chandigarh. Many people argue about it, some like it, and some dislike it. It is the biggest example in India of experimental architecture. It hits you on the head, and makes you think. You may squirm at the impact but it has made you think and imbibe new ideas, and the one thing which India requires in many fields is being hit on the head so that it may think. I do not like every building in Chandigarh. I like some of them very much. I like the general conception of the township very much but, above all, I like the creative approach, not being tied down to what has been done by our forefathers but thinking in new terms, of light and air and ground and water and human beings. Therefore, Chandigarh is of enormous importance. There is no doubt that Le Corbusier is a man with a powerful and creative type of mind. For the same reason, he may produce extravagances occasionally but it is better to be extravagant than to be a person with no mind at all.

The social functions of today bear on our architecture. We may not, even if we have the capacity, build a Taj Mahal. It does not fit in with the society of today. In the ultimate analysis a thing which fits in with the social functions is beautiful.[25]

Poised clearly to forge ahead into the modern, technical world, and possessing creative élan and a linear sense of history, it would have been unnatural for Nehru to opt for a typically "Indian" or traditional solution for Chanidgarh. The modern city of Chandigarh would be his legacy to modern, independent India as Fatepur Sikri had been to Akbar in his time. Yet the city would have the Indian essence.

The duality of the man was implicit in his birth and upbringing. There was the romantic Nehru, who found meaning in continuity and tradition; and there was the other Nehru, who was mesmerized by everything modern and scientific and who rebelled against a tradition that held people in ignorance and superstition. On one occasion he rightly observed that "the fundamental problem of India is not Delhi or Calcutta or Bombay but the villages of India, and something has to be done to raise the level of life in villages.... We want to urbanize the village, not take away the people from the villages to the towns. However well we may deal with the towns, the problem of the villages of India will remain for a long time and any social standards that we seek to introduce will be judged ultimately not by what happens in Delhi but in the villages of India."[26] On another occasion, he declared: "While the rest of the world progressed in many ways, we remained Narcissus-like, looking at our own beauty of countenance, our culture and so on, which no doubt had much beauty in them. But even beauty grows old and stagnates." Blaming India's backwardness on her obsession with her faded past, he added: "The moment you, as an individual or as a nation, think that you are wise enough and do not want to learn any further, you are doomed. You stop growing. That was what happened to India, China and the whole of Asia and we suffered from it."[27]

It is easy to see how Nehru's personality influenced the development of Chandigarh. Acutely conscious of his place in history and eager to transform Indian society, he felt obliged to act in all spheres and at every level. Reinforcing India's dependence on Nehru, particularly since 1947, as one of his biographers has noted, was "partly the authoritarian tradition of India, partly Nehru's status as Gandhi's successor, and partly his own towering position among his colleagues."[28] Imperious, but with courtly manners, he alone had the courage, independence, and self-confidence needed to challenge India's past. But despite the generous hope he offered in things modern, even Nehru could not fully repudiate deep-rooted and intricate Indian traditions, and he recognized that. As early as 1948, long before any concrete decisions had been made on the new capital, he cautioned the premier of East Punjab that "the main point in building a city should be to keep the social aspect always in view. This is usually completely forgotten and people think in [terms of] putting up a number of imposing official buildings.... Another point to be borne in mind is that as far as possible the material to be used for construction should be locally available."[29] In the same letter he recommended

Koenigsberger, praising his work for Orissa's capital Bhubaneshwar. Although recognizing India's handicap in town planning, Nehru was stoutly opposed to securing a planner for Chandigarh from the West without first fully exploring the possibilities at home.

It was therefore at Nehru's behest that the East Punjab government simultaneously opened negotiations with Otto Koenigsberger and Albert Mayer. Accordingly, P. N. Thapar, the administrator in charge of the Capital Project, met Koenigsberger at New Delhi on December 13, 1949. Engaged with the development of Faridabad at the time, Koenigsberger was a full-time employee of the government of India. He could therefore be loaned to the Capital Project, saving expenses in salary for the Punjab government. The Punjab government, however, would have to pay his traveling and expense allowances, which would not amount to much. Koenigsberger was interested in the project and promised to complete the master plan within three months, provided the Punjab government could loan him a planning unit. He expressed his preference for working from New Delhi, periodically visiting the Chandigarh site.[30]

Later in the same month, Thapar met Albert Mayer at New Delhi. A graduate of Massachusetts Institute of Technology, Mayer[31] had started his career as a civil engineer in New York City. His early engineering work on commercial and apartment buildings stimulated his interest in architectural designs and layouts, which later led him to become a registered architect. His close association with such eminent architects and planners as Frederick Ackerman, Catherine Bauer, Robert Kohn, Lewis Mumford, Clarence Stein, and Henry Wright shaped his views on urban planning, and he came to regard planning as being more than just physical design of buildings. He came to regard it as a means for creating environments conducive to community life. This led Mayer to become actively involved in President Franklin D. Roosevelt's New Deal program on new federal housing policy—a policy that led to the institution of the United States Housing Authority in 1937. Throughout the 1930s, Mayer was involved in building several housing and community complexes, and in 1935, with Julian Whittlesey, he founded the New York architectural firm of Mayer and Whittlesey (later Mayer, Whittlesey, and Glass).

World War II took Mayer to India as a United States Army civil engineer. Building airfields in Bengal for operations in the China-

Burma-India Theater, Mayer was drawn to Indian life and culture by its seductive character. Drawing on his experience with the New Deal housing policies of the United States government and motivated by his concern for improving rural life in India, Mayer started his Indian career by proposing a program for model villages to the new Congress party government of Pundit Nehru. At the time Thapar approached Mayer, he had already been associated, in addition to the Etawah rural development project in the United Provinces, with several of the postwar town planning projects in India, and had completed, with Municipal Engineer N. V. Modak of Bombay, two preliminary studies for the master plan for Greater Bombay. He had also served as an adviser for the city of Kanpur.

Like Koenigsberger, Mayer welcomed the idea of building a new city from scratch, which at the time was considered an "architect's dream." Considering Koenigsberger's primary commitment to the Faridabad project, his primary training as an architect and not as a town planner, and his difficulty in not having his own planning unit, the East Punjab government, on recommendations from Thapar and Koenigsberger himself, in late December 1949 appointed Albert Mayer to plan Chandigarh.

Mayer offered two different arrangements under which the Punjab government could sign an agreement with him. Both arrangements provided that Mayer would prepare the master plan in America. The difference between the two was that, under the first arrangement, all detail work was to be done by Mayer's staff in New York, and implemented by him and his assistant; under the second arrangement, the detail work was to be done by a planning unit composed of Indian architects and planners under the direct supervision and direction of Mayer. Mayer's fee in the two cases would be $50,000 (rupees 210,000) and $30,000 (rupees 126,000), respectively. Both figures included $10,000 that Mayer might require for consulting any outside experts for the project.[32] Mayer agreed to accept 40 percent of his total fee in rupees. He promised to complete the plan within six months, provided the Punjab government gave quick decisions. His plan would cover an area of fifty square miles, but the detailed planning would be limited to about 8,500 acres. Considering the lesser amount and the benefits of training that would accrue to Indian architects and engineers, the Punjab government opted for the second arrangement with Mayer.

Accompanied by Chief Engineer Varma, Mayer visited Chandigarh on January 11, 1950. He found the site very picturesque and was particularly impressed by the large number of mango groves, which he felt would add to the character of the new city.[33] Accordingly, Mayer promised to return from America in early summer (1950) with different master plans for the Punjab government's selection, while the Indian architects and engineers prepared detailed building plans and made arrangements for the construction work at Chandigarh. Upon his return, Mayer would review the work of the Indians to ensure that it was within the spirit of his own architectural ensemble sketches and would then make necessary revisions.[34]

Assisting Mayer in the preparation of the master plan would be, in addition to his associates Julian Whittlesey and Milton Glass, James Buckley, a consultant in the field of city economics and transportation, Ralph Eberlin, an expert on utilities, roads, and site engineering, Clara Coffey, an expert in landscaping, and H. E. Landsberg, a climatologist. Mayer also requested his good friend Clarence Stein to join the Chandigarh project as a general consultant, but cautioned him against expecting any major compensation for his services as the Indian government "really cannot afford appreciable cost, and even the relatively small number of dollars involved are a terrific effort for them to find."[35] Later, on Stein's recommendation, Matthew Nowicki, the Siberian-born, Warsaw-educated architect, joined the Chandigarh project to work out the problems of architectural design and control. This architect's work, however, remained on paper as he died in a plane crash near Cairo on his way back to America.

Nehru welcomed the selection of Mayer as the planner for Chandigarh and hoped that the new ideas that he would bring with him would help revitalize Indian society. Not everyone in the Indian government shared Nehru's enthusiasm for Mayer's appointment, however. Knowing Nehru's impatience with unpleasant dissent, most critics of Mayer remained discreet about their feelings. But N. V. Gadgil, a member of the Council of Works, Mines and Power, later made a pointed expression of his feelings to Dharam Vira in the Prime Minister's Secretariat: "Mr. Modak, the Special Engineer of the Bombay Corporation has drawn up a Master Plan for Greater Bombay in collaboration with Mr. Mayor [sic] and that Master Plan is, so to say, the basis of the present plan drawn up by Mr. Mayor [sic] for Chandigarh. The only thing is that our Indian Town Planners such as Modak, Joglekar, Manikam, Mehta, Chitale—and there are so many others—are not given to advertise." Gadgil however had the sense of administrative discretion, and added: "This does not mean that the plan drawn up by Mr. Mayor [sic] is nothing. It is quite good."[36]

Somewhat more serious was the diplomatic awkwardness caused to the Indian embassy in London by Mayer's appointment. The Indian embassy in London, on request from the Punjab government, was consulting with several well-known English architects, the most prominent among them being Sir Patrick Abercrombie. Known for masterminding the Greater London Plan, Abercrombie had taught several Indian students and was internationally respected in architectural circles. He had already given his consent to Indian High Commissioner Krishna Menon to undertake the Chandigarh project in preference to other offers, when he was informed of the Punjab government's decision to drop "finalization of agreement" due to economic reasons.

Possibly the matter would not have caused such a diplomatic flurry had Mayer not received widespread publicity in the international press and had the terms of his payment in American dollars not leaked out, which made the explanation of the Punjab government to Abercrombie seem like a bad excuse. Incensed at finding himself in a compromising position, Menon, who was quick to anger, telegraphed his resentment to Nehru: "It is deeply embarrassing for the Government of India and [for] this mission to be placed in this position of respect of a man of the eminence of Ambercrombie."[37] Citing in his letter copious excerpts from the correspondence relating to the selection of Mayer, M. O. Mathai, from the Prime Minister's Secretariat, tried to pacify Menon: "Mr. Albert Mayer, whom you probably know, did not come into the picture as an American contractor. He has been doing rural planning in the U.P. for the past several years. He knows Indian conditions well and brings in a social approach to whatever he undertakes. He has done very well."[38]

Boundless in his enthusiasm for winning the Chandigarh project and excited about the media attention he had received internationally, Mayer sent a brief introductory statement concerning the capital project to Nehru: "[T]he new city will have significance not only for the Punjab but for all India, and indeed for the world. . . . I believe there are two reasons for this kind of universal attention. In the first place we have been able to work out a plan which embodies the aspirations and techniques which have been evolving over the past thirty years and more, but for which no other similar opportunity has yet arisen. In the second place it has seemed to crystalize and dramatize the potential contribution of the 'new' countries."[39] The Indian project was to be the testing ground for ideas that could not freely be applied in the West but for which India provided an uncharted ground. The centerpiece of Mayer's plan was to be a residential neighborhood unit or superblock—a planning device developed in the 1920s through an effort to separate residential areas from automobile traffic—with the overall urban form developing from the multiplication of such units rather than from a single dominant formal concept.

Nehru shared Mayer's vision, but characteristically cautioned him: "In regard to the Punjab Capital, there is one fact to be borne in mind, and I hope it does not come in the way of your general planning. This is to make provision for the displaced persons from West Punjab. There are roughly two types of urban displaced persons. One lot have some resources at their command and given a plot of land can build on it and may even start some small or middle industries. The other lot have no resources, but given tolerably decent housing conditions, may make useful citizens. These Punjabees naturally look forward to finding a place in the new capital and we wish to give them some kind of preference. Also, there is another consideration. If these people find a place there, we can divert some funds from our Rehabilitation Budget for refugees to the new Capital Scheme, provided those funds are used for these displaced persons."[40] Similar concerns for the displaced persons had earlier prompted Nehru to suggest to the Punjab government that, in the likelihood of violent fluctuations in land values that might result from the upheavals and migrations in Punjab, "some ordinance or other legislation might be passed immediately fixing the maximum price for sale of land all over the province at the average price on a particular date."[41]

While Mayer was working on the master plan, the question of sending a couple of Punjab government officials to Europe once again came up and was brought before Nehru for his approval. Once again opposing the idea, Nehru wrote to Chief Minister Gopichand Bhargava, then convalescing after an operation at the government hospital, Amritsar, that he was surprised at the suggestion, and crisply added: "I do not understand how a person touring Europe and America, stopping for a few days at each place, can help in [the Capital Project]. It may be good for the persons concerned from an educational point of view. Specially at this time of acute financial stringency any expenditure that is not absolutely essential might be avoided."[42]

Apparently the idea of studying contemporary architectural designs in Europe and America had been suggested by Mayer to Thapar, who in turn had mentioned it to the chief minister.[43] In making his suggestion, Mayer was probably hoping the experience would provide the government officials with a much-needed sense of architectural understanding—a suggestion which he would later regret.

Always eager to visit Europe, especially after illness, the chief minister had quickly sought Nehru's approval. Irritated by the suggestion, Nehru rebuffed the chief minister. Pacifying Nehru, Governor Trivedi explained: "What we want to do is to send Thapar, the Administrator in charge of the Project, and Varma, the Chief Engineer attached to the Capital Organization, to Europe merely to select one or two good architects. What Mayer has given us is a Master Plan, and one of the architects deputed by him has given us a very detailed layout of one neighbourhood block. What remains to be done is the designing of important buildings like the Secretariat, the High Court, the Government House, the planning of plots in other areas, and the general architectural treatment of various blocks, squares, parks, etc. Our idea is to have an organization consisting of assistant architects and town planners recruited from India, but headed by one or two . . . good architects from abroad. We really cannot get good architects here."[44]

Because the selection of architects involved discussion and negotiations which possibly could not be settled satisfactorily by correspondence, the governor requested Nehru to withdraw his objection. Furthermore, it was not likely that prominent architects from the West would come to India for preliminary talks; and inviting them at government expense would have meant heavy expenditure. Should it be possible to recruit good, full-time architects in England, the governor reassured Nehru, it would not be necessary for Thapar and Varma to go to Europe and the whole exercise could be completed within a week in England itself.

The Punjab government's stress on a visit to England is yet another reminder of the belief that if economic independence follows slowly on political autonomy, cultural independence lags even farther behind.[45] This is because, first, the new elites of the newly independent country are imbued with metropolitan values and, second, the apparatus of the colonial state is not easily dismantled or changed. Despite the natural antipathy that might exist between the decolonized and metropolitan societies, the information channels persist between them and the exchange of personnel goes on. The years of dependence on metropolitan social, political, and cultural models makes it difficult for the decolonized society to find their replacement, especially from its traditional past.

Mayer had provided the master plan for Chandigarh. For designing the government buildings, for planning of plots, and for the general architectural control of the city, the Punjab government had three choices: 1) it could accomplish the task through a government instituted unit, made up of all Indian personnel; 2) it could set up a joint arrangement between the Indian unit and a foreign private firm; or 3) it could farm out the job to a foreign private firm on a certain percentage of cost basis.

The first choice would have been the cheapest, but it required that the Indian unit be headed by an experienced architect-planner. Such an expert, according to the Punjab government, did not exist in India, and therefore had to be hired from the West. The Punjab government rightly concluded that it would be difficult to hire a prominent Western architect for any length of time at a reasonable salary, unless, of course, he was an "idealist."

The second choice seemed more likely to work, and the officials felt that a couple of prominent Western architects could be hired "from America, England, France or Scandinavian countries from about £2,500 to £3,000 a year."[46] This arrangement provided that the preliminary architectural planning of buildings (such as the Secretariat, the Assembly, the Government House, the Town Hall, etc.) and the treatment of a couple of superblocks (such as the shopping center, public parks, residential houses, etc.) were to be entrusted to a foreign firm and the finishing and detailing of the work was to be done by the Indian unit. The cost for this method was estimated at about rupees 7 lakhs for a foreign firm and about another rupees 8 lakhs in local expenditure spread over three years, during which time, it was hoped, most of the designing and planning work would be completed.

The third choice was estimated to be the most expensive at about rupees 40 lakhs, under which most of the work would be done by a foreign firm in its home office, its representatives visiting Chandigarh occasionally. The main disadvantage of this arrangement, it was rightly argued, would be that, beside being expensive, it would not provide full-time architectural supervision to Indians at the time of the construction of the buildings; and any modifications that became necessary, as they do at the time of translating plans into concrete structures, would have to be done by the Indians themselves. Even more important, this would deny the opportunity of training and developing local talent. The Punjab government felt that "it would be a pity if the present opportunity of organizing and developing an architectural 'school' in India was [lost], particularly when the achievement of this objective leads to economy also."[47]

While the subject of hiring an architect-planner from the West was still under discussion, some other events took place, making it possible for Thapar and Varma to visit Europe in search of one. On August 31, 1950, Matthew Nowicki's plane, a TWA Constellation, crashed in Egypt sixty miles from Cairo, leaving Mayer without an architect-assistant. Nowicki's death shocked Mayer and the Punjab government alike, and it became abundantly clear that Mayer would not be able to implement his master plan single-handedly. Experiencing an adverse rate of currency exchange with the United States, the Indian officials decided to take advantage of this situation by procuring Nowicki's replacement in a country where India enjoyed a better rate of exchange. It has been suggested that because of the American dollar the Indian officials not only dropped Mayer from the Chandigarh project like a hot brick but also did not consider Frank Lloyd Wright—Le Corbusier's contemporary rival—and the famous Finnish-born, American-resident Eliel Saarinen.[48]

Nehru was informed about these developments. Somewhat reluctantly giving his permission, Nehru wrote to the chief minister, "In the circumstances I think you might send your officers abroad for [selecting architects] if you think this is necessary."[49] Accordingly, Thapar was instructed to prepare for a four-week trip to Europe, accompanied by Varma. They were to visit the United Kingdom, Holland, France, Italy, Sweden, Belgium, Germany, and Switzerland,[50] and after interviewing several architects, were to hire the most suitable one. The new architect was expected to meet two specific Indian demands: one, that he would be willing to move to India for a period of three years and, two, that he would be willing to accept a yearly salary not to exceed £3,000. Time permitting, Thapar and Varma were further instructed to study the organizational framework for city planning, and the latest research, material, and equipment available for constructing new buildings and townships.[51] The inclusion of the three-year residency-in-India requirement was inspired by the reasoning that, beside being necessary to get the city under way, it would provide the necessary on-the-job training to Indians in the theoretical approaches and working methods of an experienced designer.

The entire European trip was to cost the Indian government rupees 15,000, excluding salaries of Thapar and Varma. Nearly half the amount was to be paid in rupees for air passages, the remainder to be paid in foreign exchange. Except for one minor obstacle, when Secretary of Economic Affairs K. G. Ambegaokar from the Finance Ministry objected to the expenditure in foreign currency which had not been approved by his department—an error which was subsequently corrected[52]—all arrangements for the trip went off smoothly. With Mayer's plans and detailed budget for Chandigarh under their arms, Thapar and Varma left India on November 5, 1950.

Indian missions abroad, on instructions from the External Affairs Ministry, had already made the necessary arrangements of identifying prospective candidates for the job through architectural institutes and local government agencies. Trained in the colonial bureaucratic tradition, the Punjab government officials thought this to be the most efficient way of screening the applicants. Not everyone agreed, however. Pointing to the drawbacks of this technique, the English architect B. Lubetkin wrote to Dr. C. L. Katial, director general of the Employees State Insurance Corporation, New Delhi: "I . . . doubt . . . the soundness of the technique of finding a suitable architect through such official channels; I take it that the government of East Punjab wants to create buildings of a bold contemporary character, incorporating all the latest achievements of architecture, art and science, and combining them with a dignity fitting to the purpose they are to serve. If that is their aim, then it seems to me that they are going about it in the worst possible way by approaching the official institute, where only superannuated ideas and personalities are likely to be recommended." He added, "If above all they

want to play safe, and aim at complete insignificance, then probably they will achieve their purpose."[53]

On the other hand, Thapar and Varma had the difficult task of convincing a brilliant designer to move to India at a ridiculously low salary for three years. Moreover, there were enough reconstruction programs in progress throughout war-ravaged Europe to keep most architects gainfully employed for a long time. First Secretary P. L. Bhandari in the Indian embassy, the Hague, had the wisdom to recognize this fact. Accordingly, he advised Thapar that it might be more suitable to appoint a consulting architect, who would initially visit India for an extended period but would return to Punjab periodically, leaving "practical details in the hands of one or two assistant chief architects."[54] The assistant chief architects would remain in India until the completion of the project. This was a valuable suggestion and was to prove useful for Thapar and Varma in their negotiations.

Their first stop in Rome proved unsuccessful in finding an architect willing to commit himself to Chandigarh for three years. In Paris, Auguste Perret declined to leave France because of his involvement in Le Havre (Saint-Malo) reconstruction. Their disappointment was beginning to mount, when French Minister of Reconstruction and Urbanization M. Claudius Petit (1948–53) first recommended Le Corbusier. The minister also recommended the inclusion of Pierre Jeanneret, Corbusier's cousin and a longtime associate, in the team, describing him as a "good detail man."[55] At the time, rumor has it, the two architects had been estranged over a woman they both liked. The Chandigarh project would mitigate their human differences and rekindle the spirit of cooperation in which they had worked together in "perfect friendship" on several projects.

When Thapar and Varma first knocked on the door at 35 rue de Sèvres in Paris on a bleak November day, Le Corbusier's initial reaction to the Indian proposal was negative. At age sixty-three, he was already weary of disappointments from his unrealized schemes, and he strongly doubted the chances of success for the Indian project. He was equally contemptuous of the proposed honorarium and the time allowed for the completion of the city. When the Indians proposed the idea of moving to India for three years to build the city, Le Corbusier retorted, "Your capital can be built right here; we, at 35 rue de Sèvres, are perfectly capable of finding the solution to the problem."[56] A man with a profound ego and full of dreams, he had been working out a revolutionary philosophy of town planning—a philosophy of "sun, space and quiet"—but had never been offered the opportunity of building a city from scratch. Later, when Thapar and Varma saw Le Corbusier's housing development (called a *unité d'habitation*) in Marseilles, their own enthusiasm for the man faltered and they questioned the applicability of his ideas to India.

With matters left unresolved with Le Corbusier, Thapar and Varma arrived in London. Their reception by the Indian high commissioner, who had not yet forgotten the embarrassment caused him by the Punjab government, was lukewarm. However, in London they called on the office of Edwin Maxwell Fry and his wife Jane Beverly Drew. They asked the architect-couple to supervise and organize the architectural aspects of the Mayer plan. Fry found the plan well advanced, demonstrating the clear intentions of the government to construct a modern city on a site selected to serve the state at the highest level of design and execution, setting a new standard for India.[57]

Imbued with the new revolutionary architectural spirit of the 1930s that called for a functional analysis as preceding the act of creation, which was codified in the Charter of Athens by CIAM (Congrès Internationaux d'Architecture Moderne), the husband-and-wife team had already spent a considerable time in West Africa developing architecture suitable for "heavy rain, high humidity and mosquitoes."[58] Using the CIAM approach, their architectural designs in West Africa incorporated the dominant factors of the local climate, economy, and social customs. The Indian project offered yet another opportunity for the application of their revolutionary ideas. However, Fry and Drew had different responses to make to the Indians.

Impulsive by nature and romantic at heart, Jane Drew was enthusiastic about the new capital and wanted to go to India.[59] A conservative pragmatist, Fry, on the other hand, was not enthusiastic about dropping everything and decamping to India for three years. "I was slightly prejudiced against India and Indians," he later reminisced, "and half-wished that they [Indians] had not arrived in my life to upset the plans I had for building, after a long interval, in England."[60] Fry and Drew were already committed to the Inter-University-sponsored Ibadan University project in Nigeria, and Drew had an additional involvement in the Festival of Britain program. For Jane Drew, who courted challenge in her profession with passion, the opportunity was too tempting to let go. Finally, on the intervention of Sir Alexander Carr-Saunders, head of the Inter-University Council and chief client of Fry and Drew, they were freed from their commitment to the Ibadan University project, delegating their responsibilities to Lindsay Drake and Denys Lasdun.[61] Drew, however, could not leave for a few months as she felt bound to finish her share in the Festival of Britain program.

This put the Indians "in the dilemma of having two jobs to offer with only one filled."[62] Determined to fill both posts before returning to India, promising to accommodate Drew in the project when she later arrived at Chandigarh, and viewing the advantages of hiring a team of architects as opposed to a single architect, Thapar and Varma at this point asked Fry for the first time what would be the effect of introducing Le Corbusier to the team. "Honour and glory for you," reparteed Fry, "and an unpredictable portion of misery for me. But I think it is a noble way out of the present difficulties."[63] Fry later conjectured that "if Jane Drew and I had been able to drop every other obligation and had accepted the appointments, Le Corbusier would not have been approached."[64] However, "reflecting on the immensity of the architectural program for a three-year contract" and thinking "the Capitol group of buildings would be a fitting commission for the great man,"[65] Fry accepted the inclusion of Le Corbusier in the team. Temperamentally, however, the two architects were to remain separated during their work at Chandigarh, their differences bridged by the presence of the agreeable Jane Drew.

Jane Drew, who had first met Le Corbusier at the CIAM meeting at Bridgewater in 1947 and had developed a bond of friendship with him,[66] offered to phone him to arrange a meeting in Paris. Early in December, Thapar and Varma, accompanied by Fry and Drew, met Le Corbusier once again at his office. Considering the potential of creating a city and finding the opportunity of finally implementing his life-long ideas, Le Corbusier by this time had had time to review the Indian project. He had also been encouraged by Claudius Petit, the French minister, to undertake the project. But he would not accept the assignment without the inclusion of his cousin Pierre Jeanneret, with whom he had apparently been reconciled by this time. Thapar and Varma, after some hesitation, agreed.

On December 3, 1950, Thapar communicated the outcome of the negotiations to the chief minister of Punjab in a telegram. The agreement that followed provided a three-year contract with Maxwell Fry, Jane Drew, and Pierre Jeanneret to serve as senior architects at Chandigarh at yearly salaries of £3,000 each; Le Corbusier was appointed architectural adviser, with a yearly salary of £2,000, plus furnished transportation and £35 in daily expenses while he was in India, subject to a maximum of £4,000 per year (including honorarium). He was to receive, additionally, 4 percent of the cost of any building he designed.[67] In return, he was to make two visits of one month duration to India each year and design the buildings in the Capitol Complex. Altruism was clearly a strong motive for these noble men to undertake the challenge of the Chandigarh project. As Le Corbusier later put it: "It had to be decided that there would be no financial gain, but instead we would give all our time, all our hearts, all our energy, all our knowledge."[68] The sentiment was endorsed by Maxwell Fry, who gave up a £40,000-a-year practice in England to go to India: "What attracted us in these men [Varma and Thapar] who visited us and made us throw aside what we were doing to go to India and work for them on the site was the mixture of idealism with what I hold to be the divine principal of energy with which they put their case."[69] As time was to show, however, the coalition of four Western architects was not to be harmonious, and their conflicts with the Indians nearly jeopardized the project.

If Le Corbusier and Fry showed initial hesitation about working in India, there were other European architects who actively sought the assignment. In Belgium, for example, M. Lacoste actively, but unsuccessfully, negotiated with the Indian embassy.[70] Although Chandigarh held out no remunerative rewards, it offered the chance to realize a dream of creating a city. Regardless of the outcome, Chandigarh promised a place in the history of city building to all those connected with it. Each aspiring architect viewed the potential of Chandigarh from his own vantage point. The English architect Clive Entwistle best explained his and perhaps the interest of others in Chandigarh, when he wrote to Thapar, "The fact that India offers the best possible resources for the initiation of what has become a chief preoccupation of mine, which is 'mass-building' or building with volunteer labour organized on a big scale."[71] Although his ideas were never implemented in Chandigarh, they were used in a limited way in some other Indian refugee towns and found a fuller, though modified and thus far unsuccessful, expression thirty years later in Arcosanti—a city in the Arizona desert, seventy miles north of Phoenix, designed by the Italian-born visionary Paolo Soleri.

Meanwhile, not aware of the new arrangements between the Punjab government and Le Corbusier and Fry, and eager to implement his plan, Mayer wrote to Thapar inquiring about the Punjab government's decision, and added, "Of course we are anxious to do the work."[72] To his disappointment, Mayer was informed that a group of new architects had been engaged, but as a reassurance was told that all architects hired endorsed the principles of his plan.[73] This, however, was not to be the case. Le Corbusier introduced his own ideas, retaining nevertheless all the distinctive features of the Mayer plan. Although Mayer's association with India continued intermittently until 1960, his role in Chandigarh was overshadowed by the indomitable and eclectic personality of Le Corbusier—a personality that meshed well with that of Prime Minister Nehru. Mayer did put up a good fight to keep his plan intact, but Le Corbusier, who endowed every aspect of his life and work with high drama, intense fatalism, and mythic size, eventually prevailed. With Mayer reduced to a simple footnote in the history of Chandigarh, it would be Le Corbusier who would be popularly remembered as the creator of the city. Like the two men, the two master plans were to be interpreted differently.

·3·
THE MAYER PLAN

Albert Mayer's master plan for Chandigarh was to convert fifty square miles of rich agricultural land, famous for its lush mango groves, into the modern equivalent of the *to kinon asti*, the glorious city. Just as Mayer's early experiences in India were to influence his personality, so too his American training and experiences were to leave an indelible mark on his master plan for Chandigarh. But Mayer was not the first American to receive the rare commission of building a planned capital city overseas. American architect Walter Burley Griffin before him drew up the plans for Australia's Canberra, which replaced a sheep station in a wide, shallow river valley. Unfortunately for Mayer, however, fate was to deny him this claim. Coming first in contact with India as an officer in the United States Army Corps of Engineers in World War II, he was nevertheless to become one of India's strongest supporters in America.

Brought up and educated in a society enjoying a relative absence of hereditary or arbitrary class distinctions or privilege, Mayer, like most Americans, believed in geographic and social mobility as an article of American faith. Even though segregated ethnic neighborhoods in American cities—Irish, Italian, Jewish, Polish, black, Latino, and Asian—continue to serve as constant reminders of the imperfect implementation of this belief, Mayer found the segregationist thinking of most Westerners in the already caste-structured Indian society unacceptable. Recounting his early military days in India, he noted that Americans in India, in the overwhelming majority of cases, experienced an increase in their national and Anglo-Saxon feeling of superiority and isolationism. And the British generally had their sense of insularity reinforced. "Too many Americans came back with less sympathy for India, and certainly with less understanding of it, than they had before they went." Although endorsing the preventive measures taken by Americans to avoid illness or epidemic, he felt that most Americans in India lived "in a sort of *cordon sanitaire* . . . becoming virtual hypochondriacs." He blamed the United States Army and the Red Cross for deliberately creating and preserving "an all-American atmosphere."[1]

Unwilling to confine himself either to the "all-American atmosphere" or to the "foreigners' clubs," Mayer, by independent efforts, which were neither supported by the ruling British-India government nor encouraged by the local American army authorities, sought out "friendly" Indians.[2] It was Mayer's Indian friend Humayun Kabir, a nationalist Muslim, who first arranged a meeting in 1945, shortly before Mayer's scheduled departure for America, with Pundit Jawaharlal Nehru, who was destined to become India's first prime minister.

At Nehru's invitation, Mayer spent a few days at Anand Bhavan, Nehru's ancestral home in Allahabad. Reminiscing about his meetings with Nehru, which many times lasted late into the night, Mayer noted that he, prompted by "American habit," offered his services to India after her "inevitable freedom" at the end of the war—a sentiment in agreement with John Quincy Adams' declaration that America was "the well-wisher to the freedom and independence of all," but in violation of Adams' injunction that America "is the champion and vindicator only of her own." Mayer proposed to try out various pilot projects just as fast as they could be thoroughly thought out, formulated, and carried out to prepare for a "later big, inevitable program" after independence.[3] Most of the projects proposed by Mayer were based on the methods used by the extension services of the United States Department of Agriculture.

It was at one of these meetings that Mayer was to receive his first object lesson in Indian culture—a lesson which was to make him more sensitive to Indian life and was to prove useful in his many Indian projects. At Nehru's urging, he accompanied Nehru's daughter, Indira, to Kamala Nehru Hospital, erected in memory of Nehru's wife. Returning from his tour, he exclaimed to Nehru that he was unable to see how patients could get any rest while their relations and friends "swarmed noisily in the corridors." On later reflection he apologized to Nehru for his rash and insensitive remarks, realizing that "if this practice were not permitted, the Indian people, with their close family feeling, would simply be frightened of coming [to the hospital]." He even considered "that there might be something, after all, in this Indian practice that we might adapt over here [in America], where our hospital atmosphere is often too rigorous, sterilized, and boring to the patient." He admitted "how obtuse a foreign observer may be even though his attitude and intention are sympathetic, and how willing and even anxious Nehru is for criticism, even when it is fairly foolish, as mine was."[4]

After discussing with Nehru "the possibility of starting . . . some 'model' villages which would emphasize good housing, sanitation, and community structure," Mayer returned to New York to settle down to his work. Six months later, Nehru wrote Mayer inviting him "to build up community life on a higher scale without breaking up the old foundations" of India. "We want to utilize [Western technology]," Nehru continued, "and fit it into Indian resources and Indian conditions." Nehru admitted that this was "not an easy matter, for the resources are limited at present and the conditions are often very different from those in Western countries." But he added that "from the talks we had in Allahabad I feel that not only your technical knowledge and experience, but even more so your psychological approach to these problems will be of great help." Pointing out that "the average American might well feel disgusted with many things in India which are entirely new to him and which do not fit in with his scheme of life," Nehru felt that Mayer "will not feel that way." He cautioned Mayer, however, that "just at the beginning some people, used to the old type of authoritarian British expert, who neither understood nor cared to understand Indian conditions, might view any foreign intrusion with some suspicion. Our people have naturally developed a number of complexes during these past generations of foreign rule and foreign exploitation. But we can get over them given the chance."[5]

Returning to India in the fall of 1946, Mayer thus wrote: "The number and kinds of people I've seen; their ability, outlook, energy, and devotion; the tingling atmosphere of plans and expectations and uncertainty; and yet the calm and self-possession—what it adds up to is being present at the birth of a nation."[6] By the end of that year, however, he was to write home to his American friends: "I am still blowing hot and cold on my prospects of accomplishment, sometimes actually glowing with excitement (not often), more often, and more realistically, depressed at the prospects."[7] The depressing factors for Mayer were absence of trained personnel in India, lack of enthusiasm among Indians, and a sense of personal inadequacy. Equally depressing was his experience with Indian bureaucracy, notorious for its delays and lack of action. Working against such odds he wondered whether it was possible to launch and maintain a scheme which required much longer investigation than he had time or resources to conduct and which demanded greater commitment from its participants.

Even before his meeting with Nehru, Mayer had expressed his detailed thoughts on postwar planning in India in a seminar paper read at a meeting in 1944 in Calcutta. Mayer noted that, because India was about to start planning, it could profit from the experiences of other countries. In addition to suggesting "specific" planning for India because of her diversity, Mayer recommended training design and building technicians by either sending them to the West or inviting Western instructors to India and developing methods of building cheaply to meet Indian conditions. "While the foreigner has the handicap of lacking intimate knowledge . . . of a local culture," Mayer noted, "I believe you will in any case need some of them." This was because, according to him, there was a vast difference between "large-scale thinking," which the Indians were thoroughly able to do, and "large-scale planning-execution," for which Indians lacked the actual experience. Citing the example of Russia as a country that had to depend on foreign experts, Mayer noted that in the Indian case, "the number, the type, the length of time you need them will depend on how many people you have, how many you develop and how quickly you develop them."[8]

Trained as an architect and town planner, Mayer recognized that his assignment of planning new villages in India rather than towns in the West would involve new sets of factors to be taken into consideration. Even more formidable was "the disparity between what they [Indians] expect and what I believe I can do," Mayer wrote, adding that he "realistically considered telling them my deep doubts, apologizing, and going home." He was honest in admitting to his lack of experience and grounding in India as his major handicap, noting that "what others have accomplished or failed to accomplish seems to be due to much larger factors in the social and economic conditions than I can possibly control or influence, and which I don't know that I thoroughly grasp"[9]—a sentiment which stands in marked contrast to what Corbusier would say later.

Despite the odds, Mayer was to remain undeterred in his efforts for the development of India. That he was genuinely concerned for the welfare of India and understood her potential importance in world affairs is reflected in his detailed note to Ralph Chapman of the *New York Herald Examiner*. Lamenting the American indifference toward India, Mayer noted: "By far the largest chunk of our Asian help—which is fairly small in total anyway—is going to Indo-China. India is of course twenty times as large, twenty times as influential, desperately in need of just the kind of help we are best at supplying. . . . While they are certainly not going to rubber stamp our foreign policy and while their picture of domestic democracy differs in detail from ours, there is no question that Nehru's government is trying to tread the path of determined democratic gradualism." He continued, "We will not be able to get the military or equivalent *quid pro quo* on the dotted line that our present pattern seems to inevitably tie up with our help, but the value of a free gesture from us—the value to us, to India, and to the world—will be far greater and more electrifying than any well-negotiated bargain."[10] That his plea has remained unheeded has been unfortunate for both countries.

As it turned out, however, Mayer's first assignment in India was not to the remote villages but to the city of Kanpur, largest urban center in Uttar Pradesh. The population of Kanpur had tripled during World War II when it became one of the most important industrial centers in India. Kanpur urgently needed planning to be saved from "chaos and overcrowding." In addition, there existed a book of postwar projects over three hundred pages long, proposed by the various departments of the Uttar Pradesh government. Thus, Mayer spent "the early autumn of 1946 . . . in laying down outlines of a master plan for the city of Kanpur, in preparing proposals for a provincial housing and town planning office, and in other tasks concerned with urban growth and reconstruction."[11] He was, however, later able to free himself by recommending Dudley Trudgett to the Uttar Pradesh government as its provincial town planner.

During this time, Mayer also met with Mahatma Gandhi and received "his blessing" for the rural project in Uttar Pradesh. However, he found Gandhi's program for reviving cottage industry, especially hand-spinning and weaving, "archaic." He found the whole cottage industry sick and in dire need of drastic remedies to be restored to a "viable mode of production." Mayer also studied the works of missionaries in India, and examined some of their technical contributions: hospitals in Fatehgarh and Vellore, modern elementary and secondary schools at Moga in Punjab, a social contribution in the Indian village service of Uttar Pradesh, and others, all of which were to influence him. At the end of these three months of exploration, he emerged a much wiser man about India. However, it would be another three years before he would get the Chandigarh assignment.

Before his Indian assignments, Mayer had designed Fort Greene Houses, Bellmawr Housing for Mutual Defense Homes Division, and New Rochelle public housing projects; and as a consulting architect, he had been responsible for many of the best features of a New Haven Housing Authority project. He had also served as a consultant to USHA (United States Housing Authority), FWA (Federal Works Agency—abolished in 1949), and the New York State Housing Division. He had been a member of the Committee on Post-War Housing, the National Association of Housing Officials, and had served as a director of the National Public Housing Conference. He had also edited the special housing issue of *Survey Graphic* and contributed articles to the *New York Times*, *American City*, *Architectural Forum*, and other publications. Mayer's concern with the city had developed slowly out of a private interest—his experience as a builder of individual New York apartment houses, making small innovations under the municipal and financial conditions that limit success in this field. It was only after 1930 that his sense of public responsibility turned from private philanthropies to the public offices of housing and city design.

The Second World War had introduced Mayer, first, to wide areas in the United States as a consultant on wartime housing, and, later, to Africa and India. Before Nehru brought him to India to look freshly at Indian villages and plan their development, Mayer had worked with Henry Wright, Allen Kamstra, and Henry Churchill on the design of Greenbrook, one of the projected Greenbelt communities of the second Roosevelt administration. A prolific writer, Mayer recorded the story of the planning of Greenbrook,[12] which provides insight into his later works. He was to use his experiences from Greenbrook, first in 1950, with Matthew Nowicki, to prepare the first master plan of Chandigarh, thus giving to Le Corbusier, who replaced him, his first initiation into the principles of the Radburn plan—the neighborhood idea, the separation of pedestrians and vehicles—and later, with Clarence Stein as consultant, to design the new "aluminum-manufacturing town," Kitimat, in British Columbia, and Maumelle in Arkansas.

Through his prolific writings, Mayer started articulating his thinking early in his career, all of which culminated at the end of his career in his book *The Urgent Future* (1967), which Lewis Mumford characterized as being "not merely an able treatise on contemporary city planning, but a vital contribution to the politics of regional development."[13] Although respecting Patrick Geddes' warning, "survey before planning," Mayer also recognized that a total reliance on the statistical method can only be exercised at the peril of ignoring the lessons of history. Writing on the failure of American cities and the challenges of building new communities during the war years, Mayer noted:

> There are two reasons for the failure. In the case of most architects, their education and previous practice has not equipped them for this work. However big the previous job—whether skyscraper, museum, state capital or small houses—it has always been one building or two buildings, within an existing framework of streets, grades, sewers, roads. Now we are called on to create the very framework itself—the grading, the roads, the street layout, the traffic, the sewers, the water, and the whole civic ensemble. *This is as difficult an undertaking, mentally and technically, as there is*. But—and this is the second reason as I see it—the architect blithely takes on the most serious and important job of his life or of his generation, never questions *his* ability to handle it, doesn't pre-qualify himself by serious study of other projects or of the desires and aims and backgrounds of the people he's serving, and doesn't feel the need of associating himself with someone who knows a good deal about it: though if he had the far simpler job of a school or a hospital to design he would almost certainly employ an experienced consultant as his first step![14]

Looking at American cities in the early 1940s, Mayer identified four basic problems germane to all of them. First, he blamed inflated land prices for the land-crowding tradition. As a solution he recommended "open spaces, green spaces, good light and good view in our homes and offices." He made a strong case for providing a greenbelt of forest, agricultural land, parks, and golf courses for new towns because, according to him, a) it limits the ultimate growth of the towns to avoid the social defects and wastes in municipal plant common to the indefinitely growing city, and b) it also keeps the residents in reasonably close reach of the countryside. Second, he blamed the cities for not properly developing and exploiting the types of amenities peculiar to them—the out-of-door places where "people can meet and dine." He urged the use of "hedges, window boxes, street trees, backyard planting" as city developers' gadgets for achieving urban livability. Third, he blamed the automobile for widening "roadways in the centers of our cities, [narrowing] sidewalks and generally [bumping] the pedestrian around." To make room for pedestrian traffic on downtown streets, Mayer recommended that the pressure of automobile traffic be relieved by supplying off-street parking and loading facilities. Fourth, on the basis of the Radburn plan, he made a strong case for a well-integrated community with nearby shopping and service facilities, easily available recreation, and the opportunity to live near one's work, claiming that these features help create "a socially and economically stable neighborhood."[15]

Mayer's conviction in his beliefs was to be reflected in all his works, including Chandigarh. Although proclaiming "to create a thoroughly Indian city and thoroughly modern city," he noted that "the neighborhood concept is ... even more [valuable] in India where so many people are villagers at heart." He continued: "The nature of our neighborhood is intimate. The local shopping centre preserves, as far as we can [be] consistent with orderly development to do so, the excitement and gaiety of the bazaar—the people undisturbed by traffic in their social preoccupation with shopping and visiting."[16]

His neighborhood superblock, with its elementary schools, shopping centers, playgrounds, sitting parks, and with its thousand or so families, was to be one element in a three-block unity, called the district or an "urban village." Each superblock was to cover a rectangle approximately 3,000 feet long and 1,500 feet wide. The three-block district, containing about 3,500 families, was to provide local public buildings, boys' and girls' high schools, health center, and a town square "very much the same as the market square of the medieval town." The reason, Mayer explained, "is that the functions are much the same, meeting, gossiping, shopping, listening to speeches."[17]

In addition to the above facilities, the district was to contain a pool, whose reflecting beauty and sense of coolness are such a heavenly gift in the Eastern tropics. Only footpaths and bicycle and bullock-cart paths were to cross the superblocks, all the automated vehicular traffic going around them. For direct traffic to the capital from outside the city, two wide highways, called greenways, were to run from end to end of the city. A rivulet running through the valley was to be dammed at one end for a lake, in which would be reflected the capitol buildings. The ultimate town was to be built up from the three-block districts.

In essence, Mayer was validating in his Chandigarh plan the principles that he had already tried at Greenbrook, and to a limited extent, in Kanpur and Bombay. While working on the plan for Greater Bombay—a plan that he prepared with Municipal Engineer N. V. Modak and American traffic engineer W. J. Cox—Mayer had described the use of a neighborhood idea suitable for "any new area [or] replanning of any old area."[18] The casual variety of his plan was meant to avoid the monotony often sensed in planned cities. The purpose of his plan was to provide a framework in which people could carry on their corporate activities and yet satisfy their need for serenity and individuality. Starting in Chandigarh with "just a blank sheet of paper," Mayer noted that "we can do as wonderfully or as badly as we can. It's an architect's dream."[19] Never losing sight of the American city, Mayer declared on May 10, 1950, in Washington, D.C., before an august audience of planners and architects, his aims for Chandigarh:

> In a modern advanced country . . . [like] the U.S.A. . . . we are so surrounded by vested achievement, by so many facts and figures and well-developed techniques, so many highly developed technical means of one kind or another, that we are almost never able to shake ourselves loose from them, not able to put them out of the way while we concentrate on ends and objectives, not able to consider calmly and think completely through. We can in a sense really only improve. We cannot re-shape things entire and mold them to the heart's desire. And if we are not very careful, we even get further confused by piling complicated ingenious means on top of each other, still further burying the ultimate causes and objectives. I need only call your attention to the futility of our superhighways and our 3-level crossings, which never for more than a short time catch up with themselves. You all know of our hand-

some parkways in the New York region. What you may not know is that various organizations have published directions on how to avoid them because they are overcrowded. These detours are of course the poor old inferior roads they replaced.

In planning *de novo* as we are doing in India, we are free to formulate ideas and objectives as clearly and boldly as our creative spirit permits. We call in facts and techniques as we find we need them, and in sequence with our developing thought and study —but they are simply handy tools; they do not clutter up our thinking. . . .

We want to create a beautiful city. . . . Since the City Beautiful concept was thrown out fifty years ago, and the functionalists and the sociologists took over, the concept of a large and compelling and beautiful unity has not been enriched by these important later additional and integral concepts, but has rather been replaced. . . . We have creatively fused them, but we are unabashedly seeking beauty. . . .

Can anybody who has studied our proposed new civic centers here—such as for example Foley Square in New York, or the Chicago Civic Center, seriously claim that they have an abiding harmony or sense of scale or humanity. . . . We have turned to some of the great exemplars—to the Concorde in Paris, the Piazza San Marco, St. Peter's, and studied them . . . to extract the essence.

Our basic purpose is to create a sense of pride in the citizens, not only in this his own city, but in India, its past and its potential imminent future. . . . We are seeking symbols, to restore or to create pride and confidence in [the Indian] himself and in his country.[20]

Chandigarh was thus to represent beauty and serve as a symbol of pride for "frustrated" Punjabis. It was not to be "a city of bold winged engineering and cantilevers, but a city in the Indian idiom fused with modern simplicity, functional honesty and imaginative sweep."[21] By this time Mayer had acquired enough experience in India to feel confidently that, as a Westerner, he was uniquely suited to accomplish these objectives. Believing that practically all "forward-looking" Indians educated in the West were still dazzled by Western ideas and lacked the cultural self-confidence and self-understanding to do Indian work, he declared, "We can really enter into their [Indians'] spirit."[22] One overriding thought comes to mind from Mayer's remarks in Washington: Because Chandigarh was to be planned from the very beginning, it was to cast a light on work in the United States, illuminating and clarifying "the very basis of things which over here [in America] are so heavily overlaid with vested achievement that we don't recognize them.... Thus, if President Truman's Point IV [program] ever eventuates, we will find we are not entirely on the giving and instructing end, but if we are sensitive we shall get as good as we give."[23]

Considering the responsibility of creating a city and its far-reaching consequences for both India and the world for generations to come, Mayer decided to enlist the support of the best available minds in city building in the United States. In addition to his partners, Julian Whittlesey and Milton Glass, helping Mayer were Clarence Stein, James Buckley, Ralph Eberlin, Clara Coffey, and Matthew Nowicki. Of special significance were the services of microclimatologist H. E. Landsberg. Through him, Mayer hoped to achieve in Chandigarh what Major L'Enfant had failed to accomplish in Washington: an arrangement of buildings that will catch any stray breeze, providing much-needed relief from the scorching sun.

By arranging the buildings so as to minimize the harshness of climate, Mayer was hoping to avoid the costly benefits of artificial ventilating, air conditioning, and heating systems. Working closely together in the initial stages of planning—a method which Mayer termed "holistic"—the members of the Mayer team sought to avoid the "over-scale sterility and stiltedness of New Delhi and the overmonumentality of Washington, D.C." One aspect of their design was "to provide a looseness and tolerance in the plan to allow for a future [growth] that can never be entirely imagined from the past or the present."[24] Moreover, not knowing "what forms or to what degree services to citizens will increase as India develops her resources and adds to her wealth so as to be able to give to its people the kind of life and opportunity its leaders wish to," Mayer reasoned that Chandigarh "must allow open spaces and interstitial spaces for unknown future buildings and functions."[25]

The master plan that Mayer finally produced was based on two principles, both of which were widely prevalant at the time in America. First, the basic unit was to be the neighborhood, the groupings and the variations of which were synthesized into the city. Second, the elements of site, topography, and location in the region were to determine the overall character of the city—the road system, the location of the main architectural and functional foci, the park system, and so forth. As a third consideration, the plan was to give sufficient importance to direct observations of the region and its people. As such, the plan had to provide for locally heavy bicycle traffic, schools of different sizes, the main business district—and other needs which "flow from functional and statistical studies and experience in . . . North India."[26] However, absence of any substantial scientific, statistical, and demographic data was to remain an inherent drawback for the planners.

Fan-shaped in outline with the handle end to the north to contain all the government buildings as well as Punjab University, the Mayer plan placed the town between the two rivers. A large business district was placed in the center of the city so that when the city expanded southward it would continue to maintain a central position. A smaller industrial area was set aside to the southeastern side of the city and was connected to the Kalka-Ambala railway line. As opposed to a gridiron pattern, a curving network of main streets adapted to the existing terrain surrounded the residential superblocks. To be completed in about five years to accommodate a population of 150,000, the first phase of the city was designed for the northerly portion of the site. In its second phase, the city was designed to expand southward, ultimately accommodating 500,000 people. The detailed work in the Mayer plan, however, was confined to an area of approximately eight thousand acres. It was estimated that ten thousand workmen would be needed to complete the first phase of the city at a cost of rupees 10 crores.

The houses in the plan were concentrated in superblocks, and were graded according to L (lower), M (middle), and U (upper) income groups, with population densities of seventy-five, fifty, and twenty-five persons per acre, respectively. Considering the high cost of streets, water and sewer and electric lines that a modern city requires, it was argued that the old practice of providing large bungalows for the well-to-do could only be met by depriving the poorer areas of these facilities and by drastically curtailing their space allotments. Accordingly, it was provided that in the new capital private sites would be restricted to one acre. Compared to the prevailing densities of population in other Indian cities, including New Delhi, this was to be a most liberal arrangement. However, the houses were to be so designed that a second story could be added later when the owner could afford it. The houses were confined to the outer edges of the residential neighborhoods, leaving the centers free for playgrounds, parks, and agricultural plots.

Taking into account the strong sunlight in India, "the variation of streets, offsetting and breaking from narrow into wider and back," seemed to Mayer an important element of planning. At the narrow points, the house design prepared by Mayer involved an inner court for ventilation, so that there were only small openings on the street side and privacy was not invaded. "We loved this little inner courtyard," Mayer wrote to Maxwell Fry, "for it seemed to us to bring the advantages of coolness and dignity into a quite small house." Another element in planning was "to place a group of houses around a not very large court, with the ends somewhat narrowing, which could serve as a social unit—i.e., a group of relatives or friends or people from the same locality might live there, with the central area for play, gossip, etc."[27] The neighborhood units were to contain schools and local shopping centers.

The Mayer plan seems to reflect, it has been rightly suggested, "the romantic picturesque tradition of civic design which originated in the nineteenth century as part of a reaction against . . . the sterility and monotony of the classical-geometric approach to planning."[28] What this amounted to was the discrediting of the geometric grid, which had become the favored device for laying out cities during the rapid growth of industrialization, in favor of a picturesque aesthetic and an updating of Camillo Sitte's nineteenth-century *Town Planning According to Artistic Principles*. "Sitte had proposed that the architect should compose the city like a Beethoven symphony; it should become a great dramatic experience to walk through a sequence of urban spaces pulsating in scale on either side, mixing new with old, monuments with parks, all unfolding on a series of axes and contained vistas into exploding crescendi."[29]

City space was to be contained, not fragmented. This philosophy, combined with the English Garden City Movement, became the major orthodoxy and mode of design, expressions of which in the United States are reflected in Radburn (1929) and the Greenbelt towns of the 1930s. These examples, together with the Los Angeles suburb Baldwin Hills—a superblock development of 1941—were to serve as inspirations for Mayer, whose humane ideals seemed to spring from his almost antiurban aesthetic. Mayer's complete nexus of attitudes fully culminated in his Chandigarh plan. If the economic stringency of the Great Depression and the subsequent disruption caused by the war years had restricted Mayer in giving full expression to his ideas at Greenbrook, the Chandigarh experience at the beginning of the 1950s offered the opportunity of fully realizing "all those creative elements in city planning and civic design which [had] been discovered and talked about . . . for the last generation."[30]

The problem of planning for an efficient, convenient, and safe transportation system had particularly concerned Mayer in America, where there is mainly one type of vehicular traffic with essentially the same speed characteristics. In India, where modes of transportation vary from automobiles to bicycles to animal-drawn carts, each with varying speeds, the problem of traffic presented an even greater challenge to Mayer. To meet this challenge, he devised a "three-fold system."

First, by arranging land use for living, business, industry, and entertainment, and by providing self-contained neighborhoods and districts, he sought to minimize the impact of peak-hour traffic. Second, by segregating different and often incompatible traffic to separate roads, wherever possible, he sought to provide maximum efficiency and safety for each type of vehicle in its own characteristic way and sphere. For example, separate provisions were made for fast-moving automobile traffic, slow-moving animal-drawn vehicles and bicycles, and for pedestrians. Third, the overall road system was so arranged that each of the "most important through or arterial roads" paralleled one another (about a quarter of a mile away from each other), to relieve peak conditions. By using such devices as the cul-de-sac and by positioning buildings adjacent to abundant open space, Mayer sought to provide safety for both the pedestrian and the motorist. The plan also provided for pedestrian circulation through the parks and schools. Recreational and shopping facilities were placed within the pedestrian area. Also, enough diagonals and loops were provided to supplement an essentially "rectilinear system." Keeping in view any future increase in the population of the city, land was reserved for the expansion of roads, parking facilities, and business and shopping centers. Likewise, in each superblock, several acres of land were reserved for undetermined future needs, such as social services, public buildings, clubs, and so forth.

Considering the "dramatic qualities" of the ridges with hills in the backdrop, Mayer placed the Capitol Complex—containing the provincial government buildings, the Assembly, the Governors's House, and the Secretariat—at the upper edge of the city, to the north. The Capitol Complex was surrounded by the two branches of the Sukhna Cho River, which Mayer proposed to keep supplied with water through a series of inexpensive dams, thus serving as "a sort of glittering necklace encircling the group."[31] Fearing that the capitol area would not grow in proportion with the rest of the town, and considering that "spiritually" it should remain in a separate area, Mayer vetoed James Buckley's idea of moving the Capitol Complex to form the center of gravity for employment. Also vetoed was the proposal of Clarence Stein, who visualized Chandigarh as a "regional city," to be developed during its first phase as a "government city," later to be surrounded by satellites, containing their own industries. In rejecting Stein's proposal, Mayer felt that "the First Town was not large enough to have satellites of this sort, as these satellites may well develop into 'poor cousins' of the First Town."[32] The recent proliferation of satellite towns around Chandigarh seems to have borne out Mayer's fears.

By placing the capitol area at the edge of the city to the north, Mayer was breaking from the Indian tradition of placing the main government offices in the center of the city. Yet by placing the "thinking" function of the city analogous to that of the head in relationship to the body, Mayer was reaffirming the allegorical reference to the Indian caste structure in the story of Purusha (the Cosmic Man), in which his head represents the Brahamin (the priest-thinker), his arms represent the Kashtriya (the soldier), his thighs represent the Vaishya (commoner), and his feet represent the Sudra (the slave). One writer has compared Mayer's symbolic placement of the Capitol Complex of Chandigarh to the location of the administrative center in Le Corbusier's La Ville Radieuse. "The division of La Ville Radieuse into sharply defined zones of commercial, residential, and industrial activity seems also related to Mayer's Chandigarh plan."[33]

Although Mayer's contract did not call for detailed architectural schemes, he felt that he had to "adumbrate solutions [to] various problems, both because we couldn't develop a three-dimensional Master Plan without thinking [through] the building architecture, and [because] we also were charged in our agreement with the duty of setting up and establishing some 'architectural control.'"

One problem that Mayer faced in planning for the Capitol Complex was in regard to the relative architectural importance of the legislative hall in relationship to the Secretariat and other governmental buildings. Imbued with democratic tradition and representing the general mood of the time, when monumentalism had been discredited by the fascist states of Germany and Italy, Mayer felt that "spiritually and morally the hall of the people's representatives should dominate," even though functionally the buildings of the bureaucracy required more area and volume. Not wishing to repeat the mistakes of New Delhi, "where the two Secretariat buildings dominate in size . . . because of their elevated location," or the mistakes of the United Nations, "where the Secretariat of forty stories . . . dwarfs the Assembly building," Mayer decided against the use of height in the Secretariat and the departmental buildings.[34] Moreover, he felt that, according to the sight line studies, tall buildings in the Capitol Complex would compete with the ridges in the background. Considering the sun and the light conditions, the Mayer sketch for the Assembly, though modern in form, was inspired by the famous Buddhist stupa in Sanchi. Mayer found blending Indian idiom with modern techniques to be "a happy solution [for India], where it is . . . most important for national pride and self-respect to tie in their past with the modern and the future."[35]

For the same reasons, all government buildings were to be constructed of native limestone, ranging from creamy pink to deep red. This stone had been popular for centuries in northern India, where it was used extensively during the Mughal period in the sixteenth and the seventeenth centuries. Like the residential neighborhood, the Capitol Complex was based on the superblock, unpierced-by-traffic principle. By carrying the main road from the city beyond the capitol group to a main distributing road north of it, all internal communication was left undisturbed by traffic, "though at the same time vehicles [could] arrive and park adjacent to whatever building they [were] appurtenant to."[36] By the device of allowing the main road to pass the group of buildings before branching out, it was possible to provide for later expansion of the building area without getting into any traffic-crossing difficulties.

Mayer strongly doubted that, considering the administrative nature of the city without any large-scale industry, Chandigarh could "reach its initial [population] of 150,000 . . . let alone [the ultimate population of] 500,000."[37] Arguing that the history of railroad cities —where the station through warehouses, shops, small industries, and, in the case of Indian railroad towns, housing for employees close to the station—shows a generation of urban population, he chose to place the station at Chandigarh on the west side, even though the nearest railroad line lay east of the Sukhna Cho River. Because of the high administrative cost that it would involve, Mayer, on Buckley's recommendation, ruled out the idea of creating two separate "passenger and freight stations."[38] By consolidating the functions of a station into a single unit and by providing a small shopping area near it, Mayer hoped that an approximate population of 75,000 would be attracted to the city, ensuring for Chandigarh the status of a full city.

By suggesting that Chandigarh had no "naturally compelling [reason] for the growth of a city—i.e., [it was] not the center of raw materials, or of a large purchasing area, or [situated] at a natural and much used transportation cross roads, or river confluence,"[39] Mayer was echoing the sentiment expressed earlier by A. L. Fletcher, officer on special duty (capital project), who had argued that to envisage a population of 500,000 for the capital was "unrealistic." Accordingly, Mayer rejected the original plan of the Punjab government to locate the university outside the city in a separate community on an eastern plateau area. Once again marshaling his American experience in support of his argument, he noted that in the "American experience, a state . . . capital without any particular attraction other than Government, is usually a deadly dull place, and stays a small insignificant place."[40] Feeling that the university would help bolster and stabilize the population of Chandigarh, Mayer placed the university at the extreme north, where it could enjoy both beauty of location and a degree of aloofness from the hustle and bustle of the town.

Also, to stimulate population growth, the industrial area was placed in the southeastern portion of the city. The location was convenient to the railroad station, but, according to Mayer, disadvantageous from the point of view of prevailing winds. Through the help of climatologists, Mayer proposed to correct this situation by establishing a belt of trees and parkland about six hundred feet wide between the industrial area and the city as insurance against pollution.[41]

Although functionally efficient, the Mayer plan lacked originality. The centerpiece of the Mayer plan, the neighborhood idea, was also not without its detractors. Even among its supporters, the response sometimes was ambivalent. For example, Clarence Stein, one of the most celebrated supporters of the idea in the United States and also Mayer's collaborator at Chandigarh, stated at one point that "at the present the Neighborhood Unit is generally accepted as a basis for the purposeful design of new communities." However, he quickly added that "the planning theorists differ not only as to the validity of the Neighborhood Unit but even to its proper size."[42]

Born as a reaction to the deteriorating conditions of Western cities in the aftermath of the Industrial Revolution, the neighborhood idea was popularized by Clarence Arthur Perry's famous monograph, "The Neighborhood Unit,"[43] published in 1929. In describing the neighborhood unit, Perry was both rediscovering the values of early urban communities and grappling with the modern menace of the automobile. By scaling the geographical size of the neighborhood to put various facilities within walking distance—within a perimeter surrounded by traffic but not internally crossed by the automobile— the neighborhood was to be safe for children, free of the tensions induced by the crisscrossing automobile, and with internal distances scaled to easy walking. He found the formula for meeting all these requirements in an area which had the elementary school as its focus, with a constituency of about one thousand to fifteen-hundred families—an area also able to support daily-shopping facilities and other amenities. Its traffic-free form was called the superblock, and a relatively large neighborhood might be composed of several superblocks.

Perhaps the most compelling factor for the conception of this idea was demographic: "Remake our cities so that they will be places in which responsible parents will desire to have children."[44] In the 1940s, the positive answer to this advice was believed by many to be the planned residential neighborhood.[45] Sociologically, the neighborhood idea has been defined to mean "Neighborliness"[46] or "The Community Sentiment,"[47] that is, a feeling of belonging together, which, when analyzed to depict characteristic group attitudes, shows the elements of communal collectivism. Community sentiment so described is, as far as the modern city is concerned, nonexistent and certainly on the decline in rural communities as they become more integrated in the urban world. More conclusive, however, is the fate of actual experiments for creating communities with neighborhood sentiment. The utopian communities of Sunnyside (New York), designed by Clarence Stein and Henry Wright in 1924, and Radburn (New Jersey), in 1929, did not live up to their creators' expectations, nor did the new towns in Russia.

Although it remains debatable whether physical planning conceived on a neighborhood unit basis can revive social integration in the same sense as it existed, if at all, in ancient times, the idea implicitly acknowledges the incapacity for expressing and incorporating the functions of such modern developments as the automobile, the airplane, radio, television, and so forth, in an urban milieu in which they have to be separated from the main functions of the city. However, to Mayer the neighborhood idea seemed "a permanent positive attribute of human living [in which] modern resources promote the neighborhood concept, rather than destroy it."[48] Inspired by humane considerations, Mayer's goal in Chandigarh was to create "a peaceful city, not one where complications must be counteracted by other complications."[49]

Other theorists of city planning—Plato, Aristotle, and so forth—have subdivided their Ideal Cities, but there is also a marked consciousness of the unity of each town as a whole. Mayer's neighborhood idea, restricting the individual's life in a parochial society, on a spot of the earth's surface with a half-mile radius, in an expanding world with a mobile population, was not likely to provide the monumentality to the capital that the Punjabis sought. It was also to prove unsuitable for the religiously divided people. Neighborly association is, for deep reasons, important in the life of a civilized people, but its radius is short. Moreover, the success of the neighborhood idea presupposes a degree of communal harmony in a society, which Punjab has historically lacked.

Likewise, the Mayer idea of providing for a greenbelt around the city to discourage outside elements from making unauthorized encroachment into the city's boundaries and to contain the haphazard overspill of its population was bound to run into difficulties in a country where antiquated land-use laws were matched only by rapidly growing populations and jealously chauvinistic claims. "By means of its greenbelt of farms and woods," Mayer believed, the city "achieves an integration of urban and rural life." Unlike typical suburbs, which ruin adjacent city life by indiscriminately spreading its least desirable features, Mayer argued that greenbelt cities, in addition to preserving rural life, break cultural "isolation of the farmer and provide him with a direct market for his produce, while at the same time giving the urban worker immediate contact with countryside and nature."[50] By protecting the surrounding countryside, the prices of urban land and fresh produce can also be stabilized. However, to the cosmopolitan Punjabis seeking to achieve in their new capital the lost splendor and excitement of Lahore, the idea of resuscitating village life within urban communities through neighborhoods and greenbelts was to remain mystifying.

Even before Le Corbusier revised the Mayer plan, Matthew Nowicki, the architect Mayer had included in his team to do detail architectural planning, suggested several changes in the central business district, in the railroad station, and in the housing and bazaar areas. The Siberian-born, Warsaw-educated Nowicki had collaborated with such noted designers as Eero Saarinen and William H. Dietrick. His most noteworthy contribution had been to the Livestock Pavilion in Raleigh, North Carolina, where several of his original designs appear with some modifications. The Chandigarh project offered him the opportunity to express fully and freely his creative genius. Although hired to supervise architectural control rather than doing the detail designing himself, Nowicki, upon his arrival in India in June 1950, found the Indian planning unit in disarray and the Punjab government in the midst of a heated political controversy on the question of the capital site.

As Mayer learned earlier and Le Corbusier was to learn later, Nowicki learned of the Indian bureaucracy. Instead of finding himself concentrating on designs and drawings for the new capital, Nowicki was deluged with paperwork and administrative meetings. Frustrated by administrative delays, exasperated over the truancy of his staff, and unable to understand local political squabbles, Nowicki wrote to Mayer that "it is difficult to decide in one's mind whether one likes more their interest in the work or the lack of it."[51] By the end of his brief stay in India, however, his Western-trained mind was to transcend the mundane physical problems of planning to comprehend the more complex and compelling matters of Indian philosophy, the essence of which he communicated to Mayer in a letter written, ironically, two weeks prior to his fatal accident: "I have found at least the exact words of Krishna. 'Indifferent to pleasure and pain, to gain or loss, to conquest or defeat, thus make ready for the fight . . . as do the foolish, attached to works, so should the wise do, but without attachment, seeking to establish order in the world.'"[52]

If Mayer was "unabashedly" seeking beauty in his plan, a reflection of his secure democratic origins, Nowicki was more in favor of a plan with the "logic" of economy, perhaps a reflection of his own uncertain immigrant origins from politically unstable Eastern Europe and keeping more in tune with India's limited resources. Sharing his views with Mayer, he wrote: "It seems to me that the only unquestionable element in our thinking is cold logic and its striving for the utmost economy. Within this logic, which corresponds to our present (and therefore passing) problem, one must secure the greatest possible flexibility for unpredictable future changes. . . . The concept of economy and beauty derive from the same sources and the utmost economy is the utmost beauty. This is the only surviving human appraisal of beauty."[53] Reminding Mayer that "every conscious planning effort was to create an order," perhaps again a reflection of his regimented upbringing in the communist world, but which must have been reinforced during his apprentice days with Le Corbusier who worshiped authority, Nowicki concluded that "it would be a mistake to attempt to create a perfect city" based on the notion of diversity. Continuing, Nowicki reasoned: "A logical and true city plan is always a modular diagram expressing a certain philosophy and principles of life (true for a certain period) applied to specific conditions. The amount of sensitivity in applying the diagram will be responsible for legitimate variations. But the main objective should be order and not diversity." Believing that only through "order" could a truly great plan be achieved, Nowicki felt that "up to now none of our plans have approached this standard."[54]

As an alternative to the relaxed informality of the Mayer plan, Nowicki offered "the leaf plan." Based on the organic form of a leaf, the stem of the leaf represented a commercial axis cutting across the center of the city, with a vinelike system of traffic arteries flowing from it. Viewing the city as an organic body, Nowicki placed the university to the west of the Capitol Complex—"the thinking part of the body" consolidated at the top—and the industrial district at the opposite end. Providing a touch of artistry and monumentality to the Mayer plan, Nowicki observed: "In the design of the main centers—the capitol, the business center, [the] civic center, [the] railway station and the local district centers—an important element is height.

In the flat terrain of this city, few if any buildings will stand high enough to be seen from anywhere but fairly nearby. The need therefore is for the tower, the tall monument, which, symbolic of aspiration, will also be visible from many points and considerable distance. They will give a definite idiom to the town."[55]

Nowicki's recommendations for Chandigarh stemmed from his view of the city and its role. For him, the city had two main functions to perform: 1) the everyday function amounting to "dwelling and work," and 2) the holiday function amounting to "recreation." Although admitting that "the everyday function is responsible for the pattern texture of the city plan," Nowicki felt that "it is through the diagram of the holiday function that one can best express a plan of a city." Believing that it is the holiday function which unites the city, he lamented that the importance of the holiday function had been "underestimated in the recent city planning" and that "the element of recreation [had been] decentralized and confined within the texture." To restore the holiday function to its rightful place, Nowicki recommended "to strive for magnifying the space which means that there should be a complete continuity of one composition instead of dividing it into unrelated parts." Accordingly, for Chandigarh he recommended "a continuous park system tying all parts of the city with the hills, the great park, the public forum, and the capitol area. The holiday function can depend very largely on a mass pedestrian movement, just as the everyday function depends on mass transportation."[56]

For Nowicki, the capitol area represented the holiday function of the city, "where utilitarianism could give way to symbolism and ceremony."[57] Nowicki rightly felt that for the displaced people and the homeless government of Punjab in search of unifying symbols, the capitol area had inspirational importance. The question perplexing the planners was how to give a dominant profile to the Assembly in the complex, when, considering the modern demands of bureaucracy, it is the Secretariat that deserves more space. One solution proposed by Nowicki was to place "the legislative hall physically on top of the Secretariat structure, as a crowning shape above it." Mayer, however, rejected the idea calling it "too much of a tour de force."[58]

Nowicki ultimately resolved the problem by placing an assembly hall of "very powerful parabolic-domical shape, with heavily accentuated structural members and deeply cantilevered horizontal rings,"[59] in a monumental plaza, and giving it a focal point of attention in relationship to other buildings in the complex. The assembly hall was inspired by the Buddhist stupa in Sanchi, which Mayer thought would be an important source of national pride. However, one observer of the Mayer plan has rightly expressed his doubt about how a Buddhist-inspired structure could serve as a source of inspiration for the predominantly Sikh and Hindu population of the Punjab.[60] The Nowicki scheme for the Capitol Complex was based on a "loose and expansive cross axial composition" in which widely separated structures were related by extended sight lines,[61] taking advantage of the mountains in the backdrop.

For the central business district, Nowicki produced two tentative plans. In the first plan two loop-shaped roads are introduced into the superblock. The principal buildings, either square or circular in shape, are set apart from one another. A scheme of footpaths raised above the level of the street connects these buildings, with a parklike mall running through the center of the superblock. In the second plan, in the interest of order and uniformity, the number of circular buildings is reduced. The civic center, conceived as an irregularly shaped plaza, is flanked by civic buildings and contains a decorative pool in the middle. A provision for a slender tower is also made immediately to the right of the central business district to provide monumentality.

However, Nowicki's talent is best reflected in the planning of the residential superblock. Finding the variation in sizes and shapes of the superblocks unacceptable, a result of the irregularity of street patterns in the Mayer plan, Nowicki argued that any "departures from a logical standard are against the clarity of the concept and the beauty of the plan" and that "diversity of [the] plan should be secured not through the diversity of the size of the superblocks, but [through] the diversity of their space treatment."[62] He urged "qualitative" diversity, not "quantitative" diversity. Designated L–37, Nowicki's plan for the residential superblock was designed to accommodate 1,175 families of low-income government servants. Covering an area of seventy-five acres, the plan offered many of the communal features of Indian village life: a temple, six nursery schools for fifty students each, one middle school, a shopping area (restricted to pedestrians), apartments for shopkeepers, office buildings for communal activities, a provision for an open meeting space with an ampitheater, and a provision for hawkers.

Enunciating the underlying principles of his plan in his report entitled "Supplementary Notes to the Architectural Study of Superblock L-37," Nowicki wrote:

> In deciding on the low height and specific character of our solution, we had to discard the metropolitan beauty of tall, freestanding structures separated by large areas of verdure. This dream of some modern planners depends entirely on a high degree of necessary mechanization on elevators, steel construction, electric kitchen equipment, etc., and a way of life alien to that of India. Some other kind of beauty had to be striven for—contemporary to the same degree as the first, equally expressing a trend of our country and yet better suited to our conditions and better expressing the character and the spirit of this country.[63]

Nowicki's intention in all his designs for Chandigarh was to blend modern architectural solutions with the Indian way of life. Accordingly, Indian businessmen and artisans, who are used to having living quarters on their business premises were given ample space. The bazaars, although modern in form, contained all the Indian features: shops with provision to sit on the floor, merchandise in the shops protected by overhanging balconies or by canvas roofs, and a separate area for street hawkers. Keeping with the Indian tradition, houses were designed around the courtyards, creating privacy. Instead of open windows, *jalis* or screens were provided to further assure privacy. Considering the Indian habit of sleeping out in the open during the hot summer nights, the houses were provided with terraces.

However, Nowicki also included a design for a four-story apartment block built around a center courtyard—an idea which is not popular in India but which is gaining acceptance under the increasing pressure of population. To avoid "the drab appearance of the well-known refugee housing groups,"[64] Nowicki used variation in his designs by using setbacks, curving streets, courtyards, crescent groupings, and sequences of closed and open spaces. Using water and greenery, he tried to emphasize variation. For building material, Nowicki rightly concluded that, notwithstanding the use of new methods of precasting reinforced concrete, "brick may prove to be the cheapest medium"—a conclusion that holds true even today in India. "The tradition of the familiar workmanship coupled with the small price of labor [has been] the decisive argument for using brick in most cases."[65]

So well did Nowicki's designs capture the spirit of India that, even though Mayer's contract did not call for architectural details, the Punjabi administrators offered Nowicki a full-time position as an Indian government employee to supervise the development of Chandigarh.[66] The reason for offering direct employment was that the Indian government was finding it difficult to make payments in scarce and expensive American dollars. It is believed that Nowicki, exhilarated at the opportunity, had given his consent. Had fate willed the future of Nowicki differently, it is likely that Mayer's master plan would have been fully implemented. Unfortunately, however, the TWA Constellation flight in which Nowicki was returning to America crashed on August 31, 1950, abruptly terminating the promising career of this young architect.

It should be viewed as a meaningful compliment to Nowicki that many of his ideas—order and regularity in planning, provisions for monumental axes related to the Capitol Complex, parks unifying the city visually with the hills in the backdrop—were respected by the later planners of Chandigarh. In his brief career he had won the respect of his colleagues in the West and had endeared himself to the Indians. Perhaps the best tribute to this prodigious architect on his Chandigarh work was paid by his colleague-friend Mayer, when he wrote to Nowicki's brother, Jacek, in his native Poland: "Nowicki showed great awareness and sensitivity for indigenous feeling and idiom, and grasp of its functional rationale, including ways of living and climatic considerations. He also caught the essential richness, the gaiety of the village and of the bazaar; and the spontaneity of its craftsman-like and sub-craftsman-like ornamentation. These all came out fully in his sketches."[67]

·4·
THE LE CORBUSIER PLAN

The year 1951 did not bring good news for Albert Mayer. Nowicki's death the previous year had left Mayer without a competent architect to execute his master plan for Chandigarh. The relationship between Mayer and the Punjab government had also taken a turn for the worse. Mayer's own long absences from Punjab encouraged the Punjab government to search for alternative means for building the city. The shortage of expensive American dollars only added to the discomfort of the Punjab government in wanting to retain Mayer. By the end of January 1951, Mayer had been served notice by the Punjab government that the work for the architectural development in Chandigarh had been given to a group of architects from France and England.

Mayer, although disappointed, put the best face on the situation and explained to an American audience that the negotiations with the Punjab government had broken down because of "the cost and dollar problems which mounted severely as the work became more detailed in connection with the architectural development" of Chandigarh. "For this further work," he added, "the Punjab Government have sought architects outside the dollar area and have retained Le Corbusier and P. Jeanneret and Maxwell Fry." He, however, graciously offered to send a member of the Mayer and Whittlesey firm "to India . . . to consult and work with them on architectural and planning matters."[1] It was nevertheless an unceremonious ending to his year's work marked with exciting press conferences, news articles, radio talks, and guest lectures on the development of Punjab's new capital. It would be even less gratifying for him to watch the new team dismantle his work and replace it with its own ideas. In the course of time the name of Mayer would completely disappear from mention in any private discussions of Chandigarh.

That the relationship between Albert Mayer and the Punjab government had been a tenuous one is reflected in P. N. Thapar's letter to Mayer, in which Thapar pointedly notes, "I am aware that these negotiations have been difficult and have involved concessions on your part."[2] Primarily the concessions that Mayer had made were in his fee. Not only had he accepted a lower fee for the master plan, but he had accepted 40 percent of the fee in Indian rupees. He was willing to make similar concessions for implementing his plan and for the architectural work at Chandigarh. Although important, the shortage of American dollars was only one reason making the Punjab government uncomfortable with wanting to continue with Mayer. The other factor contributing to the unhappiness of the government was Mayer's unwillingness to live in India to complete his assignment, even though in the end the Punjab officials failed to secure a resident architectural consultant for Chandigarh. Had Nowicki lived to accept direct employment of the Punjab government, the Punjab officials would have solved the dollar problem and would have had a resident architectural consultant. Nowicki's death, however, closed all such possibilities. The Punjab government's mistake, which the governor of Punjab later admitted to, had been "not to employ planners and architects as one."[3]

The new team, in addition to the three names mentioned, also included Jane Drew. The arrangement reached with these four architects turned out to be far better than the Punjab government had hoped for and certainly better than Mayer was willing to offer. Although limiting himself to only two visits per year to India for the next three years of the development of the city, Le Corbusier was to remain dedicated to Chandigarh for the remaining fourteen years of his life. Fry and Drew committed themselves to staying in India for a period of three years. Jeanneret, who also committed himself for three years, remained in India to serve as the first chief architect and chief town planner for the city until the end of 1965, when he had to return to France because of ill health.

Experienced, opinionated, and different in temperament, these individuals made up an odd group. Jeanneret had been a collaborator of Le Corbusier since 1922, when he had left Auguste Perret's office to join his cousin in the demanding task of developing the conception of the *ville contemporaine* for three million people on the right bank of the Seine. But Fry and Drew had no working experience with either Le Corbusier or Jeanneret, although they were all part of the CIAM group. Dividing them further were their language differences, of which Fry has sardonically noted, "Jeanneret was . . . narrowly Parisian, with no aptitude for languages; as a consequence my French improved while all else deteriorated."[4]

Beside their own differences, their unequal relationship with the Indians was not much help either. Fry found Thapar an able administrator; but he considered Varma to be "evasive and autocratic" and throughout his stay in India remained distrustful of him. Le Corbusier in particular forced his view in total disregard of others. As these individuals thrashed out their differences "in French or English, but mostly in French, and much of it bad French,"[5] the Indians watched in bafflement. It was a difficult situation, best described by Fry: "My French was unequal to the occasion. Jeanneret was supernumerary, and Thapar only half aware of what was going forward. Le Corbusier held the crayon and was in his element."[6]

Although hired to execute the Mayer plan, it would have been out of character for Le Corbusier not to introduce his own ideas. Moreover, there were many elements in the Mayer plan that needed further refinement before implementation. Fry, who reached Simla in early February 1951, was first to recognize the shortcomings of the Mayer plan. He found Nowicki's drawings "rather romantically based on Indian idioms." He also found Mayer's proposed capitol buildings ill-sited and similar to "Lutyen's Viceregal Palace at New Delhi, largely eclipsed by the profile of the approach road." Fry was equally doubtful about the workability of the Radburn-like path system of the Mayer plan, which he found "to be out of scale with the enterprise." He was also unhappy about the "generally sloppy form of its sector planning."[7]

Troubling Fry further was his experience with the Indian bureaucracy and the Public Works Department (PWD). The condition on which he had accepted the Indian assignment was that he would not work under engineers, as had been the practice in the Indian Public Works Department. At the beginning of his stay in India he felt "the onset of a trial of strength with Varma, neglect by Thapar, and a general feeling of lassitude in the organization."[8] He came very near resigning and returning home, but on Thapar's pleading stayed on. It was Fry's negative experiences with the PWD that later prompted him to recommend to Nehru that the PWD be reorganized, to which Nehru agreed. The work in Chandigarh, however, was to remain moribund until Le Corbusier arrived on the scene in late February 1951.

That Fry should have agreed to work with Le Corbusier presented a paradox. Their ideal cities contrasted with each other as opposing variations on the same utopian theme. For both of them industrialization was the culprit that had irrevocably altered the character of contemporary cities so that new forms in city living had to be developed to mitigate the pernicious effects of industrialization, new forms that would herald the beginning of the Second Machine Age. Their beliefs were rooted in the experiences of their youth: Fry's in Liverpool, as yet uninvaded by the automobile, representing "a coherent background of well-mannered order";[9] and Le Corbusier's in La Chaux-de-Fonds, a harmonious and orderly community of prosperous artisan-watchmakers near the French-speaking region of Neuchâtel in Switzerland.

But whereas Fry, believing in the inalienable rights of man, wished to subject cities to a "scrutiny" that would reveal "their underlying function in terms of the human and mechanical working of them, the circulation in and about them, their contact with the elements as with the surrounding in which they were set,"[10] Le Corbusier, recognizing the city as the natural home of centralized power, wished to exalt it. For Le Corbusier, the existing cities were not dense enough. They offered too much expression to "anarchic individualism" and too little scope for planning. He visualized the city of tomorrow to be a Radiant City of glass-and-steel skyscrapers set in parks; it would be the beautiful and efficient city restored to order and harmony through total administration of society by a great bureaucracy.

For these reasons, Fry, with his profound humanistic values and deep moorings in the "family," found Le Corbusier to be "authoritarian" in his style.[11] Long before he was presented with the prospect of working with Le Corbusier at Chandigarh, Fry had characterized Le Corbusier's blueprints for the city of tomorrow as fit for living in "only by a race of robots."[12] He also considered Le Corbusier's Plan Voisin (1925)—with its cruciform-plan skyscrapers—repelling, proclaiming it to be "inhuman," especially for him, a housing architect "basing his plans on family life."[13] He equally doubted the efficacy of the "self-containedness" of the *unité d'habitation*, although he saw "it as a thrilling work of architecture and Le Corbusier a master." As for Le Corbusier's modular system that he developed after years of research as a tool of measurement, Fry remained unconvinced that he personally could use it.[14]

Comparing Le Corbusier to Mikhail Bakunin, a nineteenth-century Russian nobleman turned anarchist, Fry felt that Le Corbusier's attitude "led him . . . into indisciplines and disregard of anything but the grandest interpretations of his beliefs." For that reason, Fry never "enjoyed" the Chapel of Notre Dame, Ronchamp, Haute-Saône (1950–55), built by Le Corbusier. The same reasoning would later make Fry express his disapproval of the legislative building in Chandigarh, proclaiming it to be "confused in internal functioning." Fry's temperament took him more toward the other two masters of modern architecture, Walter Gropius and Ludwig Mies van der Rohe, who answered for him the "principal" questions he put to architecture and whose styles he found to be "less romantic and declamatory."[15]

The fundamental basis of their differences lay in their respective training. Whereas Fry had gone through a formal training in architecture, Le Corbusier had received no formal training in the profession he helped revolutionize. Since both men came to maturity in a world irrevocably altered by the Industrial Revolution, they had different responses based on their values and the artistic traditions of their respective pasts. In his *Autobiographical Sketches*, which he began writing during his recovery from an operation performed in the Christian Missionary Hospital at Ludhiana, India, at the time he was building Chandigarh with Le Corbusier, Fry described his "boyhood as a voyage through time within the inescapable topography of the city . . . [where] the vision fades and the city resumes life, year by year in pace with my own, so distant from it, so out of time with the endless struggles to maintain itself against the new pressures time brought with it, the groundswell functions of fortune originating beyond the knowledge of planners or the planned, beyond the power of the ageing organism to resist it."[16] In another place he admitted that "this sense would have been harder to come by had I been born in Wolverhampton or Leeds."[17]

That industrialization had had a profound impact on the thinking of the young Fry is clearly brought out in his prolific writings. He wrote: "If you mentally survey the growth of a machine you will see how it tends inevitably towards the anonymous package. The early steam engine of Trevithick was an inspiring demonstration of steam power. . . . But as time brought the turbine this demonstration of power receded, until it ended in a cased package with a small face of recording dials." He continued: "Motor cars had a shorter history of relative individuality . . . until finally traffic moved, whether swiftly or slowly, in an undifferentiated mass of little interest, from which the human element had been withdrawn behind plate glass, so the road and the pavement became separated."[18] He wondered what kind of city it was today where a conversation begun indoors could not be continued on the street. In contrast with present times, he noted that in his youth "the minuteness of life compared with the vastness of the city is obscured by the self-importance of the life and by a capacity to live that life in the midst of the city. Yet occasionally something of its size and identity was felt and an attempt made to establish some possible, if not meaningful, relation with it."[19] Elsewhere he noted, "The circumstances that confront an architect today interpose between him and the natural world a system based essentially upon abstract conceptions of mechanical perfectibility flourishing in a medium from which human considerations have been largely removed."[20]

If the winds of the Industrial Revolution had conditioned young Fry's thinking toward the pernicious effects of uncontrolled materialism, the harsh climatic realities of England to which he was exposed as a boy walking a mile and a half to and from school made him appreciative of the significance of weather in design principles, the meaning of which was to be reinforced later on the Gold Coast of Africa and then at Chandigarh. Fry recalled doing well only in his art class as a boy, an interest that would eventually lead him to the Liverpool School of Architecture, rated the "finest" school in the world. There Fry got the opportunity for an internship for a summer in New York at the offices of Carrère and Hastings, noted for building the Forty-Second Street Library in New York, the Standard Oil Building in lower New York, and the Devonshire House in Piccadilly, London. Out of college, Fry's first assignment was making drawings for cottages for a model village near Sittingbourne. It would be a while, however, before he would get the commission to build Petsamo (1938), a new town in Finland, and later yet, with Jane Drew by his side, the architectural designs for West Africa and Chandigarh.

Fry had been deeply marked by his exposure to, and subsequent reaction against, the Arts and Crafts Movement. His introduction to the movement came through his participation in the Design and Industries Association, a group composed of artists, architects, businessmen, industrialists, and writers, all trying to counteract the deteriorating standards of the industrialized world. Through this group Fry was exposed to the ideas on the Continent, which stimulated his imagination. Through Wells Coates, who later was noted for his Lawn Road Flats (1934) in London, Fry came in touch with the Congrès Internationaux d'Architecture Moderne (CIAM), an organized body of European architectural thought. It was at the La Sarraz meeting in 1928 that Fry first met Le Corbusier, who had been one of the founding members of CIAM. The forum of CIAM would later serve to bring Maxwell Fry and Jane Drew together.

The contact with CIAM further stimulated the debate over architecture in England, leading to the formation of Modern Architectural Re-Search (MARS) in 1931, the English wing of CIAM. The men responsible for founding MARS included Fry, Wells Coates, F. R. S. Yorke, D. Pleydell-Bouverie, Amyas Connell, Basil Ward, Colin Lucas, Godfrey Samuel, R. T. F. Skinner, the poet John Betjeman, P. M. Shand, and H. Hastings. Later, B. Lubetkin and C. Sweet joined MARS, and it became known for its support of cultural renewal as well as for its social commitment. After 1934 the group participated in all the major architectural exhibitions in England. A particularly significant contribution of the group was its 1942 plan for the urban reconstruction of London, prepared by the group's planning committee under the stewardship of Arthur Korn, who had left Germany for England in 1937. The plan, however, had to be suspended because of the war. Fry later characterized the role of the MARS group as a "humanistic response" to industrialization.[21] Driven by these humanistic considerations and backed by Elizabeth Denby, an English philanthropist, Fry designed flats for the London poor, and, despite the controversial press reports, called the project a "wild success."

If the exposure to CIAM had molded Fry's thinking on architecture, the emergence of fascist states in Germany and Italy influenced his political outlook. By his own admission, Fry "hated" dogma.[22]

The political events in Germany motivated Fry and other likeminded architects to use the MARS group to offer bogus employment to architects from the Germany of rising National Socialism, where they were increasingly finding it difficult to get work. It was Fry's associates, Morton Shand and Jack Pritchard at MARS, who managed the flight of Gropius from Germany to England, ostensibly to build apartments in Manchester and Birmingham. The same humanistic considerations propelled Fry to denounce the English Foreign Secretary Sir Samuel Hoare and Premier Pierre Laval of France for the "dirty compromise" that gave away northern Ethiopia to Mussolini. Fry was later to become a founding member of the Political and Economic Planning Group (PEP), a group committed to propagating new ideas free from any special interest.

Fry developed a special relationship with Gropius, with whom he collaborated to produce Impington College in Cambridgeshire (1936), a secondary school with space for adult education. The Gropius influence is reflected in Fry's earlier works: the Sunhouse in Hampstead (1935) and the Sassoon House in Peckham. Gropius, who became director of the Staatliches Bauhaus in 1919, spoke of man's enslavement to the machine. He propagated new thinking, based on teamwork, which would reintroduce craftsmanship into industry, thereby salvaging the values of the old artistic tradition and reintroducing them into the life cycle of modern society—stripped of all class characteristics—so that all society could partake of them. Gropius launched a school in which artists and craftsmen collaborated in producing objects of high quality that would serve mankind. Fry came to view modern architecture through the eyes of Gropius. "Modern architecture," wrote Fry, "and its extension into town planning, has above all this task of interpreting applied science in humanistic terms. Of making industrialism fit for human use; building cities that ennoble life instead of degrading and destroying it; and of creating everywhere, out of the disparate and anti-social manifestations of machine production and centralized power, unities of resolved thought and feeling, in the form of buildings, groups of buildings and large aggregations, in which life may know its bounds and flourish."[23]

It might have been the *Werkbund* principles of Gropius that later led Fry to accept a joint commission with Le Corbusier at Chandigarh in the greater interest of mankind and art. Although Le Corbusier himself in his book *Vers une architecture* (translated from the French edition by Fredrick Etchells as *Towards a New Architecture*) talked about the need for collaboration and the debt architects owed to industrial form, Fry felt that only Gropius and Mies meant it and acted accordingly: Gropius by founding the Bauhaus School, and Mies by using nearly exclusively the products of industry.[24] Whereas Le Corbusier said *"Brisez le* moule," Mies said "it is unnecessary to have a new idea every [Monday morning]. Two different temperaments."[25] Eventually, both Gropius and Mies left for America. It was indeed a sad day for Fry when Gropius accepted an offer from Harvard University. Fry recorded his sentiment thus: "I suffered under no misconceptions of wearing a crown discarded. I knew that when he left I should turn back upon myself as I had done before, and do only what was possible for me and no more. I stood upon a shore, my own, from which the rich native hues were fading, listening with half my mind to the low murmur of ominous winds, and took my leave of him."[26]

After the heady experiences of the European intellectual movement, arrival in West Africa with Jane Drew in 1942 placed Fry in "a colonial life relatively untouched by time or war,"[27] where they would spend intermittently some fifteen years developing architectural forms suitable for the harsh climate of the region. Recognizing quickly that climate, which had not been so important in the architecture of Europe, was a determinant in the order of building, much like in other dry and humid zones, Fry and Drew discovered "the . . . necessity for moving air passing under shade across buildings held like open fingers to receive it." To eliminate the menace of termites rampant in that part of the world, they employed concrete; and, to prevent the reinforced concrete roof from cracking open under great ranges of diurnal temperature, they developed "a perforated architecture of cast concrete screens held into the prevailing trade winds, colcured in the non-bleaching shade, and diversified in texture by the use of a low-grade granite rock."[28] That these experiences in West Africa were to introduce a new element in their repertoire of design principles is reflected in their two books[29] on the subject and in the new School of Tropical Architecture they founded with the help of their friend Otto Koenigsberger. The experiences gained in West Africa were to serve them well in Chandigarh.

If the Quaker background of Fry led him to trust in the basic goodness of man, making him anti-dogmatic, anti-institutional, and anti-hierarchial, the Calvinistic upbringing of Le Corbusier provided him with a strong calling for the restructuring of society in a godly social order. Le Corbusier's unequivocal respect for authority is a direct result of his Calvinist background. Unlike Fry and Drew, who put limitations on the scope of industrialization and hoped to sublimate its pernicious materialistic effects by making it accountable to human functions, Le Corbusier, reacting to industrialization, never ceased searching for an industrial society that would be as harmonious and orderly as an artisan community, of which he had once been a respectable member. The Industrial Revolution had been a personal experience for Le Corbusier; his adolescence and early manhood were dominated by a crisis and decline in the old way of life caused by industrialization. Born in the traditional but prosperous handicraft community of the Swiss watchmakers of La Chaux-de-Fonds, Le Corbusier did not consider his background to be an advantage. Although proud of the region's revolutionary history stretching back to the time of the Albigensian Wars, when religious minorities from southern France moved to the Jura Valley in the twelfth and thirteenth centuries to escape persecution, he found it convenient to revive his remote links with his French ancestors in order to ease his way into the Paris establishment. It was with this consideration that in 1923, at the age of thirty-six, he dropped his given name, Charles-Edouard Jeanneret, to assume the name of Le Corbusier, which belonged to one of his French ancestors. He nevertheless inherited all the characteristics of his people, being reserved, cold, arrogant, sarcastic, and suspicious.

Le Corbusier's introduction to architecture came through art, and he never forsook art. His extraordinary ability and his insatiable capacity for absorbing visual images throughout art history became evident at a very early age. At thirteen, he qualified for the Ecole d'Art at La Chaux-de-Fonds, a kind of technical high school set up for the express purpose of training engravers for the watchmaking industries in the town and second only to the academic Gymnase in prestige. For the next sixteen years the art school in La Chaux-de-Fonds provided Le Corbusier's education, where the dominating influence of L'Eplattenier, the eclectic young director of the school, was to steer Le Corbusier's interest from art to architecture. Through L'Eplattenier, Le Corbusier became exposed to the arts and crafts program, and he was only eighteen in 1906 when he designed and decorated a house for a local citizen named Fallet—an assignment arranged through his mentor. In 1907, Le Corbusier embarked on a long series of travels that took him to Italy, France, Germany, Eastern Europe, and the Mediterranean, and back to La Chaux-de-Fonds several times, before he finally settled in Paris in 1917.

Two principal characters played an important role in Le Corbusier's youth in shaping his feelings toward life, work, and social responsibility. His Calvinist mother with her Protestant morality constantly reminded him that "whatever you do, do it [well]."[30] Although Le Corbusier never developed attachment to the religion of his parents, he nevertheless received their full support for his talent for drawing. His teacher L'Eplattenier, who had become director of the art school in 1903 at the age of twenty-five, instilled in the young boy a passion for ideas. More importantly, he impressed on Le Corbusier that all true art must have as its ultimate aim the regeneration of society—a lesson that Le Corbusier took seriously. There is yet a third influence that became part of Le Corbusier's personality; from his father he inherited a love of nature that he later tried to incorporate in the sterile world of industry.

L'Eplattenier had taken over the directorship of the school at a time when the popularity of expensive, engraved pocket watches had been replaced by mass-produced wristwatches from Germany, making him realize that industrialization had irrevocably altered the traditional curriculum of arts and crafts taught at his school. L'Eplattenier passed on this feeling to Le Corbusier when he selected the young boy for his prestigious postgraduate program called *Cours Supérieur d'Art de Décoration*. For L'Eplattenier there were three immortal periods of architecture: ancient Egyptian, with its lotus leaf; Greek, with its acanthus; and Gothic, with its flowers, animals, and chimera.[31] Passing on this piece of information to his students, he explored with them the countryside of the Jura region with the hope of developing a genuine Jura style based on natural forms. That never happened. But he told young Le Corbusier, who strongly wished to be a painter, that "you will be an architect." Le Corbusier later acknowledged his indebtedness to his teacher by observing that "he would have remained a watchcase engraver all his life were it not for Charles L'Eplattenier, his teacher of drawing."[32]

L'Eplattenier also exposed Le Corbusier to the ideas of John Ruskin and Owen Jones, the proponents of Art Nouveau and the champions of Victorian morality. On the eve of Le Corbusier's 1907 trip, L'Eplattenier gave him a copy of Edouard Schure's *Les Grands Initiés*, a popular book of the time preaching that Rama, Krishna, Hermes, Moses, Orpheus, Phythagoras, and Jesus were all "initiates" who had penetrated the veil of matter and grasped the truth of the Spirit. Le Corbusier eventually came to identify himself with these figures, seeing himself as a prophet too, in the realm of art and architecture. Through the writings of Henri Provensal Le Corbusier came to view art as "the religious conscience of nations" and seriously started thinking about a cubist aesthetic in architecture.[33]

Spending much of 1907 in Italy and Austria, where he was exposed to the white stucco forms and learned of the Art Nouveau movement through Joseph Hoffmann, Le Corbusier arrived in Paris in 1908 to discover the revolutionary properties of reinforced concrete and the meaning of technological rationalism under the guidance of Auguste Perret. But Le Corbusier was still sufficiently under the influence of L'Eplattenier and, guided by his inclinations, he never enrolled at the Ecole des Beaux Arts, and therefore never acquired the right to put the letters D.P.L.G. (*Diplômé par le Gouvernement*) after his name, the title of an academically trained architect. The Paris stay in 1908 was to be the beginning of his love-hate relationship with the city as it was also to complete his transformation from naturalism and Art Nouveau to classicism. As he informed his teacher at La Chaux-de-Fonds, "Paris is . . . death for dreamers,"[34] but on another occasion admitted that it is still "a place where genius emerges through incessant competition."[35]

Even though the scientific, rationalist teachings of Perret ran counter to the spiritualized revivalism of the ancient arts taught by L'Eplattenier, Le Corbusier never rejected one teacher for the other. Although his ultimate position came closer to the ideas of Perret, Le Corbusier sought a synthesis: a medium to incorporate the values of the old arts with the technology of the future. The dualistic pattern in Le Corbusier's thinking was part of his upbringing, reinforced by the readings of Friedrich Nietzsche. The need for a synthesis was further occasioned by his acute observations, which he meticulously recorded (there are more than seventy volumes of pocket-size diaries covering Le Corbusier's full span of life). Everywhere he traveled he saw science and technology replacing the old artisan ways: a handcrafted pocket watch by a wristwatch, an earthen pitcher by an iron bucket. He reasoned that the art of the future must be an art of the Machine Age, or it would not survive. He recognized that the machine must be confronted directly, and its inherent potential for beauty and order discovered.

The other important contact in Le Corbusier's educational training was with the German Peter Behrens, a functionalist. Several factors point to Behrens' importance in Le Corbusier's life. First, like Le Corbusier, he had started as a painter and craftsman in the Art Nouveau manner, ultimately rejecting it. Next, Behrens had turned to the classical tradition for some of the discipline he found lacking in Art Nouveau. Finally, and most importantly, Behrens had concentrated upon industrial work—factories, and so forth—and upon the design of the industrial products of those factories. Because of Behrens' emphasis on utilitarian buildings, his studio in Berlin became the center for advanced work in the field in the years immediately preceding the First World War.

Mies, Gropius, and Le Corbusier were among those who apprenticed with him. Each of the three apprentices was to learn something special from Behrens: Mies about classicism, Gropius about the potentialities of an industrial civilization—a lesson that he successfully applied at the Bauhaus ten years later—and Le Corbusier about organization and Machine Art. Le Corbusier, like many others of his time, had been driven into searching for new architectural forms because the doors to old architecture appeared closed to him. These men searched for a new language—a language that could be used to deal with the challenges of the Industrial Age. They found the vocabulary for this new language in geometric forms—cubes, spheres, cylinders, cones, and so on.

The discovery of a new world of geometric forms affected Le Corbusier in another way: He became somewhat antinaturalist. The city, he said, is man's "grip" upon nature. "It is human operation directed against nature. . . . It is a creation."[36] To him the idea of integrating architecture and nature, in the manner of Art Nouveau, became anathema. A building must be a clear, sophisticated statement, he felt, and it should stand in contrast to nature, rather than appear as an outgrowth of some natural form. By their differences, nature and architecture should enhance each other, creating a sort of harmony by contrast. Just as the Art Nouveau designers had argued that nature is "honest" and therefore forms taken from nature must be "honest" too, so Le Corbusier and others who shared his views argued that machines are "efficient" and therefore forms borrowed from machines must be "efficient" too.

By the time Le Corbusier had concluded his apprenticeship with Behrens late in 1910, his ideas had already formed—ideas that changed little in the following years. First, he had committed himself to the new world of form which the Cubists had begun to paint, and which the architect-engineers of Perret's and Behrens' conviction had begun to manipulate. Second, he had committed himself to a laissez-faire attitude toward nature, believing that nature and architecture should never be mixed. Third, he had committed himself to reinforced concrete, preferring it over steel. Finally, he had committed himself to the tradition of the Mediterranean, not as interpreted by the Beaux Arts, but as represented by the vigor, strength, and grandeur of Greece, Rome, and the Renaissance. His commitment to the Mediterranean tradition was the result of a deliberate cultural choice, not of a natural condition.[37]

Until 1923, Le Corbusier, known only as a "dilettante architect," principally survived by selling his paintings. Apart from the Fallet villa at La Chaux-de-Fonds—a commission that financed his first trip outside Switzerland—he had completed two small houses: one at Vaucresson, the other—a studio for his painter friend Amédée Ozenfant—in Paris. Among the projects of the war and postwar years, there were two that stood out: the Domino Houses (the 1914 plan for mass-produced houses) and the Citrohan House (1922).

Two principal events at the beginning of the 1920s established him as an architect. In 1922 he entered his designs for a city for three million inhabitants at the Salon d'Automne in Paris—designs emanating from his love-hate relationship with Paris. This project laid down in complete detail the principles of city planning, from which Le Corbusier never deviated. It was his plan for a completely new city that would take hold first in the imagination and then in fact. The plan was based on four basic principles: first, decongestion of the city center; second, increased density of the city; third, enlargement of the means of circulation; and fourth, enlargement of the landscape areas. He proposed to accomplish his objectives by providing elevated highways to handle all fast-moving automobile traffic, never to be crossed by a pedestrian. These crisscrossing highways, joined at their ends by a peripheral highway system completely bypassing the city, placed the city center within easy and quick reach of a motorist. All pedestrian traffic was placed on the normal ground level and passed through open spaces and parks. Most of the buildings were placed on stilts, or *pilotis*, leaving pedestrians to walk freely anywhere, everywhere, and without danger from automobiles.

The center of Le Corbusier's *la ville contemporaine* was to be a group of skyscrapers, cruciform in plan, fifty or sixty stories in height, and spaced far apart so as to permit the development of generous park spaces between them. The cruciform towers were to contain offices for the city administration, businesses and the professions, with a nearby civic center. The next ring of the *ville contemporaine*, which was designed in a series of rectangular belts, was a development of high-rise apartment houses. These apartment houses were to be built in the form of long, continuous "walls," wandering in and out, changing direction, and thus creating spacious garden courts and parks for the use of the residents. As these buildings were also to be raised on *pilotis*, there was free movement between adjoining courts, underneath, and through the various structures. Finally, there was to be an outer ring of garden apartments of a special kind—Le Corbusier called them *villas superposées*—which were to be grouped around inner courts laid out as recreation areas. The city was to be protected by a massive belt of greenery, several miles thick, beyond which would be located industrial districts, perhaps a port, a sports arena, or a small suburb of individual houses.

The second event that established Le Corbusier as an architect was the publication in 1923 of his book *Vers une architecture* (*Towards a New Architecture*), a collection of articles written earlier with Ozenfant and published in *L'Esprit nouveau*, the magazine founded by him in collaboration with poet Paul Dermée in 1920. The book is more than a simple tract on aesthetics; it is a social commentary on his times. The book is an eloquent rationalization of the new "machine aesthetics," and a realization of the fact that mass production would demand an adherence to certain dimensional standards. Le Corbusier made two novel observations concerning the inevitable standardization. First, declaring that the time for individual, egocentric expression in architecture had passed, he made it obligatory upon every architect to design in a vocabulary that would one day fit into a mass-production vernacular. He also spoke of an authority that must exist capable of coordinating standardization. Second, he went back to the traditional Renaissance rule of measure and proportion for a guide of some sort to a modern unit system and produced what has been called a modular system, a basic principle in building with the idea of the Greek Golden Section. The modular system, with its proportionate scale, makes possible an infinite number of variations within a unit system of construction, and can thus be used to break the monotony which is inevitable in mass production.

Le Corbusier never deviated from his ideas reflected in *la ville contemporaine* and *Vers une architecture*, and his subsequent plans—Voisin (1925) and the Radiant City (1935)—are simply variations of the same principles. The duality of Le Corbusier also became clear at this time. He sought urban density as a premise of cultural progress, and, like the exponents of the Garden City Movement, hoped to bring back greenery and nature into urban life. The two competing goals appear as aspects of the same postulate. His preference after 1930 for materials like rough stone, fair-faced brick, raw concrete, unfinished timber, and so forth, point to yet another change in Le Corbusier—a shift to Brutalism. According to one study of Le Corbusier, this shift was prompted by his "rediscovery of natural orders, primitive societies and sexual relations with women unconstrained by conventional etiquette, sophistication or snobbism."[38] It has been further suggested that, although Le Corbusier had denounced the use of a curve as a "pack-donkey way," his renewed interest in women in the 1930s led him to the use of a curve and can be seen in buildings like Ronchamp and the Carpenter Center at Harvard, where "one can also find the curves of buttocks and shoulder arches."[39] That his interest in women and curves was to sustain itself is borne out by the slightly curved impression of the lateral streets in Chandigarh and by his unsuccessful efforts at seducing a European journalist, Taya Zinkin,[40] who was working in India in the early fifties—although in Chandigarh Le Corbusier must have been influenced by the ideas of Maxwell Fry and Jane Drew.

Le Corbusier's ideas generated public interest in his plans, but they failed to get him a commission. For the realization of his ideal city, Le Corbusier was willing to turn for help either to communists, capitalists, or anyone with sufficient money. He firmly believed that, regardless of the political system, an industrial society must be centrally controlled, hierarchically organized, and administered from above by the most qualified person or group of qualified people—once again pointing to the influence of Nietzsche and to his earlier Calvinist background. Like Max Weber, Le Corbusier believed that the industrial era would be an age of rationality dominated by a centralized bureaucracy.[41] Le Corbusier's ideal city was to be a City of Administration. Thirty years later he would get his opportunity to build that city at Chandigarh, not for a highly industrialized nation of the West, as he had perceived, but, paradoxically, for a predominantly agricultural society just recently emerged from colonial rule.

When Thapar and Varma first met Le Corbusier in the winter of 1950 in Paris, he was a disappointed man. Only three years earlier, in 1947, he had declared his "despair," noting: "Men are so stupid that I'm glad I'm going to die. All my life people have tried to crush me. First, they called me a dirty engineer, then a painter who tried to be an architect, then an architect who tried to paint, then a Communist, then a Fascist. Luckily, I've always had an iron will."[42] Most of Le Corbusier's despair stemmed from the failure of his life's work, both in France and abroad. His post–Second World War commission to rebuild Saint-Dié, an industrial town in France destroyed during the war, had run into opposition. His commission for the replanning of La Rochelle-Pallice had never materialized, as the town had escaped destruction by the Germans. His success in the redevelopment scheme for the southern area of Marseilles had been limited to one apartment building; and in South America, the Bogotá plan, developed with Paul Lester Wiener and José Luis Sert, had been postponed because of a local controversy.

The failure of the Western nations to cope with the economic depression of the 1930s, just when Le Corbusier had perfected his plan for the ideal industrial society in *La Ville radieuse* (1935), had already eroded his faith in parliamentary democracy. A critic of laissez-faire, he had become a Hamiltonian in his political dispositions. Although he had talked about "individual liberty"[43] in *La Ville radieuse*, the book itself was dedicated to "Authority." Disillusioned by Western democracies, he looked to Stalin's Five-Year Plan, to Hitler's promise of full employment and to Mussolini's political posturings as proofs of future hope and authority. Even the American New Deal appeared to him as a presidential dictatorship over the legislative branch. His belief that the important task of building a city could not be entrusted to the masses predisposed him to authority. However, his efforts to gain Mussolini's support in 1934 for his plan proved abortive. His earlier efforts in Moscow had met with a similar fate, just as his later efforts for the *Plan Obus* failed in Algiers. The tactless tenor of his pronouncements on his first visit to the United States in 1935, reflected in the title of his book *When the Cathedrals Were White: A Journey to the Country of Timid People*,[44] failed to produce either friends or new commissions for his ideas in America. Likewise, his mostly unsolicited renewal plans for Barcelona, Stockholm, Antwerp, Geneva, Buenos Aires, and various other cities had failed to produce any commissions. Since 1930, his consuming passion had been to build a city. Had it not been for the Indians, Le Corbusier's search for the absolute authority that would say yes to his plans would probably have never materialized. That authority was Nehru.

Le Corbusier recorded his sentiment in his diary of that fateful moment when he, after some hesitation, accepted the Chandigarh assignment: "It is the hour that I have been waiting for—India, that human and profound civilization—to construct a capital. Urbanism is the activity of a society. A capital is the spirit of a nation. . . . Le Corbusier is an optimist. His name is not mentioned, but in twenty years of urbanism, Le Corbusier is in all of the projects."[45]

Clearly, Le Corbusier's overriding concern had been to establish himself as the prophet of modern architecture. Chandigarh offered him that opportunity. He told Fry and Drew at their initial meeting in Paris: "We will rectify the pilot plan after our trip to India. . . . We must begin from the beginning."[46] Already familiar with India through his diverse readings, he quickly diagnosed the problem: "India had, and always has, a peasant culture that exists since a thousand years! India possessed Hindu temples (generally in carved stones) and Muslim temples in red stone, the architectural beauty of which is very geometrical. But India hasn't yet created an architecture for modern civilization (offices, factories, buildings)."

Nothing could be more appealing to Nehru, who saw in this modern-day prophet of the Second Industrial Age his own desire of ushering India into the technocratic world without repeating the mistakes of the urbanized nations of the West. What Le Corbusier wanted to produce was an architecture that would be "neither English, nor French, nor American," but "Indian" of the second half of the twentieth century. The sentiment is quite similar to that of Mayer, but with a difference. Whereas Mayer looked to India's past—bustling bazaars and closely-knit village communities—Le Corbusier looked to India's future, an India with all the paraphernalia of industrialization. This was intrinsically more appealing to Nehru and to the Punjabi officials. To this end, he hoped to give "some basic principles concerning habitation, which will be as clear as the basic principles of . . . the plan of Chandigarh."[47]

So when Le Corbusier caught up with Fry and Jeanneret in a rest house on the Simla road in late February 1951, the new plan of Chandigarh was "as good as done in four days," with Le Corbusier, Fry, Jeanneret, and Varma round a table. Although Fry has argued that the plan that finally emerged for Chandigarh "owes nearly everything to Le Corbusier,"[48] many points of the first plan that coincided with Le Corbusier's own thinking were retained. That the entire credit for Chandigarh has been conferred on Le Corbusier has less to do with the originality of his plan than with the controversial ideas associated with his mythic personality. Moreover, the process of transition from one team to the other was also not without its own rancor.

Familiar with Le Corbusier's ideas and knowing his forceful and uncompromising temperament, Mayer recognized that the change of teams also meant a change in plans for Chandigarh. Whereas Mayer's thinking was rooted in the Garden City Movement and in the ideas of Camillo Sitte that placed urban design on the random forms resulting from the growth of medieval cities, Le Corbusier believed in the gridiron plan as the only correct way of approaching the modern problems of city planning. In support of his belief he pointed to the gridiron pattern of the thirteenth-century bastides in the south of France and to American colonial cities of the seventeenth, eighteenth, and nineteenth centuries, including the plan for Washington, D.C., by Pierre L'Enfant and Benjamin Banneker. Le Corbusier felt that Sitte was "an intelligent and sensitive Viennese who simply stated the problem badly."[49]

Preferring the rigor of geometric forms, the axis, Le Corbusier argued that "man walks in a straight line because he had a goal and knows where he is going; he has made up his mind to reach some particular place and he goes straight to it. The pack-donkey meanders along, meditates a little in his scatter-brained and distracted fashion, he zigzags."[50] For him, the classical equilibrium of rectangles and pure volumes was "a symbol of perfection," and the disequilibrium of curved lines, jagged surfaces and unclear decoration represented an inferior effort of an equally inferior civilization. Some of these ideas appear more suited to the Islamic nation, where religion exhorts men to walk on a straight line with a purpose, rather than for the Hindu nation having a circular view of life, the concept of samsara.

However, it was only natural that Mayer should have come to the defense of his plan. Finding his French inadequate for the occasion and perhaps identifying more with the Anglo-Saxon background of Fry, Mayer directed most of his defense for his plan toward Fry. Immediately after learning of the appointment of Le Corbusier and Fry as the architects for Chandigarh, Mayer wrote to Fry congratulating him for getting the assignment, and noted: "It occurred to me to write you, for I felt it was appropriate to assure you that we want to take pains to give you the benefit of our study of the multiple problems, and explain to you something more about the *basis* for the planning and its unit elements than I think you are likely to get from purely the drawings and reports that you may find." He informed Fry that the "unusually large" dimensions of "super-block neighborhoods" were particularly suited for Punjab, and reasoned that a number of aspects of the plan—placement of schools, housing types based on income, shopping areas, and so forth—in absence of proper data so freely available "in our countries," had to be planned in Chandigarh on the basis of "personal knowledge and observations."[51] He concluded the letter by suggesting that he would like to arrange his next visit to India to coincide with Le Corbusier's visit so that they could all discuss the plan in detail.

Fry's answer was noncommittal, noting that he had "not really had time in which to study the plan and report as yet."[52] Fearing that Le Corbusier might leave by the time he reached India around March 15, 1951, Mayer again wrote to Fry an eleven-page letter, accompanied by a copy of his Washington, D.C., speech of May 10, 1950, detailing in length his master plan for Chandigarh. The urgency in Mayer's letter is evident: "I need hardly say that your and Le Corbusier's architectural assignment and our town plan are very closely inter-related, and that the more we can achieve and maintain an organic relationship or oneness of the two, the happier will be the result." Once again pointing to the absence of statistical data for Chandigarh, he reasoned that the Indian situation "demanded much more in the way of creative interpretation, of transfusion and synthesis of modern principles and thinking into the Indian scene, present and future."[53] Realizing the inadequacy of design and drafting personnel in India, and possibly with a view to buttressing his position further, Mayer even offered to assist in the recruitment of such talent in America and recommended the name of one Thomas McDonald, who was apparently eager to secure an architectural job in either India or Pakistan.[54]

By the time Mayer's letter reached Fry's London office, he had already left for India, but it was redirected to him at Chandigarh by Jane Drew. Fry's reply was anything but reassuring for Mayer. Although acknowledging that it was too early for him to come to "very strong conclusions about particular features" of the master plan, Fry "questioned the feasibility of sight lines onto the capitol building," and told Mayer that he was "having some sections taken out." Fry doubted whether Le Corbusier or he would like "to go all the way" with Mayer "on details, especially on informal housing lay-outs."[55] Not having worked with Le Corbusier before, however, Fry was equivocal as to what direction Le Corbusier would take. There ensued after Fry's letter a long exchange of correspondence between Mayer and Fry in which Mayer found himself increasingly on the defensive for his master plan.

Mayer's fears for his master plan were further reinforced by a telegram from Thapar, urging him to reach India by March 25, 1951, as theLe Corbusier team had suggested "consequential changes" in his plan. He further informed Mayer that Le Corbusier had found it necessary to move the Capitol Complex, the railroad station, and the business center, and that, to reduce area and cost, density of population would also have to be increased. Thapar ominously concluded that should Mayer fail to reach Chandigarh by March 25, "the Government will be obliged to accept the changes in your absence."[56] Unable to leave for India at once, Mayer responded by telegram, expressing his surprise at the proposed changes in his plan, and ruefully noted, "As planners acquainted with India, we spent six months in re-

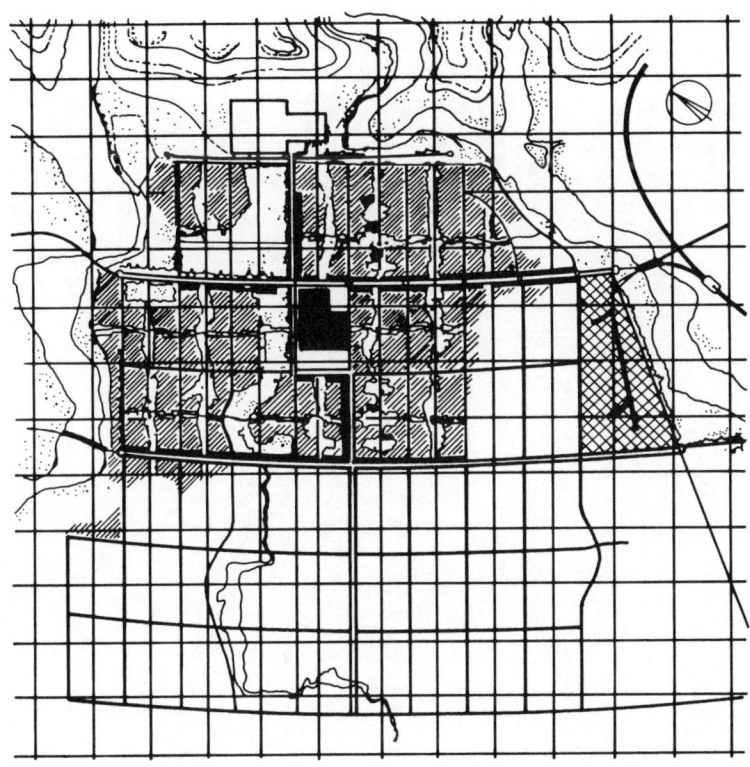
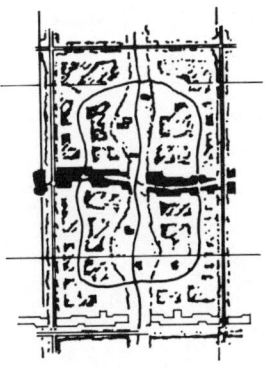

The revised Albert Mayer plan of Chandigarh, with a typical neighborhood (detail). Redrawn by Merlien Wilder King and reproduced by permission of Otto H. Koenigsberger from his article "New Towns in India," Town Planning Review *23, no. 2 (July 1952): 118.*

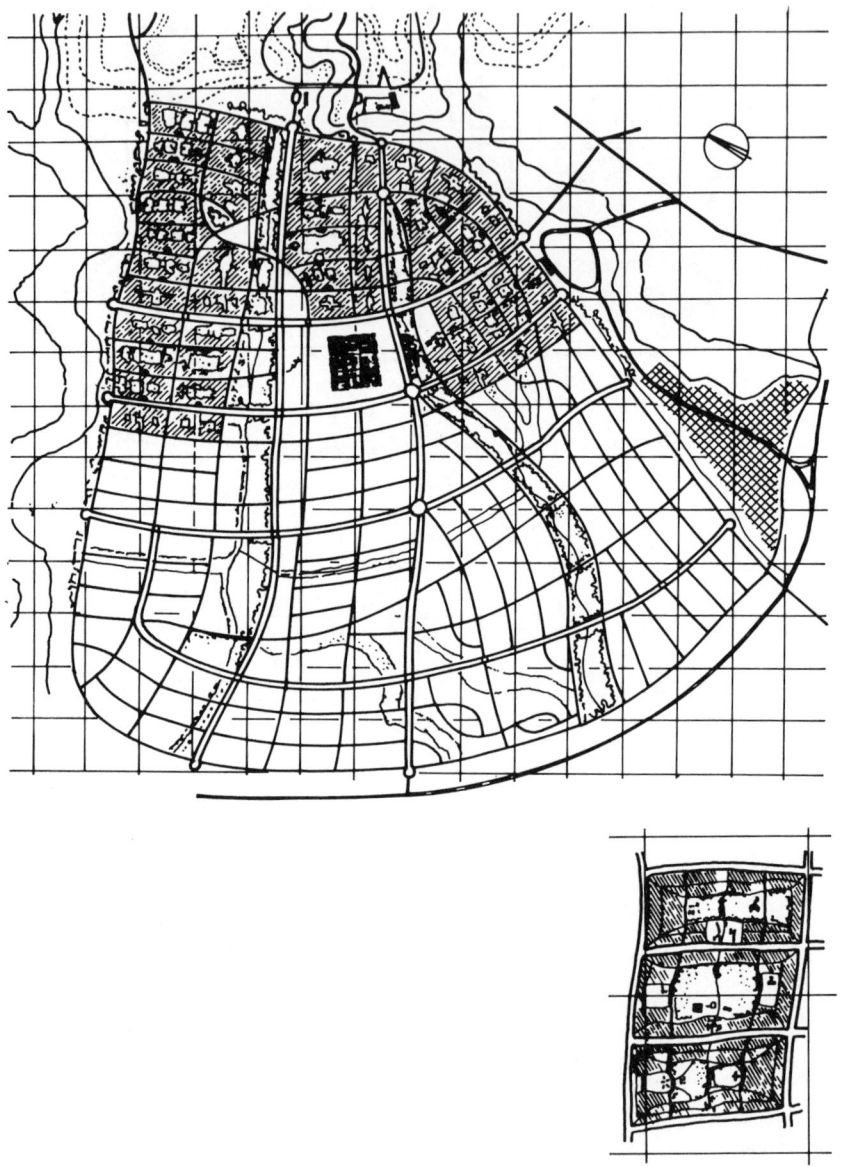

The Le Corbusier plan of Chandigarh, with a typical group of three neighborhoods (detail). Redrawn by Merlien Wilder King and reproduced by permission of Otto H. Koenigsberger from his article "New Towns in India," Town Planning Review *23, no. 2 (July 1952): 117.*

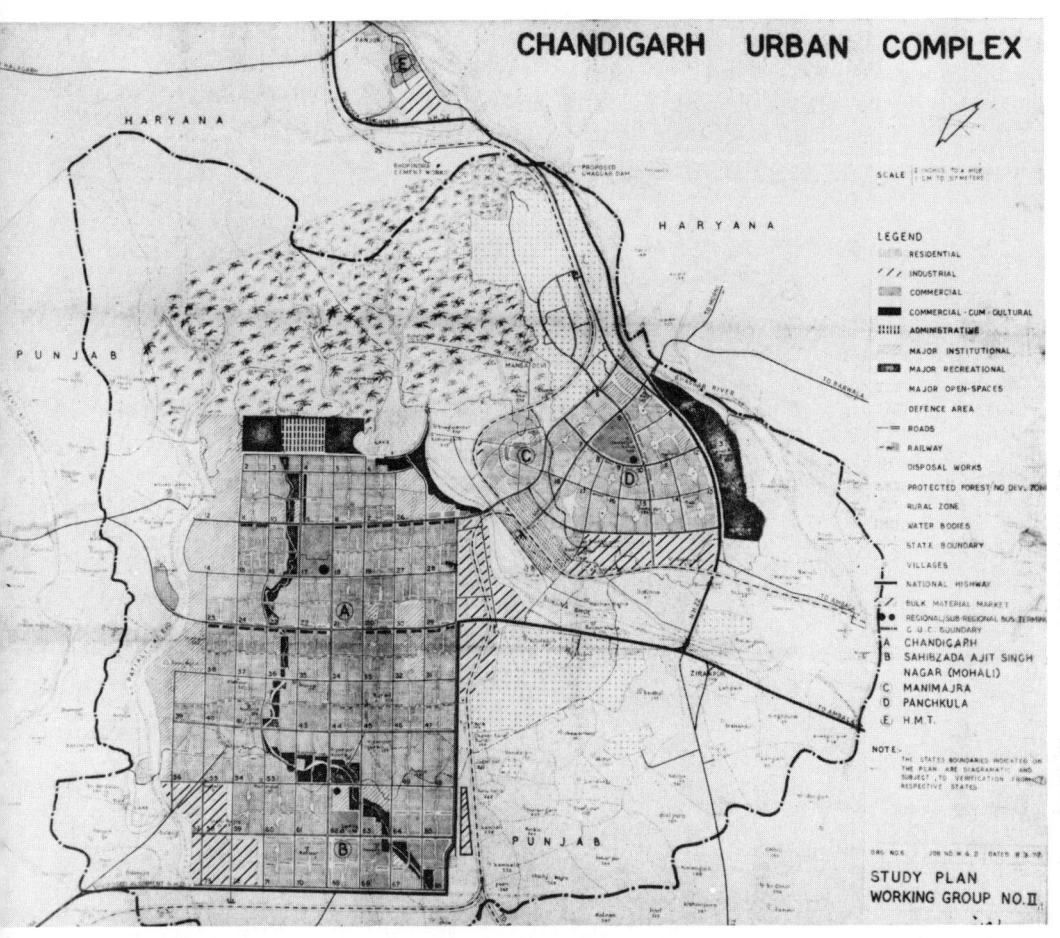

Chandigarh Urban Complex. Legend: A, Chandigarh; B, Sahibzada Ajit Singh (S.A.S.) Nagar (Mohali); C, Mani Majra; D, Punchkula; E, Hindustan Machine Tools (H.M.T.) Township. *The industrial developments (B, D), in Punjab and Haryana respectively, have aggravated the imbalance of work/residential areas in Chandigarh and are also likely to result in pollution.* Source: Town & Country Planning Organization, Ministry of Works & Housing, Government of India.

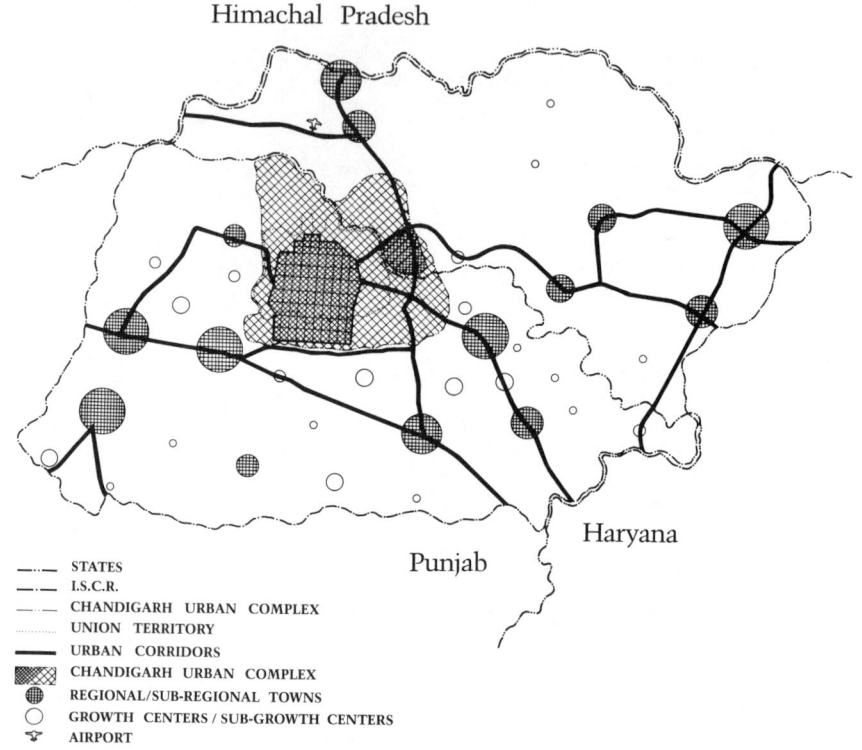

Inter State Chandigarh Region. Redrawn by Merlien Wilder King from a plan of the Town & Country Planning Organization, Ministry of Works & Housing, Government of India.

High Court Building, designed by Le Corbusier, with the parasol effect. This photograph and all others by Swadesh Talwar.

The Secretariat, designed by Le Corbusier, bears a close resemblance to the architect's Marseilles block.

The Assembly, designed by Le Corbusier, with a four-sided pyramidal prism and a hyperbolic-paraboloid form representative of the relationship between the upper and lower houses.

The City Center, which is located in Sector 17 and covers an area of 240 acres, was designed by Le Corbusier.

The Jan Marg (People's Avenue) interlinks the City Center with the Capitol Complex.

The chowk, or piazza, at the heart of the City Center.

The Madhya Marg (Middle Avenue), which, along with the Jan Marg, represent the two major cross-axial boulevards (V-2 roads) of the city.

Bicycle track, or V-8 road, in Sector 11.

The Gandhi Bhavan (House), designed by Pierre Jeanneret, is part of the Punjab University Complex. The plan of the university complex was prepared by J. K. Chowdhury.

Sukhna Lake, a result of P. L. Varma's efforts.

Low-cost housing, complete with sanitary facilities, kitchens, verandahs, and courtyards, for government employees in Sector 27. Housing in Chandigarh was mostly designed by Pierre Jeanneret, Jane Drew, and Maxwell Fry, with the collaboration of the Indian architects M. N. Sharma, Mrs. U. E. Chowdhury, Jeet Malhotra, B. P. Mathur, and Aditya Prakash.

Low-cost housing for government employees is Sector 7.

Chandigarh Railway Station.

The Railway Colony for employees

An example of an unauthorized rehri *(hawker) market colony.*

An example of an unauthorized jhuggi *(squatter) colony at Ghandidham, Chandigarh.*

search, observation and planning, and you considered the plans carefully several months more and approved the master plan, while now your architects have spent a month or so, including a short time for you to consider, and you already feel 'obliged to accept changes.'"[57]

Clearly the speed with which Le Corbusier's proposed changes were accepted had more to do with his dominating personality than with the exaggerated inadequacies of the Mayer plan. The resoluteness of Le Corbusier's purpose in Chandigarh was clearly demonstrated in his letter to the Indian ambassador in Paris: "I consider myself the only person at the moment, prepared by forty years of experience and study on this subject, capable of usefully helping your government." He added, "By participating in this project, I place the desire of my career through a work of harmony, of wisdom, of humanity in precise opposition to the chaos generally manifest in urbanism."[58] It was also likely that the monumentality of the Le Corbusier plan was more appealing to the Punjabis, who have an inclination for glitter and the grandiose.

When Mayer finally met Fry, Jeanneret, Varma, and Thapar on June 15, 1951, at the architect's office, United Services Club, Simla, he was faced with severe opposition to his plan. The new architects told him that they found his park system too "isolated," his footpath connections between parks too "tenuous" to act as links, and his loop-road system of development inadequate. Although in favor of retaining the neighborhood idea, the architects objected "to roads dominating the lay-out," instead of buildings and land use. Mayer tried to reason with them that the loop-road system gave greater privacy. The consensus that emerged from this meeting called for the development of "three sectors according to the principles underlying Mayer's plan, but with such modifications in detail as may be thought necessary."[59] Le Corbusier later noted that "sympathetically to Albert Mayer, who made the first plan of Chandigarh with sectors, I inscribed on *our* plan two 'Mayer Sectors' (Sector 8 and Sector 21)."[60]

What Mayer was hoping for by this consensus was that a real comparison could be made between his and Nowicki's ideas and those of Le Corbusier's on the question of traffic and its relationship to housing.[61] That, however, did not happen. Fry and Jeanneret found it increasingly difficult to execute Nowicki's designs. Fry explained the reasons to Mayer: "Le Corbusier, Jeanneret and I are all architects heavily involved in town planning. Any architects worth the name, and in charge of building on the scale of this city must have strong ideas on planning as being indisputably an extension of architecture. It is indeed very difficult to say where one ends and the other begins."

Fry continued, "We were therefore forced by our beliefs and ideas to present as completely as possible our conceptions in modification of what you had prepared and in view also [of] the major modifications forced upon us by circumstances." Pointing to "the detailed working out of Sector 8," one of the two sectors to be developed on Mayer's principles, Fry admitted to his inability to follow Mayer "much further than the statement of principle, because I have to build and control the buildings and for these purposes the plan and architecture are not to be separated." Fry, however, added that it grieved him that he was not able to achieve what Mayer wished because, even though "we all aim in the same direction . . . we are forced each to be ourselves and nobody else, and I can as easily fail to please Corbusier as you." Attributing much of the difficulties in designs to a lack of "joint consultation" between planners and architects in the initial stages, he recommended to Mayer to "let the matter remain at rest at the stage of agreement reached [by all]."[62]

Mayer made yet another plea to Fry for including his three-block district in the plan, claiming that "it is a moral, spiritual and ethical question," and that "you owe it fully as much to your own professional standards as to me."[63] Somewhat moved by Mayer's insistence, Fry offered as an alternative to develop sectors fourteen, fifteen, and sixteen along Mayer's principles.[64] But by this time Mayer was a defeated man, unwilling to undertake the struggles "involved in our dealings," and promised not to "further attempt to influence this plan."[65]

While Mayer was fighting a losing battle for his plan, Le Corbusier was consolidating his position with the Indian officials, particularly with Nehru, the main force behind the development of the city. To ensure that the interest of the Indians did not falter during his long absences from India, Le Corbusier wrote to Nehru regularly. On one occasion he wrote: "I have the honour and pleasure of offering you, very simply, this album concerning Chandigarh, which assumes the form of the 'CIAM Town-Planning Grid.' This album contains only a part of the tremendous work I have realized for Chandigarh . . . and I feel that I have done this task with all my soul. . . . I hope this album will still let you feel that a valuable work is being undertaken which will perhaps astonish wealthier and more powerful nations."[66]

What the CIAM Town-Planning Grid amounted to was basically the updating of the city's four functions as defined by Patrick Geddes —living, working, recreation, and communication—and coordinating these functions and determining their legitimate place in the master plan of Chandigarh. Deploring the deteriorating condition of modern cities as a result of industrialization, the CIAM charter of 1933 proclaimed to reintroduce the three basic ingredients of urbanism—sun, space, and greenery—to modern urban life. Fry explained the concept to the Indians:

> There are three main elements that operate. There is first habitation, and by the necessity of the situation this takes up the most space, but not, as so often happens, all the space. The other two elements are work—and that includes shopping and commerce, administration, Post Office, etc.—and relaxation, in which is included everything that ministers to the care of the body and the spirit, and therefore schools and playing fields and green spaces and shady walks, theatres, etc. These two elements are opposed; they do not naturally go together; each have, as it were, their time in the day.[67]

Nehru, given to eclectic tendencies, found these ideas appealing. Two days after his first visit to Chandigarh on April 2, 1952, Nehru wrote to the governor of Punjab: "I am writing this note just to draw attention to two facts: 1) that we might give thought to what M. Corbusier suggested, i.e., all our building conceptions, small or big, should be thought of more in terms of Indian conditions and 2) that our cheap housing scheme should be thought of chiefly in terms of providing sanitation, lighting and water supply. We can add to this as occasion offers and resources are available. Even good huts would be infinitely preferable with these amenities than solid constructions."[68] It is doubtful, however, whether local traditions had any significant influence on Le Corbusier. On the contrary, he is said to have remarked on one occasion, "What is the significance of Indian style in the world today if you accept machines, trousers and democracy."[69]

Meanwhile, the architectural work at Chandigarh was neatly divided between Le Corbusier and his associates. Le Corbusier, in addition to assuming the responsibility of revising the master plan and establishing architectural control, reserved the designing of the Capitol Complex for himself. Fry, Drew, and Jeanneret were given the responsibility of directing the actual construction of the city: housing for government employees, schools, shopping centers, hospitals, and other civic and housing structures of the city. Assisting them were the Indians N. S. Lamba, J. S. Dethe, and A. R. Prabhawalker as town planners; and U. E. Chowdhury, Piloo Mody, B. P. Mathur, M. N. Sharma, and Jeet Malhotra as architects. J. K. Chowdhury assumed the responsibility of designing the plan for Punjab University. Coming principally from the Indian schools of architecture with practically no experience, these young Indians made the Planning Office at Chandigarh "a finishing school, as any good office should be."[70] Le Corbusier felt that "the Indian youth must take a fundamental part in the enterprise" and he hoped to "provide them with a useful springboard to jump from."[71] In fact, Le Corbusier saw himself as the "Spiritual Director" of the entire enterprise, and outlined his role thus:

1. To provide spiritual and technical direction to the enterprise so as to give it unity.
2. To nominate two architects of our spirit, capable, devoted and sufficiently experienced who would fulfill the functions.
3. To appoint three Hindu architects to our atelier on the rue de Sèvres to carry out studies as the work proceeds in order to give them an education of the university type. . . .
4. The two foreign architects . . . will be under the control of M. Le Corbusier, receiving orders on technical and aesthetic issues.[72]

Le Corbusier's cure for the urban congestion that he saw around him rested on two things: the separation of the functions of automobile traffic and greater pedestrian movement. For him, the city was a three-dimensional organism: the space lost to the construction of tall buildings at ground level must be recaptured at the level of the roof, and converted into terrace gardens, playgrounds, plazas, and the like for the pedestrian. As the socioeconomic conditions and living habits of the Indians ruled out the idea of vertical planning, Le Corbusier had to decide on a horizontal plan more or less on the pattern of a postwar garden town. Essentially "the solution proposed rested upon the legal, and to some extent the physical, segregation of a major road-grid to fast-moving traffic,"[73] with the basic planning unit of the master plan being a sector. In Le Corbusier's own words:

"The Plan is based on the main features of the '7 V Rule,' determining an essential function: the creation of the 'Sectors.' The 'Sector' is *the container of family life* (the 24 solar hours' cycle which must be fulfilled in perfect harmony). Its [the sector's] dimensions are the outcome of studies which were made in 1929, then in 1936, then in 1939, then in 1949, at Buenos Aires, Montevideo, São Paulo, Bogotá."[74]

Providing an area of 800 × 1,200 meters to a sector, Le Corbusier argued that no pedestrians would have to walk more than ten minutes from the farthest point of the sector to the center of the sector. Self-contained in character, a sector was bound by fast-traffic roads, running on its four sides and permitting only four vehicular entries into its interior. Each sector was self-sufficient, having shops, schools, health centers, places of recreation and worship. The shops were located along the shopping street, which runs northwest to southeast across the sector. The schools and community buildings were located in the central green strips, stretching longitudinally northeast to southwest at right angles to the shopping street. The shopping center of each sector communicated with the shopping center of the adjacent sectors on both sides, thus forming a continuous ribbonlike shopping street. The central green also stretched to the green of the next sector, ultimately culminating in the surrounding farmland. In the first phase of the plan, thirty sectors were to be developed, covering an area of nine thousand acres; by the completion of the second phase of the plan, another seventeen sectors were to be added, covering another six thousand acres of land.

In the interest of scale, the market, or the hub of the sector, dominated the housing areas. Drew, who played a significant role in the planning of sectors, noted: "The architects, who had a better sense of the importance of physical environment than administrators, laid down that the main part of this centre should be three storeyed and also be strictly architecturally controlled."[75] Considering the Indian habit of open-air sleeping during summer months, and considering the socioeconomic background of the region, the height of the structures in sectors was restricted to two or three stories. House designs and sector layouts, however, could not be considered as one because there were not enough houses of any one type to enable the architects to design complete districts with but one type of house. "Inevitably there was a mixing of interests and only an approximation to a comprehensive design was achieved."[76]

Divided along social class lines, the sectors had three main density groupings of 25, 50, and 75 persons per acre. The housing plots within sectors ranged from 114 square meters to 4,500 square meters. Of the 26,000 residential plots created in the first phase and another 9,500 in the second phase, half were reserved for government construction. Fourteen different categories of housing for government employees were planned, varying from the house for the chief minister to a small, two-room house, complete with sanitary facilities, a kitchen, a veranda, and a courtyard, for the lowest-paid employee.

The next important element of Le Corbusier's master plan was the division of traffic into a series of seven categories comprising a hierarchy of circulation, ranging from arterial roads to apartment house corridors. Specifically, the V–1 represented regional roads leading into the city; the V–2 represented the two major cross-axial boulevards of the city, one of which served as the ceremonial avenue linking the central district with the Capitol Complex, while the other served as the cultural-commercial axis; the V–3 represented the fast-moving traffic roads intersecting at half a mile across and three-quarters of a mile up the planned area, thus enclosing the sectors and establishing the gridiron pattern of the city; the V–4 represented bazaar streets, were slightly irregular, were restricted to slow-moving traffic, bisected the long side of each sector, and were lined with shops on the south side to ensure shade for pedestrians and to prevent excessive street crossing; the V–5 represented a loop road and, intersecting the V–4, distributed traffic within the sector; the V–6 represented roads or paths leading up to houses; and the V–7 represented a strip of parkland that contained schools, open spaces, pedestrian paths, and connected with adjoining sectors, making it possible to cross the entire city on foot through a park. To this grouping, Le Corbusier later added the V–8, which represented bicycle trails. He reasoned that "effectively the 'two-wheels' have customs which are antagonistic to those of the 'four-wheels.'"[77]

Comparing the seven Vs to the "blood stream" function of the "respiratory system in biology," Le Corbusier believed that they created "order" in the city.[78] Although the diverse character of Indian traffic to some extent justifies the application of the seven-V rule in Chandigarh, the plan in the main is oriented for an industrialized nation of the West demanding ample space for automobile traffic. The liberal provisions for automobile traffic in Chandigarh are more or less the same as those found in the United States, where street planning is based on the ownership of two cars per family—a situation that does not apply to India.

Rectangular in form with a cross-axis in the middle, Le Corbusier's plan represents his lifelong obsession with the idea of a city as an organism. Jane Drew has described it thus:

> [The plan] is almost biological in its form. Its commanding head the capitol group, its heart the city commercial centre, its hand the industrial area, its brain and intellectual centre in the parkland where are the museums, university, library, etc. It has its stomach in its city service centre in the central market, its veins and nerves in the roads, the water, electricity. The whole is surrounded by open country but it has its internal lungs, too, its green breathing space and its structure of roads the bony system to which the flesh of the building volume of the city is related. This long simile of a town as an organism can be even further extended to the fact that allowance has been made for its growth.[79]

The City has four main work areas: 1) the Capitol in the northeast, 2) the educational zone in the northwest, 3) the City Center, and 4) the industrial area in the southeast. The Capitol is the climax of the architectural composition, interlinking the City Center through the controlled architectural developments along the Jan Marg (the People's Avenue), thus forming a focal point of the city, both visually and symbolically. The prominence given to this area symbolizes the "solidarity" of Punjab India. The City Center is centrally located at the junction of the two important axes of the city, the Madhya Marg (the Middle Avenue) and the Jan Marg (the People's Avenue). Beside the central green space of sectors, there is a green sprawling space extending northeast to southwest, designated by Le Corbusier as the "Leisure Valley," a zone of solitude and cultural activities. To the northeast of the Capitol is Rajendra Park; to the southeast of the Capitol is Sukhna Lake—a result of engineer Varma's dedicated efforts. The lake and the park are connected by the Uttar Marg (the Northern Avenue). A greenbelt extending five miles beyond the city was also provided to protect the city from unauthorized encroachment; it was later extended to ten miles beyond the city.

The speed with which Le Corbusier came up with a new master plan would not have been possible had there not existed a well-thought-out Mayer plan and had Le Corbusier not relied heavily on it. Restricting him further from introducing his ideas in Chandigarh was the nonindustrial character of India and his own unfamiliarity with the Indian way of life. In Chandigarh, Le Corbusier's idea of the vertical city was only partially realized. The plan as it has been finally applied to Chandigarh represents a compromise between the ideas of the vertical and the horizontal garden cities.

In the second plan, the Capitol Complex remained outside the city as its head, but was placed at an elevated level slightly to the northeast, offering a better view of the buildings. There were two other changes made in the Capitol Complex: the old idea of building a chain of small ponds around the Capitol was dropped for practical reasons; also dropped was the idea of a government center surrounded by housing. Likewise, in the second plan the Civic Center, railway station, and industrial complex stayed in the same vicinity. Both plans provided for traffic isolation; and neighborhood units made up the fabric of the city in both instances, with some differences. Instead of a superblock, the neighborhood unit was now called a sector, given rectangular lines, and enlarged to cover 800 × 1,200 meters, roughly the size of Mayer's three-block district. Despite the use of rectilinear axes, the second plan exhibits some curved lines, particularly in the lateral streets crossing the Jan Marg, presumably introduced on Fry's suggestion to mitigate the depressing effect of streets seeming to lead nowhere in the absence of having a terminal focus in the mountains. Le Corbusier's own revived interest in curves might also have influenced him in readily accepting Fry's suggestion.

At the philosophical level, Mayer placed greater emphasis on the socioeconomic factors of the city, its potential for future growth, the peculiarities of Indian traffic, the social customs of the people, and other related issues. Le Corbusier, on the other hand, remained concerned with the physical attributes of the city and the monumentality of the building designs. Mayer recommended the inclusion of industry in the city to stimulate its population growth; Le Corbusier felt that the inclusion of industry in Chandigarh was incompatible with its administrative character. Although both planners professed to create the city in the Indian idiom, perhaps Mayer was more sincere about it. This in itself would not have mattered but for the fact that "there were vast masses of people who were not included in the project estimate."[80] The blame for this must rest as much on the naïve planners as on the overambitious administrators.

The problems of architecture had a special significance in Chandigarh. Fry put it thus:

> Climate has been the determining factor in Chandigarh architecture, and so it should be. There is no surer way to a suitable architecture, and one that is in accord with the deepest realities of the country; for it is climate that dictates agriculture, moulds customs and affects even religion. Climate is a great element in India. . . . Climate will dictate form but economics and social custom will modify its achievement, and at Chandigarh all three operated strongly through the work of the architects involved.[81]

All architectural work was subjected to the rigorous test of functional analysis as codified in the Charter of Athens by CIAM (1933).[82] Because Chandigarh was to be a planned city, all commercial buildings were placed under architectural control as codified under the Capital of Punjab Development and Regulation Act, 1952, meticulously drafted by Fry and Drew in consultation with Le Corbusier. Initially, private housing in Chandigarh was "left to its own fate (of course, under the normal bye-laws and zoning), hoping that good taste engendered by the Government buildings will prevail and good Architects will settle in Chandigarh to fulfill the needs of private builders."[83] When this did not happen, the Chandigarh administration invoked clause four of the Act, which called for controlled development of buildings in Chandigarh. Le Corbusier himself was given to architectural control, a simplification and uniformity in building forms achieved through "standardization." For awhile Le Corbusier wanted the government architects "to work within a set of fixed modules and use the modular, but this broke down on personal grounds."[84] In general, however, government housing followed a pattern of standardized designs, private housing was architecturally controlled, and neighborhood shops were built to specified designs.

The City Center, covering an area of 240 acres, was designed by Le Corbusier, and is broadly divided into two zones—the northern and the southern. The northern zone serves the functions of the civic administration while the southern zone houses the activities of the district administration. It is connected to the Capitol Complex, to the university, and to the industrial area by fast traffic roads. At the heart of the City Center is a central *chowk* or "piazza," marking the crossing of two wide pedestrian ways running northeast to southwest and northwest to southeast in the form of a cross. Around the *chowk* are clustered the civic and commercial buildings, the Town Hall, the Central Library, the Post and Telegraph offices, cinemas, shops, restaurants, banks, and so forth. A slow-traffic road encircles the *chowk* with large areas set aside for car parking. The *chowk* itself is free from any vehicular traffic, measures approximately 360 feet × 436 feet, and is ideally suited for religious activities and other festive congregations that are so important to the Indian way of life. The *chowk* is connected to other spaces of the City Center by a network of pedestrian ways.

Architecturally, the City Center has been unified by means of standardized four-story concrete-frame buildings. The size of the buildings was restricted by the lack of elevators and the fear of earthquakes. The eleven-story Post and Telegraph Building, designed by Le Corbusier, is the tallest in the complex. It has been suggested that "the design effort [of the City Center] may have involved an attempt to balance the symbolically important Capitol Complex with another ensemble of monumental dimensions."[85] At any rate, it seems certain that the inspiration for it seems to have been derived from New Delhi's commercial district of Connaught Place. As desired by Le Corbusier, the City Center contains no provision for housing.

It is, however, the Capitol Complex, containing the Legislative Assembly, the High Court, and the Secretariat, which was to form the culmination of Le Corbusier's master plan. The Capitol Complex also had a special significance for the displaced Punjab government hoping to employ within its buildings nearly 18,000 workers, a significant portion of the 150,000 population projected for the first phase of the city. More importantly, the Chandigarh Capitol Complex was to be the Indian answer to the New Delhi Capitol, glorifying the British Empire with "its domes and colonnades, avenues and enormous squares."[86] This may be one reason for the exaggerated scale of the complex and the overmonumentality of the buildings. The bitter memory of colonial rule still alive in their minds and the wounds of partition still fresh caused the Indians to search for symbols and monuments they could call their own. Not only did the buildings in the Capitol Complex have to be the "chief" buildings of the government, but they had to look like it. Fry called it "a justifiable element of exaggeration."[87]

It is hardly surprising, then, that Le Corbusier's design proved intrinsically appealing to Indians, which is reflected in Nehru's statement: "India has many famous ancient cities and buildings. Among these reminders of the past, there now stands a new and utterly different, growing city—Chandigarh, which is, in the main, the creation of the famous architect, Le Corbusier. . . . I think, however, that Chandigarh is a great creation, which has already powerfully affected Indian architecture and brought new and fascinating ideas to our architects and town planners."[88] It is ironic, however, that the mantle of building independent India's monumental symbols should have fallen on the man who credulously believed Western colonialization to be a *"force morale"*[89] for development.

Placed at the head of the plan, occupying an area of 220 acres, cut off by a canal and a boulevard from the nearest housing, but approached directly by the wide Capitol approach road, the Capitol Complex resembles an acropolis of monuments, which radiate their dominance for miles. The composition of the Capitol is the total creation of the environment in which the natural backdrop of the Shivalik Hills is enhanced by the artificial horizons of manmade hills, by the geometric depression of vehicular roads and by the Esplanade and the paved areas for pedestrian movement. The pools, the monuments, and the trees play an important role in unfolding the visual drama of the Capitol. The main material of construction in the Capitol is raw concrete, which Le Corbusier had discovered in 1908 through Auguste Perret.

Bearing a similarity to Le Corbusier's earlier plans for Saint-Dié and Bogotá, the Capitol plan at Chandigarh once again points to his preoccupation with geometric forms. "The question of optics became paramount," wrote Le Corbusier, "when we had to decide where to put government buildings (or palaces). . . . I had to appreciate and to decide alone. The problem was no longer one of reasoning but of sensation." He continued: "Chandigarh is not a city of lords, princes or kings confined within walls, crowded in by neighbours. It was a matter of occupying the plain." For Chandigarh, he saw geometrical forms to be "a sculpture of the intellect." He further noted: "It was a battle of space, fought within the mind. Arithmetic . . . geometrics: it would all be there when the whole was finished. For the moment, oxen, cows and goats, driven by peasants, crossed the sun-scorched fields."[90] The result, however, has been termed by one critic as "compaction composition even more compacted."[91]

The three buildings in the Capitol Complex—the Assembly, the

Secretariat, and the High Court—face each other. First to be completed was the High Court. A huge parasol of concrete, held above the roofs of the courts by arched forms, slightly reminiscent of Mughal influence,[92] cools and shades the building proper. As Le Corbusier explained, "Sun and rain are the two components of an architecture." It followed from this that there must be a sunshade and an umbrella at the same time. "The roofs must be treated as problems of hydraulics," he continued, "and the problem of shade is the most important. The concept of the *brise-soleil* here acquires its full value as a breaker of acquired habits, and should be extended from the window to the whole facade, indeed to the very structure of the building."[93] The effect, however, has been that the grill of sunbreakers that makes up the wall of the High Court seems to bend forward as if to force itself forward to enter into a relationship with the other buildings. The cooling parasol also proved ineffective in the scorching heat of Punjab; as a result a concrete sunshade had to be added at the ground level.

There had been other difficulties with the layout of the High Court: a separate parking area had to be created for the status-conscious judges as they refused to park their cars alongside the rest of the people under the huge, three-pillared entrance; the operations of the courts had to be turned around to avoid the brilliant sunlight's hitting the judges in the eyes; and the acoustic-control devices for the courtrooms made up of huge woolen tapestries never appealed to the aesthetics of the judges. Le Corbusier himself designed the tapestries from various Indian motifs and had them woven in Kashmir at a cost that would have been halved if he had had them made locally. Le Corbusier received full support of Nehru, who felt that this was one way of "encouraging our cottage industries and . . . introducing new ideas, which may or may not be completely successful, but which themselves lead to other ideas."[94] When new courts were added to cope with the expanded legal system, they had to be built at the back of the High Court building, where they remain visually hidden and functionally inconvenient. The building itself is based on a simple system of columns, beams, and slabs, with courts on the ground floor and offices above each court.

The Secretariat, which bears a close similarity to Le Corbusier's Marseilles block, was next to be built. The 800-feet-long and eight-stories-high Secretariat is the tallest and the longest building in the Capitol Complex and gives the impression of a wall enclosing the northwest side of the Complex. The structure is broken in half-a-dozen places with projections, recesses, stair towers, changes in pattern, and the like. All these contrasting elements—like everything else that Le Corbusier built in Chandigarh—are related to one another through the proportionate scale of the modular system, so as to create a feeling of harmony. The top of the building is developed as a roof garden, containing necessary service structures and a cafeteria for the employees.

Le Corbusier described the building thus: "The form and attitude of the building are determined by the favourable orientation for sun and dominant winds; by its automobile access in trenches, with artificial hills made of excavated earth; by the circulation of pedestrians protected from automobiles; by various *brise-soleils* planned according to the path of the sun; and finally, by the landscape artist's role which governed its architectural silhouette in the ensemble of the capitol."[95] It seems, however, that originally Le Corbusier wanted to build the Secretariat more in the image of his ideas: a building with a tall, thin slab carrying a surface *brise-soleil*, divided by a central horizontal band, with the mass raised on *pilotis*. He even threatened to resign if his original idea was not accepted.[96] Evidently it was not a serious threat as he had an alternative plan, which was later employed.

Placed symmetrically on the horizontal axis of the Capitol Complex, the Assembly is 128 feet in diameter at its base, and rises to 124 feet at its highest point, and is the third building to have been completed in the Complex. The building is a geometric play of concrete cubes against free-form elements, also of concrete. The relationship between the upper and lower houses of the Assembly has been imaginatively expressed by Le Corbusier. The first is a small, four-sided pyramidal prism; the second is a huge, hyperbolic-paraboloid form, similar in shape to the thin-shell concrete cooling tower familiar to industry. In fact, Le Corbusier borrowed the idea from an impressive grouping of cooling towers that he saw on his visit to Ahmedabad. These two symbolic forms are placed inside a large "forum" which, in turn, is surrounded on its four sides by galleries containing offices and committee meeting rooms. The two symbolic forms are not obscured by this mass of surrounding offices, and the forum, as Le Corbusier saw it, serves as a place for the legislators to exchange ideas informally between assembly sessions.

Inside the Assembly, most of the interior lighting is derived from skylights on top. Instead of a speaker's platform, the 180 members of the Assembly have been provided with separate microphones to air their views on state matters. A massive three-stories high porch forms a monumental entrance that faces the High Court, a quarter of a mile away. Most intricate in design plans of all the buildings in the Capitol Complex, the Assembly was symbolically to represent a "coming together" of citizens. In practice, however, the building seems an elaborately contrived means of keeping them "separated."[97] As one Indian architect has perceptively observed on the functional ability of the Assembly, "It is a near impossible Parliament to deliberate in."[98] The subsequent history of the state and the unresolved political controversy over Chandigarh itself has borne him out.

The Capitol Complex plan provided for two other buildings: the governor's residence and the Monument of the Open Hand. The governor's residence was to be located at the highest point, almost touching the foothills. Five stories high, the first level of the building was to contain offices and other service areas; the second level, with the main pedestrian access, was designed as the reception area for state functions; the third level contained apartments for the governor's guests; the fourth level contained the governor's private apartments; and the fifth level was designed as a roof garden having a curvilinear outline with an upward lifting curve crowning the building against the Shivalik backdrop. Because the state government decided to use the Circut House designed by Jeanneret as the governor's residence, the scheme was dropped. But more importantly, Nehru also vetoed the scheme, maintaining that a governor's residence within the Capitol area was incompatible with democratic principles.

To maintain the visual balance in the scale of the Capitol Complex, Le Corbusier suggested as an alternative another building which he thought more appropriate to the time: a Museum of Knowledge, his "Electronic Laboratory for Scientific Decision." Like his other ideas, this museum was light years ahead of its times and resembled a modern-day video arcade. He described it thus: "Your museum becomes practicable and *capable of being used* as soon as the overwhelming techniques of electronics intervene (pictures, sounds, words, colours, diagrams, etc. . . .) manifested by magnetic tape recordings which I have called the 'Round Books,' that is to say audio-visual films. These 'Round Books' are therefore a new form of modern edition: instead of being printed on paper they are recorded on magnetic tape." He felt that these "Round Books" could be multiplied *"ad libitum"* and would be "capable of finding their decisive customers (scientists, universities, the public in general, educators, etc. . . . a whole scale of enlightenment)."[99] Nehru's response was predictable: "The proposal of Le Corbusier to have a special type of museum [as] a display of scientific progress and of electronic devices appears to me a very attractive one. It would be unique in India and will give us a glimpse of the future."[100] In a country like India, however, where 80 percent of the population depends on primitive agricultural techniques and where the literacy rate is abysmally low, Le Corbusier's idea sounded incomprehensible to the administrators and the scheme was shelved.

The idea of the Open Hand was not new with Le Corbusier, but it acquired a special significance in Chandigarh. The earliest manifestation of the Open Hand can be traced to a picture he painted in 1930, entitled *La Main rouge*.[101] Its introduction in Chandigarh symbolized, on the one hand, the beginning of the Second Machine Age, and on the other, the culmination of Le Corbusier's lifework. He no longer viewed the struggle for dominance between America and Russia relevant to the modern world. He saw instead in the modern world all things as interrelated. "The relations are continuous and contiguous around the globe, affected by nuances and diversity," he declared. "The question is man and his environment, an event of local as well as of global order."[102] Orwellian in tone and environmentalist in content, this might have been an example of Green party pontification on present-day issues. But Le Corbusier believed that India, because it had not gone through the pains of the First Industrial Revolution, was "awakening, intact, at a time of all possibilities."[103] He explained the idea to Nehru:

> India might consider precious the idea of raising in the Capitol of Chandigarh at present under construction, among the palaces which will house its institutions and its authority, the symbolic and evocative sign of the 'Open Hand':
> Open to receive the newly created wealth, open to distribute it to its people and to others.
> The 'Open Hand' will assert that the second era of the machine age has begun: the era of harmony.[104]

Whatever doubts Le Corbusier might have had left were removed by Jane Drew, who, on one of their usual evening walks in Chandigarh, urged him to build in the very heart of the Capitol Complex the "monument" by which he had come to express his ideas on "urbanism" and his "philosophic thought."[105] Drew felt that these signs "deserve" to be known as they provide the key to the creation of Chandigarh. The Open Hand, which was to be located between the governor's residence and the High Court and was to define the outer edge of the Capitol Complex to the northeast, would be an artistic sculpture upheld against the rugged profile of the Shivaliks. It was to be made of steel sheets and rigged to a concrete pedestal and be free to move on its axis, and was to create visual links between the four main structures. To provide further harmony and visual tension between the structures of the Complex, Le Corbusier also planned the Martyr's Memorial and placed it in the vast Esplanade, situated along the cross-axis between the Assembly and the High Court. That none of these monuments have been erected has been one reason for the broken visual harmony of the Capitol Complex.

Also included in the plan were provisions for a cultural center, a leisure valley, a university and an industrial area. While the leisure valley was expected to promote among the youth of the city an awareness for plays, music, dance, theater, and other cultural activities, the cultural center was expected to "harmonize" the civilization of the Second Machine Age through museums, exhibitions, and other cultural "outlets." These cultural outlets were also to be used for presenting national and local festivals to the people. As Le Corbusier noted: "The Center of Itinerant Exhibition is devoted to the 'Synthesis of the Major Arts': Urbanism, Architecture, Painting and Sculpture."[106]

In 1954, Punjab University, which had been functioning since independence with its departments scattered in Amritsar, Delhi, Jullundur, Hoshiarpur, Ludhiana, and with administrative offices in Solan, purchased Sector 14 to be its permanent home. Covering an approximate area of 306 acres, the new campus was to be a fully self-contained community: classrooms, department offices, dormitories, shopping facilities, restaurants, housing for the university staff and other employees. As in other parts of the city, housing for university employees was according to rank with employees paying 10 percent of their salary in rent. The Post-Graduate Medical Institute and the College of Engineering were to be located in Sector 12.

The plan for the university was prepared by J. K. Chowdhury, a consultant to the Punjab government. By 1958, however, the responsibility for university construction had been transferred to the joint direction of Pierre Jeanneret and B. P. Mathur, both of the Capital Project Office. By 1970, the university had acquired an additional 250 acres, and was operating nearly 40 departments and several regional centers throughout the state. It was only natural that many of the ideas and designs in the planning of the university were borrowed from the Capital Project—but the university project was one with which Le Corbusier was not directly involved. This might be one explanation for its poor planning and for its lack of community integration with the city that is so glaringly evident.

As for the industrial area, Le Corbusier was opposed to having one in Chandigarh. "Chandigarh is an administrative city," he once noted, "and consequently a 'Radio Concentric City.' It must never be an industrial city."[107] The reasons for his opposition to having industry in Chandigarh were rooted in his concept of "the Three Human Establishments," developed during the war years with the group l'ASCORAL (*Assemblée de Constructeurs pour une Révolution Architecturale*). What this amounted to was categorization of cities into three different areas with separate forms and functions for each. Thus, the Three Human Establishments of the Second Machine Age were classified as 1) the agricultural city, 2) the linear industrial city, and 3) the radio concentric city. The last was meant to be the city of exchanges, where commercial transactions take place and where administrative "authority" is established.

However, at Chandigarh Le Corbusier did make an exception by providing 580 acres of land for an industrial area at the southeastern edge of the city. To protect the neighboring residential area from smog and other pollutants, provision for a 300- to 500-feet-wide greenbelt was made in the plan, similar to what Mayer had proposed earlier in his plan. There was one restriction: only light industries powered by electricity were to be allowed in Chandigarh, such as canning, light engineering, sports equipment, hosiery, flour- and saw-mills, and building materials, and so forth. The industrial area was expected to support approximately 2,500 families by employing 15,000 people.

Ample provision was also made in the plan for developing areas as parks and green spaces. A network of narrow greenbelts was created to connect major parks, an area covering seventy-five acres was allowed for a zoological garden, and another hundred acres were reserved for the botanical gardens. A landscaping committee, consisting of engineers and architects of the Chandigarh Project, was set up in July 1953, under the chairmanship of M. S. Randhawa, a native of the region and an imaginative member of the prestigious Indian Civil Service. A chart was prepared with Le Corbusier's help showing shapes of trees and colors of flowers to be planted in Chandigarh.

The landscape treatment for the city was divided into three categories: the roads, the free spaces of the parks, and the urban spaces where landscaping would complement architectural elements, such as the Capitol Complex and the Civic Center. In July 1952, a nursery was started in Sector 23 in a mango grove, where seeds and tree saplings were collected from the old state gardens of Patiala, Amritsar, Attari, Bhunga, and the Mughal gardens of Pinjore. A provision for a rose garden was also made. However, the paucity of resources, the harsh climate of the Punjab, and the stray animals so common in Indian cities have all contributed to the deterioration of vegetation in Chandigarh. Nevertheless, the landscaping work at Chandigarh, like its architecture, was to become the basis of all tree-planting for all new towns, hydroelectric dam sites, and universities in India.

In 1952, the Periphery Control Act was passed by the Punjab government, providing a permanent greenbelt around the city. The idea behind the act was to protect the surrounding rural community from degenerating by contact with urban life and also to regulate development within a five-mile radius beyond the city. Le Corbusier called the act "a happy event" and urged the city administrators that "it must be carried out at all costs."[108] The act was later amended in 1962 to extend to a ten-mile radius beyond the city.

The effectiveness of the act, however, has been limited. Several unauthorized constructions have emerged within the periphery zone, threatening the planned character of Chandigarh. Within the city itself, it is a commonplace to find unplanned structures, tenements, and other unauthorized developments that violate the very basis of a planned city. These developments started long ago, but as long as Le Corbusier lived he fought hard to preserve the character of the city that he had planned. Nearly ten years after starting work on Chandigarh, he wrote to Nehru: "The construction of the 'Capitol' and its lateral elements has brought to Chandigarh such a marvellous landscape (lake and mountain) which no city in the world possesses. Let us not destroy it!"[109]

.5.
A PLANNED CITY

A planned city presupposes the existence of an authority or an organization sufficiently effective to secure the site, marshal resources for its growth, and exercise continued control until the city reaches a viable size. After that, the maintenance of a planned city is also on a regulated basis. Different from an "organic city," which has developed and grown without benefit of centralized planning, a planned city is attractive as a policy tool precisely because it provides the creator with the opportunity to restructure society in accordance with his or her understanding of society. At its core, therefore, the creation of a new city is a moral and social act to improve the urban condition. Its origins are in social reform and its objectives are to restructure urban form and life to achieve more balanced growth among nature, technology, and economic and social classes.

In Chandigarh, these objectives were defined by Le Corbusier and endorsed by Nehru. The two men shared a common vision of building a city that would serve as the model for the nation, if not for the world, in city planning. That these objectives have not been fully accomplished in Chandigarh can be attributed to the absence of local authority, to a lack of understanding of the local culture and values on the part of the planners, and to the subsequent history of the region. In the development of Chandigarh, authority relations, lines of accountability, and decision-making structures never became clear and, with the subsequent bifurcation of Punjab in 1966, have become even more blurred. When it became clear to the planners of Chandigarh that the Capital Project Office had limited political autonomy, and when faced with the challenge of building an innovative community with superior services and facilities within the confines of a tradition-bound, rural, and financially conservative system of government, they learned to appeal to the Office of the Prime Minister for implementation of their goals.

When P. N. Thapar, for example, was temporarily removed from the Chandigarh project in 1951, Maxwell Fry complained to Prime Minister Nehru that there was "no unity of administrative control" left, which promptly brought back Thapar to Chandigarh.[1] This practice intensified the involvement of the central government in Chandigarh, thereby further eroding local involvement and authority. Because power distribution structure changes with time, and because in Chandigarh no provision was made to facilitate orderly and adaptive changes in power structure, much of the legislation passed to ensure planned growth of the city has remained ineffective.

Recent behavior modification and learning research suggests that positive reinforcement from the environment, rather than punishment, is a more powerful determinant of behavior. This has led to the conclusion that new town designs that provide positive reinforcement for desired behavior, rather than punitive controls, are more successful.[2] The question of authority is particularly important in Chandigarh because, despite the existence of legally enforceable protective laws, the Chandigarh administration continually faces the problem of trying to ensure planned growth for the city.

There were two specific laws passed to guarantee the planned development of Chandigarh. The first of these, the Capital of Punjab Act, 1952, which controlled development and regulation, was signed by the governor of Punjab on December 17, 1952. The act empowered the chief administrator of the city to issue directions for the erection of buildings, to prevent any construction which was in violation of building rules, to enforce the provisions of the Punjab Municipal Act of 1911, to levy fees or taxes for amenities, to impose penalties and modes of recovery of arrears, to promote the preservation and planting of trees, and to control and regulate the display of advertisement in Chandigarh.[3] To ensure further that all construction in Chandigarh complied with the master plan, clause sixteen of the act empowered the chief administrator to forbid any person who was not a certified architect or engineer from certifying "any plan or completion of a building or engag[ing] in any plumbing work . . . unless registered and licensed by the Chief Administrator."[4]

The other legal instrument protecting the sacrosanctity of the master plan was the Punjab New Capital (Periphery Control) Act of

1952, which came into force on January 12, 1953, after being approved by the president of India. Section five of the act provides that "no person shall erect or re-erect any building or make or extend any excavation, or lay out any means of access to a road, in the controlled area save in accordance with the plans and restrictions and with the previous permission of the Deputy Commissioner in writing."[5] Initially the "controlled" area covered a five-mile radius extending from Chandigarh; in 1962 the law was amended to extend to a ten-mile periphery zone. The main object of the Periphery Act was to prevent the rise of urban slums in the outlying areas of Chandigarh, particularly along the roads.

The act, however, did take a liberal view of activities related to agriculture. Subsection four of section six of the act provided that "the Deputy Commissioner shall not refuse permission to the erection or re-erection of a building, if such a building is required for purposes subservient to agriculture."[6] This provision discouraged any urban development within a ten-mile periphery area of Chandigarh. However, when it was found that this act was actually retarding agricultural activities in the area, Chief Administrator M. S. Randhawa passed an order emphasizing that "it is our duty to promote agriculture, particularly horticulture and vegetable cultivation in the periphery area so that it serves as a green belt."[7]

Since their inception, the two acts have remained unchanged. However, there have been practical difficulties in implementing them, thereby necessitating more liberal interpretations. The two acts were conceived to guarantee uniform architectural control of new buildings within the ten-mile periphery of Chandigarh by making the three municipal committees—Kalka, Kharar, and Banaur—in the area seek approval for all construction applications from the estate officer, Chandigarh. This resulted in duplication of administrative work, causing delays and extra expense. To correct the situation, it was later decided that if the Chandigarh estate officer did not respond to applications within thirty days, "the concurrence of the Capital authorities should be presumed."[8] This practice substantially eroded the effectiveness of the acts.

In the wake of these acts there followed a series of other acts, ordinances, and executive orders, all directed toward maintaining the planned character of the city. For example, the Capital Administration Punjab Municipal Act (Number 27), 1952, stipulated that every house in Chandigarh was to have a "dust-bin" conforming to a specific design.⁹ The biggest violator of these regulations, however, has been the government itself. The difficulties in fully subscribing to the master plan started emerging in the very early stages of the city's development. Anticipating such difficulties, Le Corbusier had proposed the creation of the "Statute of Land," similar to Rousseau's General Will, which would regulate the development of the city. Rising from the "collective will," it was to have had the force of authority, unchallenged by any "inattentive resolutions or decisions," to control the proposed future developments of the city.[10]

The first major test of these laws and regulations came when the leading Punjab daily, the *Tribune*, reported that the Defense Ministry was planning to purchase from the Punjab government about two thousand acres of land on the northern side of Sukhna Lake at an estimated cost of rupees 29 lakhs. The land, which was to be carved out of Mani Majra, Suketra, Bhaisa Tibbi, Bilaspur, Surajpur, Dhara Karori, and Chandi Mandir villages, was to be converted into a military cantonment.[11] Calling the decision "a true crime," Le Corbusier noted in a memorandum that, first, the Periphery Control Act of Chandigarh absolutely forbade the sale of reserved land up to a periphery of five miles all around the city for any purpose other than agriculture; and second, the land north of Sukhna Lake, under the master plan, was "sacred land," the natural beauty of which was inviolable and for the enjoyment of the citizens.[12] Considering the front-line character of Punjab state, the Advisory Committee of the Chandigarh Capital Project Control Board, under the chairmanship of M. S. Randhawa, assisted by Chief Engineer P. L. Varma, concluded that objection to the cantonment scheme was unwarranted. The committee, however, recommended that all construction in the cantonment must be carried out in accordance with the advice of the Chandigarh Project authorities so as to maintain the skyline of the city.[13]

Unable to make any impression on the local authorities, Le Corbusier wrote to Nehru that he could not "permit this decision which would ruin the town planning principles of Chandigarh." Characteristically he added: "In the world, two cities are in course of construction. The first . . . is Chandigarh . . . by Le Corbusier and Pierre Jeanneret; the second . . . is Brasilia . . . by Lucio Costa and Oscar Niemeyer, both . . . friends and followers of Le Corbusier." (He neglected to mention the contributions of Maxwell Fry and Jane Drew.) Proclaiming Chandigarh to be the result of his life's work, he urged Nehru to take a personal "interest" in this matter.[14] Moved by Le Corbusier's repeated pleas, Nehru directed Chief Minister Pratap Singh Kairon not to "overrule Corbusier" as his opinion was of "value."[15]

While the fate of the cantonment scheme was being decided, another challenge to the master plan developed. Le Corbusier had argued that it would be erroneous to introduce industry in Chandigarh with a view to augmenting the city's population. The Punjab officials themselves were ambivalent about having any major industry in Chandigarh that might turn the city into a potential target of neighboring hostile Pakistan. Yet when Le Corbusier saw the plans for a linear industrial city near Chandigarh, he was quick to protest and reiterated that industry must be confined to outside the protected periphery zone.[16] He wrote in great detail to Nehru and to Punjab government officials, protesting the setting up of the air rifle factory near Pinjore.

Hardly a decade had passed since the inception of the city when considerable unplanned urban growth mushroomed within the restricted periphery zone of Chandigarh: a military cantonment, a Hindustan Machine Tools factory at Pinjore, an industrial factory near Kharar, and unauthorized urban growth near the airport. Pierre Jeanneret, who had assumed the position of chief architect to the Punjab government in February 1951, helplessly reported to his cousin Le Corbusier that although "theoretically" the periphery legislation should prevent expansion of industry in Chandigarh, "enforcement is always a problem."[17] By the close of the 1960s, Chief Architect Mrs. U. E. Chowdhury noted in a memorandum that, while on the outskirts of Chandigarh squatter colonies, slums, and tenements had sprung up, there was "over-crowding in the city itself." With the increase in population, many unauthorized shops and street hawkers, so common to Indian cities, had emerged in Chandigarh; and dwellings, meant for one family, had now "one family in each room."[18]

Further tarnishing the planned character of the city were illegal commercial shops sprouting up in different sections of Chandigarh. "Though Sector-22 is the most thickly populated area in Chandigarh," observed M. S. Randhawa on his visit to the city, "a number of illegal shops exist at the fringe and are a potent cause of unsanitation." Concluding that a visitor to Chandigarh gets a very bad impression from these structures, he cautioned the authorities that if they were not immediately "removed . . . it would be much more difficult later on to remove these stalls."[19] Clearly the local authorities had failed to enforce the existing laws. The central government was too remote to regulate development according to the master plan. Le Corbusier correctly called the situation "a crisis of authority."[20]

If unplanned growth in Chandigarh showed buoyancy, the planned growth languished because of administrative indecision, artificial shortages in building materials, and a paucity of economic resources. Visiting Chandigarh in December 1957, Le Corbusier found the Capitol Complex work site "empty."[21] Because of the integration of PEPSU (Patiala and East Punjab State Union) with Punjab in 1956, the plans for a legislative assembly had to be revised three times to meet the changed conditions of the state. The Punjab government found the provision for air conditioning in the Assembly building expensive; but Le Corbusier "absolutely" refused "to change anything in the plans."[22] The plan for building the governor's mansion in the Capitol Complex was vetoed by Nehru. The work at the Secretariat was at a standstill, while Le Corbusier found the maintenance of the High Court building "appalling." Blaming the government offices for poor communication, Le Corbusier admonished that the entire world was watching the development of the city. Let it not be said, he wrote, "India cannot continue and finish it."[23]

The merger of PEPSU with Punjab created additional demand for offices and residential buildings, forcing the government to raise the expenditure in the Second Five Year Plan to rupees 1,320.56 lakhs, and creating a deficit of rupees 484 lakhs.[24] This made the Punjab government reconsider the work in Chandigarh, leading to the postponement of some plans. Also responsible for slowing down building work in Chandigarh were other financial considerations. Faced with declining resources, accentuated by the absence of any municipal tax in Chandigarh, the Punjab government started reducing the staff of the Capital Project Organization, and even considered phasing out the organization. Jeanneret, in a letter to Secretary D. P. Nayar, Punjab government, noted that the development of the city and the reduction of the staff of the Capital Project were contradictory policies and called for a policy that would facilitate the development of Chandigarh.[25] Once again the prime minister was brought into the picture when Le Corbusier reminded Nehru that the Capital Project Organization had served as the training school for Indian architects, and that any reduction of staff in the organization would result in the reduction of valuable architectural control, so "basic" to Chandigarh.[26]

Meanwhile, poor communication links between Chandigarh and other parts of the state were discouraging construction in the city. Not until the governor of Punjab took up the matter of linking Chandigarh with other cities with Union Railway Minister Lal Bahadur Shastri was the work of linking Chandigarh with other parts of the state undertaken.[27] Private construction also languished in the city because of the poor financial circumstances of the plot holders and the black marketing of cement and other building materials. The difficulty in securing permits for construction from the scattered and lethargic government agencies in the city further added to the frustration of builders.

Despite the low-interest loans and twenty-five years of municipal tax holiday, which has still not been revoked, the Capital Project Office in 1960 estimated that there were over five thousand residential plots in Chandigarh where the owners had failed to complete building work.[28] This was in direct contravention of rule twelve of the Chandigarh (Sale and Site) Rules (1952), which stipulated that the failure to complete building within five years of acquiring land would lead to its repossession by the Capital Project under section nine of the Capital of Punjab (Development and Regulation) Act, 1952. To encourage construction, the Punjab government notified these plot holders that if buildings on their lands were not completed within a year, their plots would be repossessed and 15 percent of the money forfeited.[29]

Discouraging construction activities further in Chandigarh was the interminable Akali agitation for a Punjabi-speaking province,[30] an agitation that still remains vocal. A socioeconomic survey, the first of its kind in Chandigarh, conducted by the Economic and Statistical Organization, Punjab, in May 1957, indicated that 70 percent of respondents were unable to construct because of financial difficulties. Another 13 percent indicated shortage of building materials, particularly cement and bricks, as their reason for not being able to undertake construction. Want of time to supervise the building operations stood in the way of another 15 percent of all plot holders: they were either living abroad or serving outside Chandigarh.

Other reasons for delay included difficulties in getting designs approved by the Capital authorities, or that the designs as approved with amendments did not suit the needs of builders, the possession of plots was not yet complete, or the desire to exchange plots for those in some other area. A number of the plot holders had dropped the idea of building houses in Chandigarh, while some were waiting either to get a job in the city or for their "residential" areas more fully to develop.[31] Of the completed houses, nearly half (45.1 percent) were rented, while 17.6 percent were partially rented. Only 37.3 percent of all constructed houses were fully occupied by owners. More than two-thirds of the cost for building was met by owners themselves, either from their savings or through the adjustment of evacuee property claims. Government loans accounted for 30 percent of total costs incurred.[32]

The occupations of private homeowners provided an interesting demographic picture of the city in its initial stages. In percents, businessmen and industrialists owned 32.9 of the new homes, while retired officials owned 15.9. Again in percents, the administrative and clerical staff owned 13.4, contractors 10.7, lawyers 9.1, doctors 5.2, academic personnel 4.0, engineers and architects 3.6, and others 5.2.[33] The largest number of wage earners (27.6 percent) held administrative and clerical jobs, which reflected the administrative character of the city. The next most important occupation was manual labor, constituting about 19 percent of the earning force.[34] A majority of this class was engaged in construction activities within the city.

To control and regulate the planned growth of Chandigarh, it was decided to develop residential colonies for workers. The plots in these colonies, called "villages," were 5 meters wide and 22 meters long. Each plot was separated by a six-foot-high brick wall and contained within itself basic amenities, such as a semi-open toilet and washing area (separate from the house), and a house with a kitchen, a sleeping area, and a place for sitting out in front. The rest of the ground, approximately 10 meters deep, was reserved for lawn. The dimensions of the "village" were 200 meters by 200 meters, and it was to be enclosed by a wall, with openings provided at designated places. The roads within the village were 4 meters wide, paved in brick, and restricted to pedestrian traffic.[35] Most of the housing in the village was done by Jane Drew and Pierre Jeanneret, with the cheapest house costing rupees 2,500.

The cost analysis for plots in Chandigarh included all city services, such as schools, health clinics, stadiums, clubs, swimming pools, public libraries, museums, and so forth, chargeable to all residents, irrespective of earning power. With the bulk of the labor population earning rupees 150 to 300 a month, most were naturally priced out of the labor housing. Since construction of the city was financed by grants and loans from the central or the state governments, and as industrial activity formed a weak economic base of the city, the government housing programs became a heavy burden on the public exchequer and had to be abandoned by 1960, making it more difficult for the economically weaker sections of the population to find shelter. But rather than reassess the ability of different sections of the population to pay for various services of the city in accordance with their economic abilities, the Chandigarh administration continued to adopt the basic policy of first estimating the costs of high standards of physical development and then extracting them from residents of the city.[36]

Faced with financial constraints, the administration gave up all measures of artificially controlling land prices in 1959 and introduced instead a policy of auctioning land to the highest bidder, causing rapid shifts in land value. By 1974, the policy of freehold ownership had also been replaced by leases of ninety-nine years. Le Corbusier had earlier recommended a leasehold basis for developing future sectors in Chandigarh, arguing that such a policy had been successfully tried in Brasília, the new capital of Brazil.[37]

Resettlement schemes initiated by the government in 1958 for the labor colonies also ran into difficulties because of high costs and restrictions that prohibited slumdwellers from engaging in "informal" economic activities—commercial enterprises, poultry farming, subletting part of their premises—in their homes to supplement income. In May 1957, there were 2,396 labor huts and 655 improvised houses with no proper ventilation, sanitary facilities, water, or electricity in Chandigarh.[38] Life in the huts offered glaring contrasts to the high standards of amenities provided for the rest of the population. Maxwell Fry admitted that there was "no economy" within which to include the lowest-paid workers, not "even with the smallest house."[39]

By the beginning of the second phase of the development of Chandigarh in 1967, Chief Commissioner Randhawa noted that the city would have to focus consideration upon weaker sections of the population—laborers, untouchables, and low-paid government servants.[40] Yet in 1971, 15 percent of the population in Chandigarh lived in unauthorized settlements. The administration's efforts at providing housing failed to keep pace with the phenomenal growth rate of the city. During the 1960s, Chandigarh's population grew at a rate of 14 percent per annum; during the 1970s, it grew at a rate of 8 percent per annum. In the 1980s, Chandigarh's population is expected to grow at the rate of 6 percent per annum, making the housing problem even more severe.[41] The administration's efforts to solve the slum problem by setting up transit colonies at the villages of Karsan, Dadu Majra, Khudda Jassu, Khudda Lahora, and in Sector 26 have not been effective largely because these efforts have ignored the related issues of income, jobs, security of tenure, land and development policy, health and, above all, education. Planned as transit colonies, they have acquired a permanent character, but without the necessary infrastructure. For essential services, these colonies continue to depend on Chandigarh, putting further pressure on the city's shrinking resources.

A major factor contributing to the growth of unauthorized squatter colonies in Chandigarh was the city's poor economic base. From its inception, Chandigarh looked to state and central agencies for funds needed for development. Even though this is not unusual in the case of Indian cities, which are extraordinarily subservient to their state governments,[42] in Chandigarh it became a handicap at the local level for the improvement of the economic well-being of urban labor. Preoccupied with the administrative and the planned physical character of the city, Chandigarh's planners had paid little attention to urban labor and had discouraged informal activities. The importance of the informal sector lies in the fact that the formal sector, because of its capital-intensive base, is not only small in developing countries but its employment growth rate is also slow to absorb additions to the urban labor force. Besides, many newcomers to the job market are too ill-educated and ill-trained to participate in the formal sector. Finally, even though the number of jobs in the government sector increased rapidly in many developing countries as a result of their independence and the expanding role of government, it soon reached a plateau, forcing newcomers to the labor force to search for alternative enterprises.[43] Discouraged from using alternative means for generating income and faced with a shortage in developed plots, urban laborers were forced to squat illegally in Chandigarh.

Adding to the problems of Chandigarh was the growing lack of discipline in the ranks of the Capital Project administration. Individual rivalries, personal ambitions, and private patronage, rather than concern for the national interest, which have generally characterized Indian society, were quick to surface in the absence of established local authority. Complaining that many of his officers dabbled more in "public relations" rather than in "actual solid work"—behavior unfortunately encouraged by senior officers—Jeanneret wrote Chief Minister Kairon that he was unable to "get work from [these] officers without the backing of the Government."[44] Jeanneret's own inadequacy in English and unfamiliarity with Indian bureaucracy contributed to his predicament. He found, for example, Secretary of Agriculture K. S. Narang difficult to work with.[45] Much of his disagreement with Narang revolved around the question of promotion of officers in the Capital Project Office.

The Indian bureaucracy, a curious mixture of English and traditional Indian influences, awards promotions on the basis of seniority and internal evaluations. Jeanneret wanted to award promotions to his architects on the basis of merit, as assessed by himself. When Narang, acting in accordance with established practice, rejected Jeanneret's recommendations for promotions, Jeanneret wrote Nehru threatening to resign if the government did not "agree" with him.[46] Intervention from Randhawa averted the showdown, but not before confidence within the department had been shaken. On Nehru's intervention, however, Narang was transferred from the Department of Agriculture, to be replaced by the more agreeable Swaroop Krishan.[47]

Repeated failures of the local political elite to deal with the problems of Chandigarh were reminders of their continuing psychological and economic dependence on the political center—a familiar theme in many developing countries. There are several reasons for this tendency. First, there is a concern to provide some kind of cohesion and integrated feeling for the new nation and to prevent the growth of factionalism and regionalism that might threaten the country's unity. For an effective administration, colonial rule had created divergent competing forces within the country. But colonial rule was also instrumental in bringing these divergent forces together to rid the country of its foreign rule. However, once that goal had been achieved, there was no longer that uniting factor and new conflicts emerged over the control of power. To prevent divisive tendencies from taking hold, the political center itself exhorts federal units to rely on the central authority. "We must always realize the importance of the Center, which blends all the different states and provinces and areas together,"[48] Nehru reminded his audience in one of his speeches.

Second, the country's political elites during the colonial period have been trained at the national level, and there are only a few qualified people at the local level to take control. In instances where there is a competent local elite, it aspires to rise to the national level of effectiveness. They have no confidence in local government and think that all wisdom and competency must exist at the political center.

Third, this feeling is further reinforced when the local unit, in the absence of a viable economic base, finds itself heavily dependent upon the political center. All three elements are discernible in the history of Chandigarh.

If failure to delineate proper lines of authority at the local level and failure to create a strong economic base contributed to the problems of Chandigarh, the bifurcation of Punjab in 1966 along linguistic lines nearly shattered the unity of the city. As India moved from a colonial state to the status of an independent nation, it was inevitable that such a transformation would involve certain socioeconomic changes.

One such change was the reorganization of Indian states on a linguistic basis. Even though the Dar Commission, which was appointed to advise the Constituent Assembly on the issue of reorganization of states on a linguistic basis, cautioned that such an approach would have a "sub-national bias" and would threaten national unity, the States Reorganization Commission, on Nehru's behest, while rejecting "one language one state" theory, endorsed "linguistic homogeneity as an important factor conducive to administrative convenience and efficiency."[49] It was on this recommendation that the

States Reorganization Act was finally passed by the Indian Parliament in 1956. Although Bombay and Punjab, the two sensitive areas, were not immediately reorganized on a linguistic basis, the act stirred raw regional and linguistic sentiments, which can be felt to this day.

In postpartition Punjab, the two dominant communities were Hindus and Sikhs with two official languages, Hindi and Punjabi. The British Punjab was the original home of the Sikh religion and tradition, and there were more Sikhs living there than in any other part of India. Partition divided the Sikh homeland in two. Punjab was affected also by the process of absorption of the princely states of British India. The smaller enclaves, in and near Punjab, were first merged with it in a rationalizing of boundaries. Then in 1956, Punjab took on a population 25 percent its own size by the integration of the domains of the Punjab princes (PEPSU). This brought a series of problems, including the integration of administrative and legal systems into a common national structure. The tragic loss by the Sikhs of their homes and land in Pakistan accentuated and strained relations between this powerful, martial, and concentrated minority and the Hindu majority, whose faith came to bear strongly on the fate of Chandigarh.

Throughout the development of Chandigarh, the unity of Punjab was continually threatened by pressures from more militant Sikh groups, especially the Akalis, for the establishment of a separate Punjabi-speaking state, if not an independent nation, called *Khalistan* (Sikh "Land of the Pure"). Although the early Sikh religion represented a variation on the Hindu way of life and culture, and the literary language of Punjab was a mixture of Braj, Rajasthani, and Punjabi, written in Gurmukhi script, the growth of Sikh heterodoxy and Hindu revivalism later polarized the two communities. In postindependence Punjab, the *Tribune* reported as early as 1951 that the Sikhs failed fully to adjust themselves "to the national setup and the reasons are to be found in the privileged position they used to enjoy under British rule and frustrations resulting from the displacement of those among them who had been in West Pakistan."[50]

In this context, Sikh religious frenzy was also the result of deeper insecurities of modern Sikh politics and the schism created in the community by caste and urban-rural disparities. Although economically prosperous and, based on the 1981 census, having a higher life expectancy (66.8 years against the national average of 53.87 for men, and 61.9 against 52.93 for women), a higher literacy rate, and a higher per capita income than the national average (rupees 2,098 against rupees 1,516), and though their faith stringently prohibits caste discrimination, urban Sikhs suffer from insecurities resulting from their minority status. Because the urban Sikh, unlike the rural Sikh, has not been able to translate his economic power into political power, and because 75 percent of the Hindu population in Punjab is concentrated in towns, the urban Sikh is constantly in fear of being "overwhelmed by Hindu values." This has led one scholar to conclude that "extremist" Sikh movements, such as their demand for Khalistan, are "a purely urban middle-class phenomenon."[51] Also, economic prosperity for Sikhs has resulted in the decline of the birthrate, especially since 1971, but with the current population of thirteen million, nearly 2 percent of India's population, they are hardly in danger of extinction.

As long as Sikhs in the Congress party opposed the division of Punjab and as long as the moderates in the Akali party remained in power, the central government deferred any decision on the issue of creating a Punjabi-speaking state. As the demand for the creation of a Punjabi state came essentially from the Akalis, it acquired a communal character and was viewed by the central government as a threat to the unity of India. However, in the post-Nehru era the politics of Punjab underwent a radical shift, creating the need, on the one hand, to protect the moderate Akali leadership from being defeated by the extremist demand for a separate Sikh nation, and on the other, to meet the growing demand from Haryana leaders and the non-Punjabi-speaking population of hill districts for a division of Punjab along linguistic lines. Some Hindus of Punjab, afraid of being subjected to Sikh rule and reluctant to communicate in the Gurmukhi script, disclaimed Punjabi as their mother tongue in the 1961 census. The breach between the two groups was thus further widened, leading in 1966 to the creation of two unilingual states, Punjab and Haryana, out of the previously bilingual state.

The guiding principles of the Shah Commission, appointed by the central government for the explicit purpose of dividing Punjab, were to "apply linguistic principle with due regard to the census . . . of 1961," and to consider administrative, economic, and geographic factors that would not amount to "breaking up of existing tehsils."[52] According to this latest change, the hill areas of Punjab—forming forests and water resources that could be utilized for developing industries, hydroelectricity, and irrigation—fell to the share of the state of Himachal Pradesh. To the new state of Haryana went Hissar, Rohtak, Gurgaon, Karnal, and Mahendragarh districts, Ambala, Jagadhri, and Naraingarh tehsils of Ambala district, and the territories in Mani Majra kanungo circle of the Kharar tehsil of the Ambala district.[53] Together these areas contained rich mineral resources, cattle wealth, and some industrial centers.

Punjab, considerably reduced in size, was left with small-scale industries and areas which possessed greater potential for the development of agriculture. It now contained the districts of Jullundur, Hoshiarpur, Ludhiana, Ferozpur, Amritsar, Patiala, Bhatinda, Kapurthala, and parts of Gurdaspur, Ambala, and Sangrur, constituting a total area of 20,254 square miles and a population of 115.84 lakhs, of which about 56 percent was Sikh. Even more important, 85 percent of the total Sikh population in the country would be residing in Punjab.

At the epicenter of this geopolitical change was Chandigarh, which found itself caught between Haryana and Punjab, each state demanding the city as its own capital. The Shah Commission had originally awarded Chandigarh to Haryana on the basis that the population of the Kharar tehsil, of which Chandigarh was a part, had a 55.2 percent Hindi-speaking population, and only a 43.9 percent Punjabi-speaking population. Moreover, the 1961 census indicated that nearly 73 percent of the Hindi-speaking population was concentrated in the urban areas of Chandigarh, Kharar, and Mani Majra.[54]

Sensing popular Sikh discontent with this arrangement and recognizing the controversial character of the 1961 census, the central government rejected the Shah Commission's recommendation, and instead converted Chandigarh into a union territory that would include Mani Majra and Manauli kanungo circles of the Kharar tehsil in Ambala.[55] The indirect role of the central government in the development of Chandigarh had come full circle, bringing the city under its direct administration. In addition, Chandigarh was to serve as the joint capital of Punjab and Haryana, pending agreement between the two states on several elusive issues. Meanwhile, Punjab and Haryana were to share the city on a 60:40 ratio.

The politicization of Chandigarh intensified the involvement of the central government in the development of the city, subjecting it to the vagaries of the noninstitutional methods of political pressures (fasts, sit-ins, demonstrations, etc.) at the national level by the local and regional elites.[56] Immediately following the 1966 decision, both Haryana and Punjab quickly articulated their claims to the city and have so far successfully prevented the central government from reaching any decision that would satisfy the contending parties. In Punjab, the Akalis were the first to take action and were subsequently joined by other local and regional groups in demanding the city for the state. A joint communiqué of an eight-party coalition in 1969 declared that "Chandigarh, which was built by rejecting pure Punjabi-speaking people, historically, geographically, culturally and linguistically belonged to Punjab and therefore it should be handed over to Punjab immediately."[57]

Haryana's Rao Birinder Singh, on the other side, declared that "to take away Chandigarh from the state, in which the temple of Goddess Chandi lay, would hurt the religious susceptibilities of the people of Haryana." He added, "It would amount to withdrawing an 'offering.'"[58] As for the residents of Chandigarh, unofficial reports from time to time have indicated that they would prefer the city to continue as a union territory so as to preserve its cosmopolitan character, at least until such time as the raw linguistic passions aroused by "the hot heads in the Punjab and Haryana died down."[59]

In 1970, under mounting pressure, the central government led by Prime Minister Indira Gandhi made another effort at deciding the fate of Chandigarh. Before announcing the new award, the central government considered several solutions to the dispute: dividing Chandigarh on a 60:40 ratio between Punjab and Haryana, outrightly awarding the city to one or the other state, holding a referendum in the city, referring the dispute to a judicial commission, declaring Chandigarh a charter city with complete local autonomy, and maintaining the status quo. There was yet another suggestion made by Union Minister for Works, Housing and Urban Development K. K. Shah, who called for the reunion of Punjab and Haryana, claiming that a majority of citizens of Chandigarh would favor such a reunion.[60]

Finally, on January 29, 1970, Prime Minister Gandhi awarded Chandigarh to Punjab and, as compensation, sanctioned rupees 200 million (half in outright grant) for Haryana to build its new capital city.[61] The new award also gave cotton-rich Fazilka tehsil, along with

Fazilka and Abohar towns, to Haryana, even though Fazilka and Abohar were not contiguous to Haryana and would have required a 200-meter-wide corridor through Punjab to connect them with Haryana. The final takeover of Chandigarh and the transfer of Fazilka and Abohar were to take place by January 1975. The new award, however, did not alter the position of Bhakra-Nangal, which remained under the joint management of the four states of Punjab, Haryana, Himachal Pradesh, and Rajasthan.

The 1970 award was not without precedent. In 1960, Bombay was awarded to Maharashtra, and Gujarat was given economic assistance to build a new capital, although not before Gujarat had put up a strong fight for the economic capital of west India. In north India, however, the formula remains to be implemented. Failure as yet to implement the award has meant that Chandigarh became subjected to three competing interests within Punjab, Haryana, and the union territory administration. It has also meant some structural and substantive changes in the management of the city.

First, Chandigarh city, and its thirty-four adjacent villages, which had formed part of Punjab, were given a new constitutional entity as a union territory, and control over the city administration shifted from the Punjab government to the Union Ministry of Home Affairs. The union territory of Chandigarh also included the Sukhna Lake catchment area. Second, the president of India, under Article 239 of the Indian Constitution, appointed a chief commissioner as his agent to administer the territory,[62] replacing the erstwhile chief administrator, Capital Project, Chandigarh. Third, the estate office, which had been responsible for Chandigarh, was replaced by an expanded district administration, incorporating the functions of both the estate officer and chief administrator of the city. Fourth, the budget of the union territory formed a part of the union budget, subject to approval by the Indian Parliament, and Punjab and Haryana became tenant states of the central government in Chandigarh. It may be noted, however, that neither Punjab nor Haryana has paid rent on the buildings each has been occupying in Chandigarh since 1966. Finally, a separate secretariat and regulatory agencies, independent of both Punjab and Haryana, had to be developed to look after the needs of the union territory.

It was anticipated that the union territory administration in Chandigarh would be perceived by various factions as evenhanded and neutral and would help resolve the differences. Instead, the result has been continued intransigence by Punjab and Haryana, and their refusal to accept any solution offered by the central government. The fate of Chandigarh was no longer subject to local conditions alone; it became directly linked to the national government and its limitations. For the central government the decision proved economically expensive and politically inexpedient. This was to become abundantly clear when in 1973 Sikh leaders included Chandigarh as one of their demands in the Anandpur Sahib Resolution, which aimed at securing greater political autonomy for the Sikhs in Punjab. The continuing conflict which followed culminated in 1984 when, in a bid to put an end to increasing Sikh militancy in Punjab, Prime Minister Indira Gandhi authorized the army to enter the Golden Temple—an action that resulted in her assassination at the hands of two disaffected Sikh bodyguards on October 31.

The latest agreement signed between Prime Minister Rajiv Gandhi and Akali Dal president Harchand Singh Longowal on July 24, 1985, which awards Chandigarh to Punjab, resulted in August in the assassination of Longowal by militant Sikh detractors. The handing over of Chandigarh to Punjab, the transference of the capital of Haryana to Ambala, and the settlement of other territorial and water disputes between the two states will need the cooperation of the Akali Dal, which came into power in Punjab in September, and the Congress (I), which continues to control the central government. The implementation of the Gandhi-Longowal accord will also require the cooperation of Haryana.

As early as November 7, 1966, the Government of India, recognizing that competing interests of Punjab and Haryana may not necessarily be conducive to the preservation of the planned character of the city, had constituted a committee for the control of the periphery area of Chandigarh. It was made up of the chief commissioner, Chandigarh; the directors of town and country planning offices from Punjab and Haryana; the chief architect and assistant estate officer from the Chandigarh Union Territory Administration; and the subdivisional officer from the Kharar tehsil.[63] Because this committee had no statutory powers, it has essentially remained a forum for heated discussions among its constituent members rather than serving to regulate effectively the growth of Chandigarh.

Even though Chandigarh provided innovative ideas in architecture and town planning, the rival political claims between Punjab and Haryana have rendered them useless. The artificiality of the manmade environment of Chandigarh became subjected to the natural influences of the local sociopolitical culture and tradition. Today the city region is dotted with the new satellite towns of Parwanoo, Punchkula, Sahibzada Ajit Singh (S.A.S.) Nagar, Hindustan Machine Tools (H.M.T.) Township, and Chandimandir Cantonment—none of these originally included in the master plan for Chandigarh. Punjab, to strengthen its claims to Chandigarh, developed S.A.S. Nagar, an industrial town, covering an area of approximately 5,800 acres. This area, southwest of Chandigarh, was originally reserved for a greenbelt for the city. Planned on the same grid as that of Chandigarh, S.A.S. Nagar is expected to grow to a population of 3.5 lakhs. It is no accident that the numbering of sectors in this town are a continuation of serial numbers of the sectors in Chandigarh.

In response to Punjab's S.A.S. Nagar, Haryana developed Punchkula, about eight kilometers from the heart of Chandigarh, on National Highway 22. Employing the neighborhood pattern of Chandigarh, this town is expected to grow to a population of 1.25 lakhs. This town was accorded the status of an urban unit for the first time in the 1981 census. To provide the town with an economic base, the Haryana government has reserved an area of 425 acres for industrial development. Escalating land values in Chandigarh have attracted many new builders to Punchkula. However, neither S.A.S. Nagar nor Punchkula have a fully developed urban infrastructure of their own. As a result, the citizens of these two townships continue to depend on Chandigarh for vital facilities such as medical care, education, and other social services.

East of Chandigarh lies Chandimandir Cantonment, covering an area of approximately 383.81 acres. Developed in the face of opposition from Le Corbusier, the master plan for this urban unit contains provisions for open spaces, playing fields, schools, swimming pools, and a stadium—provisions which have yet to be fully realized. Other urban units in the Inter State Chandigarh Region include Kharar, Kurali, Morinda, Dera Basi, Banaur, Kalka, Naraingarh, Pinjore, and Hindustan Machine Tools Township, all lacking in proper infrastructure and all depending on Chandigarh for one service or another.[64]

In the 1971 census, the urban population in the Chandigarh union territory was 90.55 percent, which had risen to 93.60 percent by

1981—the highest percentage of urban growth to the total population in the country. During the decade 1971–81, Chandigarh's urban population recorded a growth rate of 80.84 percent, while the rural population grew at the rate of 18.49 percent, substantially below the all-India average.[65] The reason for this has been mainly the urbanization of the rural areas surrounding Chandigarh. As a result, the number of towns in the Chandigarh Union Territory rose from two in 1971 to four in 1981.[66] All of these towns form part of the Chandigarh urban agglomeration, a term introduced in the 1971 census to describe continuous urban spread on the periphery of a town,[67] even though that urban growth may be outside the statutory limits of the individual local body.

Alarmed by the unrestrained urban growth, both within the city and on the periphery of Chandigarh, the Ministry of Works and Housing, Government of India, in 1975 constituted a coordination committee for the balanced development of the Chandigarh region. Chaired by the secretary, Ministry of Works and Housing, the committee was composed of the quarter master general from Army headquarters of the Ministry of Defense; the chief commissioner, Chandigarh; and the chief secretaries of Punjab and Haryana.[68] The committee was charged with three specific tasks. One was to study the development plans for the union territory of Chandigarh, S.A.S. Nagar, and Punchkula and to suggest measures for a coordinated development of the region. The second was to study and measure the impact of S.A.S. Nagar and Punchkula on the region, and accordingly make recommendations to Punjab, Haryana and the union territory authorities. And finally, the committee was to prepare a regional plan for Chandigarh and for the urban areas falling within its zone of influence.[69] Although the committee met five times between 1975 and 1981, it was not until April 1981 that it appointed two working groups for preparing a regional plan for the Inter State Chandigarh Region. Because the committee has lacked statutory powers, much of its work still remains to be implemented.

The idea of looking at Chandigarh's growth in a regional setting was first articulated in a seminar, sponsored by the United Nations Economic Commission and the Government of Japan, in 1966. In a paper submitted at the conference, L. R. Vagale, assessing the impact of Chandigarh on new towns and settlements within a forty to fifty mile radius, argued that "the present tendency to plan the expansion of Chandigarh without considering its regional setting should be discouraged."[70] That paper ascribed two reasons for this: first, the rapid growth of Chandigarh had qualitatively transformed the basic administrative character of the city, making it a regional economic and cultural center; second, the bifurcation of Punjab, coupled with the new development projects of the fourth Five Year Plan period, were expected to bring new pressures upon the city and its region.

Subsequently, Chief Architect Mrs. U. E. Chowdhury, inspired by the regional plan for metropolitan Delhi, drafted an explanatory memorandum on a regional plan for Chandigarh for discussion at the meeting of the North-Zonal Council. Contending that the influence of Chandigarh extended from a seventy-five to two-hundred-mile radius, she reasoned that unless the region was also planned with the city, the administration's best efforts would fail to cope with the problems of Chandigarh. She called for metropolitan planning of Chandigarh that would include "urban, industrial, and rural integration" of the region.[71] This integration was to be multidimensional in content: economic, social, and physical. The scheme called for the creation of new towns and villages in the region that would offer complete economic and social services, thus relieving the pressure on Chandigarh. It was sound advice, but was to remain unheeded for some time.

Since then, studies and official papers on Chandigarh have repeatedly stressed that the changing pattern of development around the city, as well as socioeconomic conditions within the city, make it imperative to conceive the future of Chandigarh not as an isolated city but as a significant exercise in regional planning. The main effort in this direction has come from the coordination committee set up in 1975, resulting in 1982 in the development of a regional plan.

In its introduction, the plan acknowledges the failure of the Periphery Act of 1952 in containing unplanned urban growth in parts of the Chandigarh region bordering Haryana and Punjab.[72] "From the preliminary studies of the region," the report notes, "it is [clear] that the urban centres around Chandigarh are largely dependent on the urban amenities of Chandigarh." Even for such basic services as secondary education, health care, recreation, and cultural activities, people from these areas come to Chandigarh. Pointing out that the infrastructure in Chandigarh was designed for a total population of 500,000, the report adds that, with the establishment of S.A.S.

Nagar, Punchkula, Hindustan Machine Tools Township, and Chandimandir Cantonment, the population of the Chandigarh urban complex by 2001 is expected to reach 1,000,000. "The pressures over [the city's] amenities are already being witnessed," ominously concludes the report.[73]

Among some of the other problems of the Chandigarh region, the regional plan report lists fast-depleting underground water resources, which have so far provided the primary source of water to the city; soil-erosion and flooding along the Narkanda, Ghaggar, Tangri, Jyanti-Devi-Ki-Rao, and Siswan rivers; shortages in housing and office space; poor communications and road links; and the deteriorating ecological balance of the region with rapid industrialization. In addition, the report notes two proposed urban schemes in the north of the Capitol Complex by Punjab and Haryana, covering an estimated area of 1,923 acres on the Punjab side and 550 acres on the Haryana side. Such urban schemes are likely further to upset the ecological balance of the city region.

To provide a physically efficient pattern and socially desirable environment in the urban growth of the Chandigarh region, the report recommends incorporating all those areas of the region that are either dependent on or directly influenced by Chandigarh, irrespective of their administrative boundaries.[74] Most of these areas fall either in Punjab or in Haryana. The total area covered by the regional plan approximates 2,421 square kilometers, and includes, beside Chandigarh, four small towns—S.A.S Nagar, Mani Majra, Kharar, and Kalka—each with over 20,000 population; three urban centers—Morinda, Kurali, and Punchkula—each with less than 15,000 population; and four small urban settlements—Naraingarh, Banaur, Dera Basi, and Pinjore—each with less than 10,000 population. The plan also notes that none of these urban centers has nonagricultural employment opportunities to offer.[75] Corresponding to poor urban infrastructure, the literacy rate is also lower in these centers. Equally significant, the rural areas in the region conspicuously lack essential services: medical care, drinking water, sanitation, recreation, education, and veterinary services.

The plan also identifies 2,420 industrial units in the region, employing nearly 30,932 workers. Of these, 941 industrial units employing 15,500 workers are located in Chandigarh; the rest are scattered along the national highways. Most of the industry in the Chandigarh region is agro-based or service industry. Most of the commercial and trading activities are located in Morinda, Kharar, Kurali, Dera Basi, Lalru, and Chandigarh, making up the third largest employment sector in the region.[76]

Somewhat ambitiously, the regional plan proposes to develop in the next twenty years a hierarchy of towns and villages in the region that would be socially acceptable and physically integrated in the region. Equally ambitious is the plan's goal of developing in these urban centers the same standards of physical planning as are available in Chandigarh. The plan proposes to accomplish these goals in two phases, with an estimated outlay of rupees 85.65 crores in the first phase and rupees 81.40 crores in the second phase.[77] For the enforcement of its ideas the plan rightly places the burden on local units of the region, calling for proper legislation that would allow them necessary autonomy. But because much of this planning is expected to be financed by the central or state governments, their dominant role in the whole process is assured. The plan proposes no alternative means of generating funds locally.

Moreover, in view of the existing linkages which bind various facets of urban political life in India to the operations of state and national governments and politics, any legislation aimed at providing extraordinary local autonomy is not likely to become a popular issue either at the local or the state or the national levels. As long as the basic services in Indian cities, such as education, police, health, and public works, continue to be administered by state governments, the role of local units of administration is going to remain marginal. "The study of urban politics in India," as one scholar has concluded, "is so closely tied to the control of resources by state governments and the operations of municipal governments so dependent on the laws and administrative regulations promulgated by state authorities that even to separate the 'local' from the 'state' in analyzing urban political systems is misleading."[78] Furthermore, in light of the unsettled territorial disputes and other differences between Punjab and Haryana, it remains an open question as to whether the two states will set aside their political prejudices and cooperate in any effective regional plan for Chandigarh.

.6.
CONCLUSIONS

From its inception Chandigarh was beset with controversy. There was never any real unanimity concerning it. Some individuals in the government favored creation of a new capital for Punjab; however, others vigorously opposed the idea on economic and social grounds, and argued for the upgrading of an existing city to capital status. Psychological and administrative considerations eventually outweighed the economic arguments of the government, and the decision was taken at Simla to build a new capital that would provide shelter to refugees and new status for the displaced Punjab administration.

The authorities, however, remained divided on the questions of where to place the capital and what should be its character. There was also no unanimity on the size of the new capital. Pragmatists in the government, like A. L. Fletcher, who had no emotional links to Lahore, the erstwhile capital of the united Punjab, argued for a strictly administrative city, manageable in size and economically feasible. Visionaries like P. L. Varma, who had been romantically tied to Lahore for generations, wanted more than an administrative city. They wanted a capital of 500,000 population that would surpass the Mughal imperial splendor of Lahore, its many beautiful gardens, its bustling bazaars, and its crowded streets. They asked for a new capital that would replace the cultural, economic, and social loss of Lahore.[1]

The government, however, naively believed that the creation of a new capital would resolve other social, economic, and political problems of the state. It was forgotten that a city, an entirely man-made environment, is a unique product of a particular society and culture and its influences operate within a given distribution of power. Even where external influences are superimposed on the value structure of a given society and culture, that society over a period of time asserts its value structure. No attention was paid to the fact that there are inherent drawbacks in a method that attempts to create a totally new community within a larger cultural milieu as an answer to specific needs. This is because such an exercise threatens to transform the experience of the existing culture without first creating the necessary preconditions for such a transformation. With no previous experience in city planning and in the absence of scientific data, it is hardly surprising that no effort was made to integrate the physical planning of the city with socioeconomic conditions of the region.

With Simla, Amritsar, Jullundur, Ludhiana, and Ambala ruled out, either for their poor urban infrastructure or for their close physical proximity to neighboring hostile Pakistan, the Punjab government in March 1948 selected the site at Chandigarh, in the Kharar tehsil of the Ambala district. Indecision over the site for the new capital would have lingered longer had not Nehru personally interfered. His admonishments to the state government eventually galvanized that administrative machinery into action. Indecision and economic limitations of the state government, however, assured an active role for the central government in the development of Chandigarh.

The subsequent breakdown of the constitutional machinery in Punjab brought about president's rule (rule by the central government), and it was the Indian Parliament that first passed the Capital of Punjab (Development and Regulation) Act early in 1952, further assuring an important role for the central government in the Chandigarh project. This had two lasting effects on the city. First, it undermined local authority in effectively supervising the development of the city; and, second, the local political elite learned to appeal to the political center for their causes. As long as Punjab remained united, the central government could manipulate the local and regional political elites. But with the division of the state in 1966, the central government fell hostage to two competing interests in the region, subjecting the future of the city to the political ambitions of two antagonistic states.

The selection of the site itself was not without controversy. The acquisition of 28,000 acres of land for the new capital meant displacing fifty-eight villages with a total population of 21,000. Of the total land acquired, 22,000 acres was fertile, cultivable land. Although the displaced villagers were to be rehabilitated, that decision was unpopular. The premier of East Punjab himself admitted in a letter to Nehru that "the land is very fertile and the persons to be displaced cannot be rehabilitated elsewhere."[2] The decision was followed by widespread demonstrations by the farmers, which the Akalis and the Communists tried to exploit for their own political gains, blaming the government for creating "another refugee problem."[3] Also opposing the Chandigarh site for their own reasons were Congress leaders Baldev Singh and Rajkumari Amrit Kaur in the central government, and Bhim Sain Sachar and Lala Jagat Narain in Punjab. Casting further doubts on the Chandigarh site were questions about adequate water resources for the city, which have been justified with time.

Adding to the controversy over Chandigarh was the question of where to get architects for the city. Although having a rich urban tradition, India in the 1950s lacked technical manpower. Because of the nature of British rule and existing economic opportunities, most Indians in the early twentieth century educated themselves to become bureaucrats or lawyers. Restricting educated Indians further from entering limited trade and technical schools in the country was their upper-caste status, which prohibited any work that involved soiling the hands. In the absence of local talent, there were several Western architects and town planners working on several postindependence projects in India. However, the Punjab government officials, eager to build a unique city, were more inclined to procure architects in Western Europe. In fact, to recruit the best talent, they wanted to hold an international competition. Nehru opposed this expensive and unrealistic idea, and the Punjab government eventually contracted with the American Albert Mayer, who had been building in Uttar Pradesh, and who was later replaced by Le Corbusier.

Because Chandigarh was built as a totally planned city, it was hoped that the success of the city would influence other cities of India, creating a better urban environment. The city was to serve as a catalyst for the modernization of India. It was forgotten, however, that innovations in new towns are usually not transferable to existing cities. Also forgotten was that any government pursuing a modernization policy must consider social, economic, and physical elements of the planned community to make it a success. The initial development of Chandigarh took place in accordance with a well-drafted master plan, the principles of which were rooted more in Western experience than in local or regional socioeconomic realities.

Too much emphasis was placed on physical targets—building designs, location, green spaces, the Capitol Complex, the City Center, 7-V roads, etc.—and long-term goals of planning were practically ignored. Economic and social issues, such as productivity, economic utilization of space, reduction of the friction of space, improvement of communication to suit local needs, reduction of social tensions, integration of economically poor classes, and the achievement of collateral and overall effects, never received proper attention. Emphasis was placed on the city itself and its periphery zone extending up to a ten-mile radius, and no study was made of the impact the city would have on the region as a whole. In that sense, Chandigarh turned out to be a designed city, not a planned one.

In the typical tradition of most developing countries, Indian efforts to modernize, although regarding any association with "Westernization" as pejorative, failed to break loose of Western-inspired colonial practices. Indian "housing policy," for example, "continues to be colonial, urban land policy continues to be capitalistic, the town-planning and municipal rules and regulations continue to be based on obsolete nineteenth century and early twentieth century British legislation, and the system of city government breeding inefficiency, corruption and nepotism is certainly not geared to meet the challenges"[4] of modern-day urbanization. Benign disregard in the master plan for the aspirations of all of the people, not just the visions of the city's creators, gave Chandigarh its inequitable character. It is only natural that with the passage of time social tensions and traditional customs have surfaced, in many instances defying the very principles of the master plan.

Le Corbusier, with uncritical faith in his wisdom and with a theoretician's belief in his grand schemes, had hoped that by neatly dividing the city into four different functions—living, working, leisure, and communications—"the population will have qualified for a new condition of living."[5] In a country like India, where close traditional ties exist between working and living, reinforced by economic conditions, the demarcation of the city into single-purpose zones meant excluding a sizable proportion of the population from the master plan. The unquestioning faith of Indian planners in the benighted master plan simply prevented the total assimilation of all elements of the community. Those who could not find formal employment in the designated working areas were disinherited by the city. There was no "alternative" economy within which they could be included, forcing them deeper into bare poverty. The master plan's failure to absorb or integrate these families into the existing structure of the city forced many of them to defy established laws and authority to seek shelter and employment, while continuing to live at levels far below minimal standards of hygiene and sanitation generally acceptable for urban living.

The underlying assumption of the planners was that the city has a civilizing influence and that urbanization leads to modernization. Recent research has shown, however, that urbanization is neither a necessary nor a sufficient condition for economic growth.[6] The other assumption was that new technology and related capabilities would produce a qualitatively superior environment in Chandigarh compared to the available alternative in existing cities. The Punjab government's refusal to upgrade an existing city to the status of a capital, and Nehru's declared hope for creating a new city that would be "unfettered by the traditions of the past," attested to that assumption. The difficulties and lack of experience, however, in coordinating all the various components going into the new city and the urgencies in meeting existing housing and other urban problems instilled considerable conservatism.

The question of how the new city might perform over the long run under conditions of rapid social, technological, and economic changes was pushed to the background. Also, the planners had the conviction that the new designs, structures, and land use relationships that were incorporated in Chandigarh offered a break with the past and represented major innovations. Moreover, since Chandigarh was to offer a modern urban environment, its different assumptions, concepts, and technologies could be incorporated into other Indian cities. Finally, the planners were aware from their Western experience that the built environment of yesteryear could be reshaped, partially at least, in response to changing living conditions, work habits, and leisure time activities.

Available evidence, however, indicates that cities in South Asian countries do not necessarily have a modernizing influence. A recent study concludes that the visible Western, or supposedly "modern," attributes of a South Asian city are mere manifestations of "middle and upper class life styles."[7] In support of its argument, the study points to the family structure of these cities, which has not undergone a change normally associated with urbanization; the caste and class considerations of the people, which continue to influence marriage, joint family, occupation, and social relations; the urbanization process, which has failed to produce the same demographic trends with which it is credited in the West; urban working-class occupations, which are mere extensions of rural craft skills; the lot of the poor, which remains unaffected irrespective of their location; and the lack of proper housing and other social services, which are so glaringly apparent in South Asian cities. Elsewhere it has been pointed out that in modern India only high castes like Brahmans and Rajputs are "undergoing westernization, including urbanization, and the lower castes lack the means as well as the motivation to move into the modern world."[8]

The assumptions of the Chandigarh master plan were based on the consumption patterns of the middle classes of the industrialized countries of the West and they envisaged that opportunities would expand at the middle level and that the lower classes would be induced to climb to that level. The physical constructs of the master plan comply with these assumptions: overscaled streets for high-volume motorized traffic, single-family homes with gardens, open spaces, and the overall high physical standards of the city. Even the most economical houses developed by the planners provided two rooms, a kitchen, a bathroom, and a courtyard. The success of these exaggerated physical targets depended on the rate of growth of economic opportunities at the middle level exceeding the rate of natural increases of the middle-class population. However, the urban economy in India does not offer scope for quick expansion and absorption of new elements.[9]

Given the limitations of the Indian government to undertake mass-scale public housing and the failure of the economy to expand at a higher rate than the natural increases of the middle class, cities in India have no modernizing influence, and the lower reaches of the social strata never get a chance to improve their lot.[10] In fact, with the devalued Indian rupee, even the well-off residents of Chandigarh are finding it hard to maintain their overscaled homes and gardens. The Chandigarh administration itself has not been able to keep up with the costs of repair and maintenance. The Union Territory Administration's failure to collect rent from Punjab and Haryana has only added to the financial woes of the city. "In my rounds of the

Capital," a city officer once observed, "I saw flocks of goats grazing at a number of places," and he good-humoredly requested his staff to "please examine if we can prohibit the keeping of goats in the city of Chandigarh."[11]

The planners' other effort at social engineering included the practice of assigning homes in Chandigarh by administrative rank rather than by caste, community, or language group, and of providing a modest degree of income mix in residential sectors. Although relatively progressive in comparison to other traditional Indian cities, Chandigarh has failed to produce any visible social changes. The traditional Indian social structure, based on particularistic principles of caste, kinship, and religion, has not been compatible with these ideas.[12] As a result, Chandigarh today has acquired all the ordinary features of any other Indian city, which are reflected in all aspects of daily life—communications, social interaction, family life, consumption habits, political and community participation, and other activities.

The absence of local municipal government further restricted the residents of Chandigarh from engaging in a productive sociopolitical interaction for the management of the city. The absence of local government in Chandigarh is particularly important because there is no alternative body through which to monitor the pulse of the city. In fact, in postindependence India, municipal government did not find any mention in either the Directive Principles of State Policy in the Indian Constitution or in the five-year plans sponsored by the Planning Commission. Not until the third Five Year Plan was it marginally recognized that problems of urbanization, as the result of socioeconomic development in the country, needed attention on the part of state governments, municipal governments, and the people.[13]

Every town is, to a degree, a factor in the interplay of forces that are constantly changing the relations between its various communities, and it is also subject to the influence of the national government's attempts to manage the development of the country's social and economic life. The influence of the national government on the city would have been more intelligent than it has turned out to be had the government been better informed about the city's life, evolution, and potentialities. It is important, therefore, that each municipality should keep the government informed fully on these matters. This is not to suggest that the national government would have necessarily done what the city wished, however well the case was presented, but it is certainly more likely that it would have responded better if the local situation and its potentialities had been fully understood. Moreover, if the desires of the municipal government could not be met, the city planners certainly could have adjusted their policies better if they understood the point of view of the national government and its difficulties. Such a process, however, was lacking in Chandigarh.

The mid-1960s proved a turning point in the history of Chandigarh. The division of Punjab in 1966, although undertaken on account of mounting pressures from the Punjabis, especially from the Akalis, transformed the course of development for the city. Chandigarh became a union territory, falling directly under the control of the central government, while serving as the dual capital of Punjab and Haryana. The management of the city became subjected to the competing interests of Punjab, Haryana, and the union territory. Perhaps, none of this would have mattered so much had Nehru's death on May 27, 1964, soon followed by Le Corbusier's death on August 27, 1965, not robbed the city of its two most ardent supporters. With the departure of Pierre Jeanneret, Le Corbusier's cousin and the first chief architect of the Capital Project, in December 1965, the city was left with no individual who could advocate the convictions of its creators above the din of petty political considerations. The unplanned growth of the Chandigarh region is the direct result of the politicization of the city.

Claims by both Punjab and Haryana on Chandigarh as their capital have led to a stalemate of the future development of the city. While the central government has been unable to devise a solution acceptable to the two disputing states, a recent survey indicated that 80 percent of the city's residents would prefer Chandigarh's remaining a union territory.[14] Since the basis of the demands by the two states is political, there is no certainty that either state would be able to administer the city in a way that would be socially and economically beneficial for the people of Chandigarh. Moreover, the psychological security of being administered by the cosmopolitan central government appears definitely more attractive than the possibility of being placed under the tenuous administration of a state government based on parochial considerations. The residents of Chandigarh seem to understand that.

One reason new towns are attractive to people is for their physical characteristics, which often include novel elements. In that sense Chandigarh does provide a break with earlier Indian cities. It is both mystical and mythical. There are those who love it and those who hate it. Chandigarh began as the cherished hope for equality; it now stands charged as a socially segregated city, a fortress of privilege. Yet, it is a city with beauty, with space, with light, with clean air, and with recreational facilities. The clean, functional lines of Chandigarh, easily discernible when flying over the city, best represent the city as the symbol of modernism. Chandigarh was the dividing line between the past and the present. It is no accident that in Chandigarh, unlike other Indian cities, there are no statues commemorating India's past. "I am absolutely in opposition [to the] erection of statues in the city of Chandigarh which must breathe a new spirit," Le Corbusier once observed. The erection of statues "is a passion of the nineteenth century," he felt.[15]

Le Corbusier's primary passion was for art, and whose critical genius flourished on iconoclasm. The Capitol Complex represents that genius. It is meant to be seen, not used. It is hard to walk to buildings; there are no sidewalks, and the distances within the city are great. The ensemble of buildings in the Capitol Complex conveys a strong antipopulist feeling. The stunning monuments and public structures provoke a feeling of awe, even though the structures have come to represent concrete figures of authority, separated from the people. There are two cultures in Chandigarh—the culture of buildings and monuments and the culture of the people. The two cultures are different in content, and the monuments and buildings do not represent the spirit of the people.

The sectors, which make up the residential section, are marked by a sameness that leaves a visitor lost, without landmarks. Each sector is self-contained, providing essential services within walking distance of every dwelling. The most positive aspect of the sectors is that they provide a safety area for children. They can play, walk to school, and to shopping areas, usually without crossing a street.

Chandigarh was meant to be something beyond a new state capital. But it lacks a culture. It lacks the excitement of Indian streets. It lacks bustling, colorful bazaars. It lacks the noise and din of Lahore. It lacks the intimacy of Delhi. It is a stay-at-home city. It is not Indian. It is the anticity. But with all its shortcomings, Chandigarh provokes the interest of people far beyond the borders of India. Neighboring Pakistan wanted to consult Le Corbusier and the Chandigarh administration as it got ready to build its new capital at Islamabad. Burma, wanting to profit from the experience of Le Corbusier, sent him a prepaid return ticket to visit Rangoon. The rest of the world closely watched the development of a planned city and the results it would bring. In India the city became an educating experience for Indian architects and planners, who rushed to other parts of the country to duplicate the features of Chandigarh.

It is, of course, difficult to grasp the essence of any community, even those with distinctive characters that have been formed over many years. In the case of Chandigarh the task is rendered even more difficult because its ultimate essence has yet to emerge. No longer a mere administrative capital, Chandigarh today serves as the regional center for cultural, economic, educational, and social activities. Thousands of people from neighboring towns and villages commute daily to Chandigarh for one reason or another. Its present population is about 450,061, with a population density of 3,948 per square kilometer and a literacy rate of 64.68 percent, one of the highest in the country. By 2001, it is projected that the city region will have an estimated population of 25 lakhs, 66 percent urban, 34 percent rural. Chandigarh itself is expected to grow to a population of 10 lakhs by 2001, double the size it was planned for.[16] All this points to the fact that new towns, whatever their size or location, are not isolated and independent islands but are component subparts of society. As such, society's economic, social, and political problems limit the benefits new towns can be expected to provide.

Another reality of a community is its persistent change. The population's beliefs swing back and forth with the winds of socioeconomic change, having a strong impact on the city. There are presently in Chandigarh challenges to old values about work, family, caste, and communal integration.[17] Increases in population, pollution, and traffic congestion, and decreases in food and fuel, demand changes. Continuing social problems that have been barely touched by piecemeal restorative-rehabilitative programs demand new methods of attack. The persisting conflict among different communal and socioeconomic groups increasingly threaten the city's survival and urgently require change.

Given these demands for change, Chandigarh can no longer develop according to a fixed master plan conceived some thirty-five years ago. Without denigrating the value of the work being done by current planners of the city, their efforts are hardly likely to produce any broad understanding of the influences shaping the development of Chandigarh unless they question the validity of the information on which so many of their assumptions are based. Their basic assumption seems to be that they can create new forces of change in Chandigarh with mere physical structures and restrictive legislation. Such an approach points to their preoccupation with the existing master plan and to their own Western bias in planning. As one senior architect, who served for twenty years in the Capital Project and now owns a private practice in Chandigarh, observed, "Even though we may argue that Chandigarh is an alien concept in which people may have been forced to live, but in reality if Indian architects and town planners were given the chance to build Chandigarh or any other city today . . . we would fall into the same Chandigarh pattern as conceived by Corbusier—mainly because of the educational training, which is mainly Western."[18]

Not until positive forces for change can be identified within the community by its own people will Chandigarh reflect the full aspirations of the people. This means recognizing the limitations of physical planning in developing a new community or in regenerating an old one. What is required are programs which will be directly beneficial to the lower classes—programs such as building a network of communal services (latrines, baths, medical clinics, social and educational centers, etc.), the provision of a clean and ample water supply, cleaning the streets, and encouraging families to form cooperative production units to boost consumption levels. The weaker sections of the population have to be protected from the powerful middle classes in the community. This can be achieved by strengthening the economic base and improving the living conditions of the areas where the majority of the Indian population lives—slums, villages, and old cities.

The absolute magnitude of the Indian urban sector and its relatively small share of the total population indicates that the usual urbanization-industrialization strategies will not rapidly be able to accommodate a growing population. Two rather distinct strategies of development should be devised—one for India's rural, the other for its urban sector. As long as severe overall resource constraints remain basic facts of Indian life, trade-offs between the two sectors will most probably lead to heavy rural emphasis in planning policies.

This is not to argue for an antiurban stance in all planning. The internal management of large cities like Chandigarh is important, because of limited resources and the size of the population. But any plan for Chandigarh that fails to develop social and economic opportunities in its surrounding areas is not likely to succeed in the planned growth of the city. The success of such an effort calls for an interdisciplinary approach in which individuals from many disciplines are invited to pool ideas on the crucial issues of urban life—education, health, religion, recreation, employment, housing, and so forth—to examine successes and failures in urban and suburban communities, and to learn more about how the planning and development of the community could contribute to the life and growth of the individual and the family. The success of such a plan also presupposes greater local autonomy and greater cooperation among the concerned states in the region.

The Chandigarh experience has already served the very useful purpose of exposing India to the science of mass-scale planning for a new community in a relatively short time. It has also demonstrated that new towns, besides being spawning grounds for new ideas, are also prone to the malaise of unrealistic expectations. So far, the wrong people, which is to say those in the upper classes, who could not bear to see the city besieged by philistines, have admired Chandigarh for the wrong reasons. They have admired Chandigarh for its physical features and open spaces. Chandigarh has shown that new towns, especially when removed from their natural settings, are *new* primarily in the physical sense. New designs and construction do not by themselves, however, make the dream of planning and building better urban environments come true. A new town cannot be any better (or worse) than the people who live in it, the planners who design it, or those who manage it.

NOTES
BIBLIOGRAPHY
INDEX

NOTES

CHAPTER 1. GENESIS

1. N. S. Lamba, "Emerging Capitals and New Towns," *Journal of the Institute of Town Planners*, no. 63, June 1971, p. 65.
2. About 4.9 million refugees from West Pakistan and about 2.6 million refugees from East Pakistan came to India. These figures represent only the male population. Government of India, *The First Five-Year Plan: A Summary*, Dec. 12, 1952, pp. 129–30.
3. Ashish Bose, *India's Urbanization, 1901–2001*, 2nd ed., (New Delhi: Tata McGraw-Hill, 1978), p. 82.
4. Ibid., p. 19.
5. Government of India, *The First Five-Year Plan: A Summary*, p. 130.
6. Government of India, *Census of India*, 1941, vol. 1, p. 26.
7. Ashish Bose, *India's Urbanization*, p. 82.
8. Government of India, Ministry of Information and Broadcasting, *Jawaharlal Nehru's Speeches: 1949–53*, 2nd ed. (New Delhi, 1957), p. 10.
9. Government of India, Ministry of Information and Broadcasting, *Jawaharlal Nehru's Speeches: September 1946–May 1949*, 2nd ed., vol. 1 (New Delhi, 1958), pp. 64–65.
10. At the time of the Partition in 1947, Lahore had a bustling population of about 8.5 lakhs, covering an estimated area of 128.75 square miles. D. C. Khanna and R. N. Dogra, "A Preliminary Note on the Selection of the Site for the New Capital of East Punjab," undated, the Randhawa papers, Chandigarh.
11. *Tribune*, Jan. 26, 1951, p. 5.
12. P. L. Varma in personal interview with the author in Chandigarh, June 10, 1982.
13. Rajkumari Amrit Kaur, letter to Nehru, Dec. 12, 1949.
14. Premier of East Punjab, note to Nehru, Feb. 14, 1949.
15. A. V. Raman, letter to R. K. Sidhwa, Feb. 2, 1948.
16. Ibid.

17. P. L. Varma, "A Note on the New Capital," Dec. 3, 1948.
18. A. L. Fletcher, "A Note on the New Capital," Jan. 1949.
19. Ibid.
20. Ibid.
21. Information contained in the minutes of the meeting held in New Delhi on Nov. 23, 1947. The meeting was attended by Jawaharlal Nehru, Sardar V. B. Patel, Sardar Baldev Singh, N. Gopalaswami Ayyanger, Dr. S. P. Mukerjee, Dr. John Mathai, Rajkumari Amrit Kaur, N. C. Neogy, Rafi Ahmed Kidwai, Dharam Vira and Y. K. Puri.
22. The Committee for the Selection of the Site for East Punjab Capital included the following members: P. L. Varma, P. N. Thapar, R. N. Dogra, D. C. Khanna, Brij Mohan Lal, G. R. Garg, Dr. A. R. Mehta, and S. A. Gadkary.
23. D. C. Khanna and R. N. Dogra, "A Preliminary Note on the Selection of the Site for the New Capital of East Punjab," undated, p. 10.
24. Government of India, Ministry of Housing Affairs, Public, File no. 15/11/1948. National Archives, New Delhi.
25. Ibid.
26. Khanna and Dogra, "A Preliminary Note on the Selection of the Site," p. 11.
27. Ibid., pp. 8–10.
28. Ibid., pp. 12–15.
29. Ibid., pp. 15–17. Also see Sri Ram Sharma, *Administrative Set-up at Chandigarh* (Punjab, undated), p. 2; and Norma Evenson, *Chandigarh* Berkeley: Univ. of California Press, 1966), p. 6.
30. Khanna and Dogra, "A Preliminary Note on the Selection of the Site," pp. 15 and 20.
31. As early as 1949, Jean Chesneaux had argued that urbanization in developing countries was in direct response to industrialization. However, Ashish Bose has indicated that during the 1960s, when India's industrialization increased, no proportionate increase registered in India's urban population. (Ashish Bose, *India's Urbanization*, ch. 4.) At any rate, with the Indian urban population at 23.31 percent (1981 Census), the agricultural-rural sector continues to command political attention. Also see, Shanti Tangri, "Urbanization, Political Stability and Economic Growth," in Roy Turner, ed., *India's Urban Future* (Berkeley: Univ. of California Press, 1962).
32. S. A. Lal, letter to A. V. Pai, Principal Private Secretary to the Prime Minister, Feb. 7, 1949.
33. C. M. Trivedi, letter to the Governor General of India, July 13, 1949.
34. Nehru, letter to the Premier of East Punjab, Aug. 13, 1949.
35. Governor of East Punjab, note to Governor General of India, Jan. 29, 1949.

36. P. H. Appleby, *Reexamination of India's Administrative System* (no publisher, undated), p. 7. See also, W. R. Natu, *Public Administration and Economic Development* (Poona, 1954), pp. 11–15.
37. Nehru, letter to Bhim Sain Sachar, Sept. 23, 1949.
38. C. M. Trivedi, letter to Nehru, Mar. 11, 1948, p. 7.
39. Ibid., p. 8.
40. Premier of East Punjab, note to Nehru, Feb. 11, 1949, pp. 1–2.
41. Punjab Government, *Construction of the New Capital at Chandigarh, Project Report*, undated.
42. P. L. Varma, "A Note on the New Capital," Dec. 3, 1948.
43. Punjab Government, *Report of the Sub-Committee Appointed for Reporting on the Compensation and Rehabilitation of the Landowners of the Site of the New Capital*, undated.
44. Maxwell Fry, "Problems of Chandigarh Architecture," *Marg* (Bombay), vol. 14, no. 1, Dec. 1961, p. 20.
45. Premier of East Punjab, note to Nehru, June 13, 1949.
46. Governor of East Punjab, note to Governor General of India, Sept. 26, 1949, p. 2.
47. Government of Punjab, Press Statement, "Change Capital Site," Mar. 17, 1950.
48. Premier of East Punjab, note to Nehru, Jan. 21, 1950.
49. Chief Minister of Punjab, letter to Nehru, June 14, 1950.
50. Lala Duni Chand, letter to Nehru, May 26, 1950.
51. Governor of East Punjab, note to Governor General of India, May 4, 1949.
52. C. M. Trivedi, letter to Nehru, Feb. 17, 1952.
53. C. M. Trivedi, letter to Nehru, Feb. 21, 1952.
54. The Akali Movement, born in the 1920s, was directed against, on the one hand, the corrupt priests and other vested interests in the Sikh shrines and, on the other hand, against the repressive British administration in Punjab. The word *Akali* means "immortal." For a good recent study of the Akali Movement, see Mohinder Singh, *The Akali Movement* (Delhi: Macmillan, 1978).
55. Nehru, letter to Swaran Singh, Mar. 19, 1954.
56. Jagat Narain, letter to Nehru, Feb. 20, 1952.
57. P. N. Thapar, letter to C. M. Trivedi, Feb. 21, 1952.
58. Government of Punjab, Chandigarh, "Press note issued by the Advisory Committee for the New Capital," Feb. 29, 1952.
59. Nehru, letter to C. M. Trivedi, Feb. 24, 1952.
60. Chief Minister, East Punjab, note to Nehru, July 15, 1950.
61. Punjab Government, "Report on the Chandigarh Site," June 30, 1949.
62. Punjab Government, "Press note issued by the Cabinet Sub-Committee (New Capital) following the meeting of August 28, 1948," undated.

63. Ibid.
64. Ibid.
65. Lal Bahadur Shastri, letter to Nehru, July 11, 1953.
66. M. S. Randhawa, note dated May 16, 1949.
67. Premier of East Punjab, note to Nehru, Dec. 5, 1949.
68. Evenson, *Chandigarh*, p. 7.
69. *Hindustan Times* (New Delhi), July 20, 1982.
70. P. K. Wattal, "Report on the Population Problems in India—A Plea for Coordinated and Continuous Treatment," Apr. 14, 1949. Home Affairs, Public, File no. 2/10/49, pp. 5–6. National Archives, New Delhi.
71. Government of India, Ministry of Home Affairs, Public, File no. 2/29/49. Notification published in the *Gazette of India, Extra-Ordinary*, May 16, 1949, p. 19. National Archives, New Delhi.
72. Ibid.
73. M. W. M. Yeatts, "A report by the Census Commissioner of India," Jan. 22, 1949. Home Affairs, Public, File no. 15/17/49, p. 6.
74. Chief Minister of Punjab, note to Nehru, Nov. 20, 1952.
75. Governor of East Punjab, note to Governor General of India, Jan. 3, 1950.
76. Chief Minister of East Punjab, note to Nehru, undated.
77. Governor of East Punjab, note to Governor General of India, Jan. 3, 1950.
78. Premier of East Punjab, letter to Nehru, Dec. 5, 1949. Also see, East Punjab Governor's letter to Nehru, Sept. 8, 1950.
79. Nehru's speech quoted in *Hindustan Times*, Apr. 4, 1952.

CHAPTER 2. ARCHITECTS

1. *Hindustan Times* (New Delhi), July 8, 1950. Also, see L. R. Nair, ed., *Why Chandigarh?* (Simla: Publicity Department, Punjab Government, 1950), p. 4.
2. Rajkumari Amrit Kaur, letter to Sardar Gurbachan Singh, Apr. 27, 1954.
3. *Time*, June 19, 1950.
4. Ebenezer Howard, *To-morrow: A Peaceful Path to Real Reform* (1898). Revised and reissued in 1902 as *Garden Cities of To-morrow*. Edited, with a preface by F. J. Osborn, and an introductory essay by Lewis Mumford (London: Faber & Faber, 1946).
5. Peter Self, "Introduction: New Towns in the Modern World," in Hazel Evans, ed., *New Towns: The British Experience* (London, 1972), p. 10.
6. Shanti Tangri, "Urbanization, Political Stability and Economic Growth," in Roy Turner, ed., *India's Urban Future* (Berkeley: Univ. of California Press, 1962).
7. Hugh Tinker, *Race and the Third World City*, An International Urbanization Survey Report to the Ford Foundation (Apr. 26, 1971), p. 8.

8. *Tribune* (Ambala), Jan. 2, 1951.
9. Government of India, Ministry of Information and Broadcasting. *Jawaharlal Nehru's Speeches: 1949–53*, 2nd ed., (New Delhi, 1957), p. 94.
10. Stanislaus von Moos, *Le Corbusier's Elements of a Synthesis* (Cambridge: MIT Press, 1979), p. 215.
11. Albert Mayer, letter to Nehru, May 1, 1950.
12. Gordon Sanderson, *Types of Modern Indian Buildings* (Allahabad: Government Press, 1913).
13. E. B. Havell, *Indian Architecture* (London, 1913).
14. Percy Brown, *Indian Architecture—Islamic Period* (Bombay, 1942).
15. Madhu Sarin, *Planning and the Urban Poor. The Chandigarh Experience: 1951–75*. 2 vols. (A Research Report Sponsored by the Ministry of Overseas Development, London, at the School of Environmental Studies, University College, London, Dec. 1975), vol. 1, p. 3.
16. Otto Koenigsberger, "New Towns in India," *Town Planning Review*, vol. 23, no. 2, July 1952, p. 100.
17. Norma Evenson, *Chandigarh* (Berkeley: Univ. of California Press, 1966), p. 9.
18. Government of India, Planning Commission. "Nehru's address to the Third Meeting of the National Development Council," Nov. 9, 1954.
19. A. L. Fletcher, "A note on the Competition Idea sponsored by C.E. (Development)," undated, the Randhawa papers.
20. Premier of East Punjab, note to Nehru, Dec. 5, 1949.
21. Nehru, letter to Premier of East Punjab, Dec. 7, 1949.
22. Michael Brecher, *Nehru: A Political Biography*, (London: Oxford Univ. Press, 1959), p. 602.
23. Nehru's speech in Parliament, Dec. 15, 1952. Government of India, Ministry of Information and Broadcasting, *Jawaharlal Nehru's Speeches: 1949–53*, 2nd ed., (New Delhi, 1957), pp. 91–92.
24. Ibid., p. 93.
25. Government of India, Ministry of Publication and Broadcasting, *Jawaharlal Nehru's Speeches: September 1957–April 1963*, vol. 4, (New Delhi, Aug. 1964), pp. 175–76.
26. Government of India, Ministry of Information and Broadcasting, *Jawaharlal Nehru's Speeches: 1963–64*, vol. 5 (New Delhi, Nov. 1968), p. 100.
27. Nehru's speech in Madras at a public meeting on Oct. 2, 1953, reported in the *Hindu*, Oct. 3, 1953.
28. Michael Brecher, *Nehru*, p. 19.
29. Nehru, letter to Gopichand Bhargava, Aug. 9, 1948.
30. P. N. Thapar, letter to the Premier of East Punjab; quoted in the Premier of East Punjab's letter to Nehru, Dec. 22, 1949.

31. For the materials relating to Albert Mayer, I am indebted to the Southern Asia Reference Center, the Joseph Regenstein Library, University of Chicago, Illinois, for giving me permission to photocopy the Albert Mayer papers.
32. Minutes of the meeting of the Cabinet Sub-Committee on the Capital, Dec. 25, 1949, p. 213.
33. Premier of East Punjab, letter to Nehru, Jan. 21, 1950.
34. Mayer, letter to Varma, Dec. 28, 1949.
35. Mayer, letter to Clarence Stein, Feb 7, 1950.
36. N. V. Gadgil, letter to Dharam Vira, May 30, 1950.
37. Krishna Menon, telegram to Nehru, Feb. 21, 1950.
38. O. M. Mathai, letter to Menon, Feb. 21, 1950.
39. Mayer, letter to Nehru, May 22, 1950.
40. Nehru, letter to Mayer, May 23, 1950.
41. Nehru, letter to Gopichand Bhargava, Mar. 16, 1948.
42. Nehru, letter to Gopichand Bhargava, Aug. 30, 1950.
43. Gopichand Bhargava, letter to Nehru, Sept. 2, 1950.
44. C. M. Trivedi, letter to Nehru, Sept. 8, 1950.
45. For a good discussion of this point, see Anthony King, *Colonial Urban Development* (London, 1976).
46. "A note on Capital Project (Punjab)," Punjab, undated.
47. Ibid.
48. Christopher Rand, "City on a Tilting Plain," *New Yorker*, Apr. 30, 1955, p. 36.
49. Nehru, letter to Gopichand Bhargava, Sept. 11, 1950.
50. M. R. Sachdev, letter to the Joint Secretary to Government of India, Ministry of External Affairs and Commonwealth Relations, New Delhi, Oct. 19, 1950.
51. M. R. Sachdev, letter to P. N. Thapar, Oct. 19, 1950.
52. P. N. Thapar, telegram to K. G. Ambegaokar, Nov. 1, 1950.
53. B. Lubetkin, letter to C. L. Katial, Sept. 28, 1950.
54. P. L. Bhandary, letter to Thapar, Oct. 24, 1950.
55. P. L. Varma, personal interview with author in Chandigarh, June 10, 1982.
56. Le Corbusier in *Oeuvre complète 1946–52* (Zurich: Girsberger, 1953), p. 118.
57. Jane Drew, letter to author, Apr. 26, 1983. Also see Maxwell Fry, "Le Corbusier in Chandigarh," in Russell Walden, ed., *The Open Hand* (Cambridge: MIT Press, 1977), p. 351.
58. E. Maxwell Fry, "Problems of Chandigarh Architecture," *Marg* (Bombay), vol. 14, Dec. 1961, p. 20.

59. Maxwell Fry, letter to author, Jan. 6, 1983.
60. Ibid.
61. Ibid. See also Maxwell Fry, "Le Corbusier at Chandigarh," in Walden, ed., *The Open Hand*, pp. 351–52.
62. Fry, "Le Corbusier at Chandigarh," in Walden, ed., *The Open Hand*, p. 352.
63. Ibid. See also Fry, letter to author, Jan. 6, 1983.
64. Fry, letter to author, Jan. 6, 1983.
65. Ibid.
66. For Jane Drew's association with Le Corbusier see Jane Drew, "Le Corbusier as I knew him," in Walden, ed., *The Open Hand*, pp. 365–73.
67. P. N. Thapar, telegram to the Chief Minister, Punjab, Dec. 3, 1950.
68. Le Corbusier, *Oeuvre complète 1952–57* (Zurich: Girsberger, 1958), p. 51.
69. Maxwell Fry, "Chandigarh: The Capital of East Punjab," *RIBA*, 3rd ser., vol. 62, no. 3, Jan. 1955, p. 87.
70. Dharam Vira, letter to M. R. Sachdev, Nov. 30, 1950.
71. Clive Entwhistle, letter to Thapar, Jan. 30, 1951.
72. Mayer, letter to Thapar, Dec. 22, 1950.
73. Thapar, letter to Mayer, Jan. 8, 1951.

CHAPTER 3. THE MAYER PLAN

1. Albert Mayer, "Americans in India," *Survey Graphic*, Mar., 1947, pp. 203, 206.
2. Albert Mayer, *Pilot Project, India: The Story of Rural Development at Etawah, Uttar Pradesh* (Berkeley: Univ. of California Press, 1958), p. 5.
3. Ibid., p. 6. See also, Mayer's article, "Nehru, The Man—And India's Travail," in *Survey*, Dec. 1949, pp. 658–61.
4. Mayer, *Pilot Project, India*, p. 6.
5. Nehru, letter to Mayer, June 17, 1946, cited in Mayer's *Pilot Project, India*, pp. 7–8.
6. Mayer, from a newsletter to American friends, Oct. 27, 1946, in *Pilot Project, India*, p. 13.
7. Mayer, from a newsletter to American friends, Dec. 11, 1946, in *Pilot Project, India*, pp. 30–31.
8. Mayer, "A Note on Post-War Planning in India," reprinted from the *Calcutta Review*, Aug. 1944, pp. 112–18, the Mayer papers.
9. Mayer, *Pilot Project, India*, p. 13.
10. Mayer, note to Ralph Chapman, September 27, 1950, the Mayer papers.

11. Mayer, *Pilot Project, India*, p. 16.
12. Mayer, "A Technique for Planning Complete Communities," *Architectural Forum*, vol. 66, nos. 1 and 2, Jan. and Feb. 1937.
13. Lewis Mumford, "Trend Is not Destiny," *Architectural Record*, vol. 142, no. 6, Dec. 5, 1967, p. 133.
14. Mayer, "What's the Matter with Our Site Plans," *Pencil Points (Progressive Architecture)*, vol. 23, no. 5, May 1942, p. 245.
15. Mayer, "Horse Sense Planning," *Architectural Forum*, vol. 79, Nov. 1943, pp. 61–62.
16. Mayer, quoted in *National Herald* (Lucknow), June 5, 1950.
17. Ibid.
18. Mayer, "The Greater Bombay Master Plan", *Eastern Rotary Wheel*, Sept. 1948, the Mayer papers.
19. Mayer, quoted in *Time*, June 19, 1950, p. 37.
20. Mayer's address to Convention Symposium I, "Urban and Regional Planning," Washington, D.C., May 10, 1950, reprinted in the *Journal of American Institute of Architects*, Oct. 1950, pp. 171–73.
21. Mayer, "Report on Master Plan of the New Punjab Capital," May 12, 1950, the Mayer papers.
22. Mayer, "Urban and Regional Planning," p. 173.
23. Ibid., p. 166.
24. Ibid., p. 175.
25. Mayer, undated manuscript sent to Wilma B. Fairchild of the American Geographical Society on Mar. 6, 1950, the Mayer papers.
26. Mayer, letter to Maxwell Fry, Jan. 31, 1951.
27. Mayer, letter to Fry, Feb. 23, 1951.
28. Norma Evenson, *Chandigarh* (Berkeley: Univ. of California Press, 1966), p. 13.
29. Charles Jencks, *Modern Movements in Architecture* (Garden City, N.Y.: Doubleday/Anchor, 1973), p. 246.
30. Mayer, note to Nehru on "The New Capital City for the Punjab," July 1, 1950.
31. Mayer, letter to Fry, Jan. 31, 1951.
32. Minutes of the meeting held in Mayer's office in New York, Mar. 31, 1950, the Mayer papers.
33. Evenson, *Chandigarh*, p. 16.
34. Mayer, letter to Fry, Feb. 23, 1951.
35. Ibid.
36. Ibid.
37. Mayer, letter to Fry, Jan. 31, 1951.
38. Minutes of the meeting, Mar. 31, 1950, the Mayer papers.

39. Ibid.
40. Ibid.
41. Ibid.
42. Clarence Stein, "Towards New Towns for America," *Town Planning Review* (Liverpool), Jan. 1950, pp. 352–53.
43. Clarence Perry, "The Neighborhood Unit," *Neighborhood and Community Planning*, vol. 7, 1929, the Mayer Papers.
44. *Proceedings of the National Planning Conference, 1937*, American Society of Planning Officials, Chicago, pp. 132–37.
45. For a good discussion of the neighborhood idea, see Thomas Sharp's *Town Planning* (London, 1945).
46. R. Glass, *Social Background of a Plan or Study of Middlesborough* (London, 1948).
47. R. MacIver and C. H. Page, *Society* (London, 1949), p. 10.
48. Mayer, *The Urgent Future* (New York: McGraw-Hill Book Co., 1967), p. 103.
49. Mayer, "Report on Master Plan of the New Punjab Capital," May 12, 1950, the Mayer papers.
50. Mayer, "A Technique for Planning Complete Communities," *Architectural Forum*, Jan., 1937, pp. 21–22.
51. Matthew Nowicki, letter to Mayer, undated, cited in Evenson, *Chandigarh*, p. 20.
52. Nowicki, letter to Mayer, Apr. 16, 1950, cited in Evenson, *Chandigarh*, p. 24.
53. Nowicki, letter to Mayer, undated, cited in Evenson, *Chandigarh*, pp. 14–15.
54. Ibid.
55. Nowicki's quote cited by Mayer in his "Note on Matthew Nowicki's Work for the Punjab Capital," p. 2. Mayer mailed this note, along with some sketches by Nowicki, to Nowicki's brother Jacek in Poland. The material was accompanied by a covering letter from Mayer, dated Aug. 21, 1959. The Mayer papers.
56. Nowicki, letter to Mayer, undated, cited in Evenson, *Chandigarh*, p. 15.
57. Evenson, *Chandigarh*, p. 20.
58. Mayer, letter to Jacek Nowicki, Aug. 21, 1959.
59. Ibid.
60. Sten A. Nilsson, *The New Capitals of India, Pakistan and Bangladesh*, trans. Elisabeth Andreasson (Lund, Sweden: Studentlitteratur, 1973), p. 93.
61. Evenson, *Chandigarh*, p. 20.

62. Nowicki, letter to Mayer, undated, cited in Evenson, *Chandigarh*, p. 18.
63. Nowicki, "Supplementary Notes to the Architectural Study of Superblock L–37," undated, the Mayer papers.
64. Ibid.
65. Ibid.
66. Evenson, *Chandigarh*, p. 23.
67. Mayer, letter to Jacek Nowicki, Aug. 21, 1959.

CHAPTER 4. THE LE CORBUSIER PLAN

1. Albert Mayer, Press Release, Jan. 31, 1951, New York, the Mayer papers.
2. P. N. Thapar, letter to Mayer, Aug. 26, 1951.
3. Maxwell Fry, letter to Mayer, Aug. 18, 1951.
4. Maxwell Fry, "Le Corbusier at Chandigarh," in Russell Walden, ed., *The Open Hand* (Cambridge: MIT Press, 1977), p. 353.
5. Fry, "Chandigarh: The Capital of East Punjab," *RIBA*, 3rd ser., vol. 62, no. 3, Jan. 1955, p. 87.
6. Fry, "Le Corbusier at Chandigarh," in Walden, ed., *The Open Hand*, p. 354.
7. Ibid., p. 353.
8. Ibid.
9. Fry, *Art in a Machine Age* (London: Methuen, 1969), p. 73.
10. Fry, *Autobiographical Sketches* (London: Elek, 1975), p. 141.
11. Fry, letter to author, Jan. 6, 1983.
12. Fry, letter to Richard Neutra, Sept. 9, 1940, cited in Thomas S. Hines, *Richard Neutra and the Search for Modern Architecture* (New York: Oxford Univ. Press, 1982), p. 193.
13. Fry, letter to the author, Jan. 6, 1983.
14. Fry, *Art in a Machine Age*, p. 49.
15. Fry, letter to the author, Jan. 6, 1983.
16. Fry, *Autobiographical Sketches*, p. 61.
17. Fry, *Art in a Machine Age*, p. 73.
18. Fry, *Autobiographical Sketches*, p. 9.
19. Ibid., p. 47.
20. Fry, *Art in a Machine Age*, p. 24.
21. Fry, *Autobiographical Sketches*, p. 141.
22. Ibid., p. 151.
23. Fry and Jane Drew, *Tropical Architecture in the Dry and Humid Zones* (London: B. T. Batsford, 1964), pp. 19–20.
24. Fry, *Art in a Machine Age*, p. 123.

25. Fry, letter to author, Jan. 6, 1983.
26. Fry, *Autobiographical Sketches*, p. 151.
27. Fry, *Art in a Machine Age*, p. 141.
28. Ibid., p. 142.
29. Jane Drew, with Edwin Maxwell Fry, *Village Housing in the Tropics* (London: Lund Humphries, 1947); Fry and Drew, *Tropical Architecture in the Dry and Humid Zones*.
30. Cited by Stanislaus von Moos in his *Le Corbusier: Elements of a Synthesis* (Cambridge: MIT Press, 1979), p. 2.
31. Ibid., p. 4.
32. Robert Fishman, *Urban Utopias in the Twentieth Century* (New York: Basic Books, 1977), p. 167.
33. Paul Turner, "Romanticism, Rationalism, and the Domino System" in Walden, ed., *The Open Hand*, pp. 19–21.
34. Cited by Charles Jencks in his *Le Corbusier and the Tragic View of Architecture* (London: Allen Lane, 1973), p. 23.
35. Ibid.
36. Le Corbusier, *The City of To-Morrow, and its Planning*, trans. Frederick Etchells (Cambridge: MIT Press, 1971), p. 1.
37. von Moos, *Le Corbusier*, p. 2.
38. Jencks, *Tragic View of Architecture*, p. 110.
39. Ibid., p, 104.
40. See Taya Zinkin, "No Compromise with Corbusier," *Guardian*, Sept. 11, 1965. Also see Jencks, *Tragic View of Architecture*, pp. 100, 104, 189.
41. Robert Fishman, in Walden, ed., *The Open Hand*, p. 247.
42. Jencks, *Tragic View of Architecture*, p. 18.
43. Le Corbusier, *La Ville radieuse* (Boulogne, 1935), p. 154.
44. Le Corbusier, *When the Cathedrals Were White: A Journey to the Country of Timid People* (New York, 1947).
45. Le Corbusier, *Personal Notes* (Fondation Le Corbusier, Paris).
46. From a record of the meeting between Le Corbusier, Max Fry, and Jane Drew, Dec. 6, 1950, Fondation Le Corbusier, Paris.
47. Le Corbusier, letter to Fry, Dec. 12, 1951.
48. Fry, "Architects to the Rescue!" *RIBA*, 3rd ser., vol. 66, no. 8, June 1959, p. 285.
49. Cited in von Moos, *Elements of a Synthesis*, p. 194.
50. Le Corbusier, *The City of To-Morrow*, p. 11.
51. Mayer, letter to Fry, Jan. 16, 1951.
52. Fry, letter to Mayer, Jan. 25, 1951.
53. Mayer, letter to Fry, Jan. 31, 1951.
54. Mayer, letter to Fry, Feb. 16, 1951.

55. Fry, letter to Mayer, Feb. 14, 1951.
56. Thapar, cablegram to Mayer, Mar. 19, 1951.
57. Mayer, cablegram to Thapar, Mar. 20, 1951.
58. Le Corbusier, letter to Indian Ambassador Lachmanam (Paris), Nov. 25, 1950.
59. Minutes of the meeting held on June 15, 1951, at Simla, attended by Mayer, Fry, Jeanneret, Varma, and Thapar.
60. Le Corbusier, "The Master Plan," *Marg* (Bombay), vol. 14, no. 1, Dec. 1961, p. 9.
61. Mayer, letter to Fry, Aug. 29, 1951.
62. Fry, letter to Mayer, Aug. 18, 1951.
63. Mayer, letter to Fry, Aug. 29, 1951.
64. Fry, letter to Mayer, Sept. 5, 1951.
65. Mayer, letter to Fry, Oct. 16, 1951.
66. Le Corbusier, letter to Nehru, Nov. 11, 1952.
67. Fry, "Chandigarh: Birth of a Capital," *Sunday Statesman* (New Delhi), May 6, 1951.
68. Jawaharlal Nehru, note to the Governor of Punjab (with copies to the Planning Commission and P. N. Thapar), Apr. 4, 1952.
69. Mulkraj Anand, "Conversation with Le Corbusier," in *Le Corbusier: 80th Birthday Anniversary Issue*, ed. Santosh Kumar (Bombay: International Cultural Organization, 1967) pp. 11–14.
70. Fry, "Chandigarh: The Capital of East Punjab."
71. Le Corbusier, letter to Indian Ambassador Lachmanam (Paris), Nov. 25, 1950.
72. Le Corbusier, document ref. no. AW21, Nov. 1950, Fondation Le Corbusier, Paris.
73. Ibid.
74. Le Corbusier, "The Master Plan," *Marg* (Bombay), vol. 14, no. 1, Dec. 1961, p. 5.
75. Jane Drew, "Sector 22," *Marg*, p. 22.
76. Fry, "Problems of Chandigarh Architecture," *Marg*, p. 21.
77. Le Corbusier, "The Master Plan," *Marg*.
78. Christopher Rand, "City on a Tilting Plain," *New Yorker*, vol. 31, Apr. 30, 1955, p. 42.
79. Jane Drew, "Chandigarh Capital City Project," *Architects' Year Book*, no. 4 (London, 1953), p. 56.
80. Fry, "Chandigarh: The Capital of East Punjab," p. 87.
81. Fry, "Problems of Chandigarh Architecture," *Marg*, p. 20.
82. Ibid.
83. Aditya Prakash, "Architectural Control, Shops, Flats, etc.," *Marg*, p. 39.

84. Fry, "Problems of Chandigarh Architecture," *Marg*, p. 20.
85. Norma Evenson, "Chandigarh (1969)," in Peter Serenyi, ed., *Le Corbusier in Perspective* (Englewood Cliffs, N.J.: Prentice-Hall, 1975), p. 148.
86. von Moos, *Elements of a Synthesis*, p. 259; also see, Allen Greenberg, "Lutyens' Architecture Revisited," in *Perspective 12* (New Haven, Conn., 1969), pp. 148 ff.
87. Fry, "Problems of Chandigarh Architecture," *Marg*, p. 20.
88. Nehru's message in the special issue of the *Architectural Forum* on the 80th birthday anniversary of Le Corbusier, Apr., 1961, p. 102.
89. von Moos, "The Politics of the Open Hand: Notes on Le Corbusier and Nehru at Chandigarh," in Walden, ed., *The Open Hand*, p. 444.
90. Le Corbusier, *The Modulor II*, trans. Peter de Francia & Anna Bostock (Cambridge: Harvard Univ. Press, 1958), pp. 214–15.
91. Jencks, *The Tragic View of Architecture*, p. 154.
92. Fry, "Le Corbusier at Chandigarh," in Walden, ed., *The Open Hand*, p. 357.
93. Le Corbusier, *Oeuvre complète 1952–1957* (Zurich: Girsberger, 1958), p. 117.
94. Nehru, letter to C. P. N. Singh, July 15, 1954.
95. Le Corbusier, *Oeuvre complète 1946–1952* (Zurich: Girsberger, 1953), p. 140: cited and translated by Norma Evenson in *Chandigarh* (Berkeley: Univ. of California Press, 1966), p. 78.
96. Evenson, *Chandigarh*, p. 79.
97. Ibid., p. 82.
98. Charles Correa, "The Assembly, Chandigarh," *Architectural Review*, vol. 135, no. 808, June 1964, p. 412.
99. Le Corbusier, letter to the Government of India, Dec. 29, 1960. Extracts from this letter have been reproduced by Eulie Chowdhury in *Architectural Design*, Oct. 1965, p. 505.
100. Minutes of the meeting of the Advisory Committee on the Chandigarh Capital Project, May 10, 1960.
101. von Moos, *Elements of a Synthesis*, p. 291.
102. Le Corbusier, cited in von Moos' "The Politics of the Open Hand," in Walden, ed., *The Open Hand*, p. 447.
103. Le Corbusier, cited in Mary Patricia May Sekler's "Le Corbusier, Ruskin, the Tree, and the Open Hand," in Walden, ed., *The Open Hand*, p. 70.
104. Le Corbusier, letter to Nehru, no date, reproduced by Stanislaus von Moos in "The Politics of the Open Hand," in Walden, ed., *The Open Hand*, pp. 456–57.
105. Jane Drew, interview at her home with the author, Aug. 25, 1982. Also

see Mary Sekler in Walden, ed., *The Open Hand*, p. 71.
106. Le Corbusier, a note on the "Chandigarh Cultural Center," undated, Fondation Le Corbusier, Paris.
107. Le Corbusier, "A note on the Master Plan," June 18, 1964, Chandigarh.
108. Le Corbusier on "The Statute of Land," undated, Chandigarh.
109. Le Corbusier, letter to Nehru, May 13, 1960.

CHAPTER 5. A PLANNED CITY

1. Reference to this incident is made in Nehru's letter to Bhim Saim Sachar, Mar. 21, 1951.
2. See R. G. Studer, "Behavior Contingent Design of Non-environment Systems," in W. M. Smith, ed., *Behavior, Design, and Policy Aspects of Human Habitats* (Green Bay: Univ. of Wisconsin, 1972).
3. Chandigarh Administration, Law Department, "The Capital of Punjab (Development and Regulation) Act, 1952, Punjab Act No. XXVII of 1952," *Chandigarh Code*, vol. 3, 1972, pp. 77–90.
4. Ibid., p. 87.
5. Chandigarh Administration, Law Department, "The Punjab New Capital (Periphery) Control Act, 1952, Punjab Act No. 1 of 1953," *Chandigarh Code*, vol. 3, 1972, p. 98.
6. Ibid.
7. M. S. Randhawa, in "Development of Chandigarh, Proceedings," Dec. 7, 1966, Chandigarh, the Randhawa papers.
8. From the minutes of the meeting held at Chandigarh, Aug. 8, 1966, the Randhawa papers.
9. From minutes of the meeting, Aug. 18, 1966, Chandigarh, the Randhawa papers.
10. Le Corbusier, "For the Establishment of an Immediate Statute of Land for the City of Chandigarh," Dec. 18, 1959, Chandigarh.
11. *Tribune*, Apr. 30, 1960.
12. Le Corbusier, "A Note Regarding the Location of a Cantonment near Chandigarh," undated.
13. Minutes of the meeting of the Advisory Committee on the Capital Project Control Board, May 10, 1960.
14. Le Corbusier, letter to Nehru, Dec. 11, 1962.
15. Nehru, letter to P. S. Kairon, Nov. 4, 1960.
16. Le Corbusier, "Report on Certain Town Planning Problems of the City of Chandigarh," Apr. 27, 1964.
17. Pierre Jenneret, letter to Le Corbusier, Mar. 6, 1963.
18. Mrs. U. E. Chowdhury, Memorandum, June 30, 1969.

19. M. S. Randhawa, "Difficulties Experienced by People Who are Building in Chandigarh," Dec. 16, 1958, the Randhawa papers.
20. Le Corbusier, "A note on Chandigarh," undated.
21. Le Corbusier, letter to M.S. Randhawa, Dec. 9, 1957.
22. Ibid.
23. Ibid.
24. Annexture 1: "Financing the Capital Project During the Second Plan Period," undated, Chandigarh, the Randhawa papers.
25. P. Jeanneret, letter to D. P. Nayar, Apr. 11, 1958.
26. Le Corbusier, letter to Nehru, May 9, 1958.
27. C. P. N. Singh, letter to Lal Bahadur Shastri, July 8, 1953.
28. Minutes of the meeting of the Chandigarh Capital Project Control Board, July 18, 1960, the Randhawa papers.
29. Ibid.
30. Chief Minister, Punjab, letter to Nehru, Mar. 20, 1954.
31. Government of Punjab, Economic and Statistical Organization, *Chandigarh: Socio-Economic Survey, May, 1957*, Publication no. 13, Chandigarh 1958, pp. 16–17.
32. Ibid., p. 14.
33. Ibid.
34. Ibid., p. 27.
35. Le Corbusier, "A Report Concerning Important Points for the Development of the City of Chandigarh," Dec. 29, 1959.
36. For these insights, I am indebted to Manmohan Dayal for letting me read his unpublished report, "An Action Research of a Squatter Settlement in Chandigarh," sponsored by the Punjab State Institute of Public Administration, Chandigarh, undated.
37. Le Corbusier, "A Report on Certain Town Planning Problems of the City of Chandigarh," Apr. 27, 1964.
38. Government of Punjab, *Chandigarh: Socio-Economic Survey*, p. 40.
39. Maxwell Fry, "Chandigarh: The Capital of East Punjab," *RIBA*, 3rd ser., vol. 62, no. 3, Jan. 1955.
40. M. S. Randhawa, "A note on the Second Phase of Chandigarh," undated, Chandigarh, the Randhawa papers.
41. "Squatters in Chandigarh," Office of the Chief Architect, Union Territory Administration, Chandigarh, undated paper, the Randhawa papers.
42. Donald B. Rosenthal, ed., *The City in Indian Politics*, (Faridabad: Thompson Press [India], 1976), p. 7.
43. For a good explanation of the informal sector, see S. V. Sethuraman, "The Informal Urban Sector in Developing Countries: Some Policy Implications," *Social Action*, vol. 27, no. 3, July–Sept. 1977, pp. 195–205.

44. P. Jeanneret, letter to P. S. Kairon, Aug. 8, 1963.
45. P. Jeanneret, letter to M. S. Randhawa, Oct. 14, 1963.
46. P. Jeanneret, letter to Nehru, Sept. 29, 1961.
47. P.S. Kairon, letter to Nehru, Apr. 16, 1964.
48. Nehru's speech in Madras at a public meeting reported in the *Hindu*, Oct. 3, 1953.
49. Government of India, *Report of the State Reorganization Commission* (New Delhi, 1955), p. 46.
50. "India and her minorities," in the *Tribune*, Jan. 3, 1951.
51. M. S. Dhammi, quoted in *India Today* (New Delhi), vol. 6, no. 20, Oct. 31, 1981, p. 36.
52. Government of India, *The Punjab Boundary Commission Report* (also called *The Shah Commission Report*), (New Delhi, 1966), p. 66.
53. Government of India, Ministry of Law. *The Punjab Reorganization Act, 1966* (New Delhi, 1967), p. 3.
54. Government of India, *The Shah Commission Report*, pp. 41–42.
55. Ibid. The rural Mani Majra and Manauli were appended to the City administration on Nov. 1, 1966 on the creation of the Union Territory. Union territories are constituent units of the central government in India, enjoying a lesser level of status than states, and are directly administered by the President through his agents.
56. Yogender Malik, "Conflict over Chandigarh: A Case Study of an Interstate Dispute in India," *Contributions to Asian Studies*, vol. 3, 1973, p. 62.
57. *Hindustan Times* (New Delhi), July 10, 1969.
58. *Times of India* (New Delhi), July 23, 1969.
59. *Hindu* (Madras), Sept. 5, 1969.
60. *Patriot* (New Delhi), Oct. 9, 1960.
61. *Statesman*, (New Delhi edition), Jan. 31, 1970.
62. Government of India, Ministry of Home Affairs, Notification No. 4.1.66—Chandigarh, Nov. 1, 1966, published under part 1, section 2, of the *Gazette of India, Extraordinary*, Chandigarh Administration, Chandigarh.
63. Minutes of the meeting held on Nov. 7, 1966, in the office of the Chief Commissioner, Chandigarh, the Randhawa papers.
64. Jeet Malhotra, interview with the author, Chandigarh, June 10, 1982; also see his, "Development of Architecture: Human Settlements and Highways in Punjab," Dec. 30, 1981, Chandigarh.
65. Government of India, *Census of India*, 1981, Series 26, Chandigarh, pp. 9–10.
66. Ibid.
67. Government of India, *Census of India*, 1981, Series 17, Punjab, p. 1.

68. V. R. Iyer, letter to Chief Commissioner, Chandigarh, July 26, 1975.
69. Ibid.
70. L. R. Vagale, *A Case Study of Chandigarh and Environs in the Regional Setting* (United Nations Economic Commission for Asia and the Far East, sponsored by the United Nations and the Government of Japan, at Nagoya, Japan, Oct. 10–20, 1966) p. 38.
71. Mrs. U. E. Chowdhury, "A Regional Plan for Chandigarh City," Department of Architecture, Union Territory Administration, Chandigarh, June 30, 1969.
72. "Report on the Interstate Chandigarh Region," Chandigarh, 1982, p. 2.
73. Ibid., p. 38.
74. Ibid., p. 7.
75. "Summary Report on the Interstate Chandigarh Region," 1982, p. 3.
76. Ibid., pp. 2–5.
77. Ibid., p. 14.
78. Rosenthal, ed., *The City in Indian Politics*, p. 7.

CHAPTER 6. CONCLUSIONS

1. C.M. Trivedi to the Governor General of India, July 13, 1949.
2. Premier of East Punjab to Nehru, June 13, 1949.
3. "Change Capital Site," Press Statement, Mar. 17, 1950, the Randhawa papers.
4. Ashish Bose, *India's Urbanization, 1901–2001*, 2nd ed. (New Delhi: Tata McGraw-Hill, 1978), p. 29.
5. Le Corbusier, a note to M. S. Randhawa, on "the consideration of several problems . . . in the realization of Chandigarh," Dec. 8, 1957.
6. See Shanti Tangari, "Urbanization, Political Stability and Economic Growth," in Roy Turner, ed., *India's Urban Future* (Berkeley: Univ. of California Press, 1962).
7. M. A. Qadeer, "Do Cities 'Modernize' the Developing Countries? An Examination of the South Asian Experience," *Comparative Studies*, vol. 16, June 1974.
8. M. N. Srinivas, *Social Change in Modern India* (Berkeley: Univ. of California Press, 1969), p. 66.
9. Government of India, Planning Commission. *First Five Year Plan: A Summary* (New Delhi, Dec. 12, 1952), p. 130.
10. M. A. Qadeer, "Do Cities 'Modernize' the Developing Countries?"
11. Secretary Capital Project, letter to Deputy Secretary, July 18, 1966.
12. Victor S. D'Souza, *Social Structure of a Planned City: Chandigarh* (Bombay: Orient Longmans, 1968), p. 277.
13. For a recent analysis of the role of the municipal government in India,

see B. S. Khanna, ed., *Report of the Seminar on Municipal Government in India (April 4–9, 1965)* (Chandigarh: Punjab Univ., 1966).
14. *India Today* (New Delhi), Nov. 15, 1982, p. 76.
15. Le Corbusier, letter to P. L. Varma, Dec. 9, 1954.
16. These figures are based on the Government of India 1981 Census Report, New Delhi, 1982.
17. Several of these issues are currently being researched by Indian scholars at universities in Punjab and other parts of the country.
18. S. D. Sharma, in an interview with the author, Chandigarh, July 4, 1982.

BIBLIOGRAPHY

The unpublished sources, government records, and correspondence between officials, which are cited in notes only, include the personal papers of M. S. Randhawa at the Chandigarh Museum, Chandigarh, the Jawaharlal Nehru papers at the Prime Minister's Office, New Delhi, the Albert Mayer papers at the Southern Asia Reference Center, University of Chicago, and the Le Corbusier papers at the Fondation Le Corbusier, Paris. In addition to these sources, I interviewed several individuals, who either had worked with Le Corbusier or were connected with the development of Chandigarh. These include, in India, S. S. Bhati, Mrs. U. E. Chowdhury, J. K. Chowdhury, R. N. Dogra, Victor D'Sousa, P. C. Khanna, Jeet Malhotra, Surjeet Singh, S. S. Shafi, M. N. Sharma, S. D. Sharma, P. L. Varma, and B. B. Vohra, and, in England, Jane Drew, Maxwell Fry, and Otto Koenigsberger. For data, I have relied on the Government of India census, 1941, 1951, 1961, 1971, and 1981, the yearly statistical abstracts of the Punjab government, and news reports in the *Tribune*, the *Hindustan Times*, the *Times of India*, the *Statesman*, the *Hindu*, the *Indian Express*, the *Patriot* and the *National Herald*. These sources are also cited in notes only.

ADAMS, THOMAS. *Recent Advances in Town Planning*. London: J. A. Churchill, 1932.
AHMAD, QAZI. *Indian Cities: Characteristics and Correlates*. Research Paper, no. 102. Chicago: Univ. of Chicago, Dept. of Geography, 1965.
ALTSHULER, ALAN. *The City Planning Process: A Political Analysis*. New York: Cornell Univ. Press, 1965.
ANTHONY, HARRY A. "Le Corbusier: His Ideas for Cities," *American Institute of Planners Journal*, vol. 32, no. 5, Sept. 1966, pp. 279–88.
BARFIVALA, CHUNILAL D. *Hand Book of the Law of Land Acquisition*. Bombay: The Local Self-Government Institute, 1957.

BARRIER, N. GERALD. *The Sikhs and Their Literature.* Delhi: Manohar Book Service, 1970.
BARTH, GUNTHER. *Instant Cities.* New York: Oxford Univ. Press, 1975.
BEGDE, PRABHAKAR V. *Ancient and Mediaeval Town-Planning in India.* New Delhi: Sagar Publications, 1978.
BENEVOLO, LEONARDO. *History of Modern Architecture.* Vol. 2, *The Modern Movement.* Cambridge, Mass.: The MIT Press, 1971.
BESSET, MAURICE. *Who Was Le Corbusier?* Trans. Robin Kemball. Geneva, Switzerland: Skira. Distributed in the United States by the World Publishing Co., Cleveland, 1968.
BHALLA, J. R. "The Role of the Architect in India Today." *Royal Institute of British Architects Journal (RIBA),* Mar. 1967.
BOSE, ASHISH. *India's Urbanization, 1901–2001.* 2nd ed. New Delhi: Tata McGraw-Hill Publishing Co., 1978.
BRECHER, MICHAEL. *Nehru: A Political Biography.* London: Oxford Univ. Press, 1959.
BREESE, GERALD W. *Urbanization in Newly Developing Countries.* Englewood Cliffs, N.J.: Prentice-Hall, 1966.
BREESE, GERALD W., ED. *The City in Newly Developing Countries: Readings on Urbanism and Urbanization.* Englewood Cliffs, N. J.: Prentice-Hall, 1969.
BROWN, PERCY. *Indian Architecture—Islamic Period.* Bombay, 1942.
BURCHELL, ROBERT W., ED. *Frontiers of Planned Unit Development: A Synthesis of Expert Opinion.* New Brunswick, N.J.: Center for Urban Policy Research, 1973.
CASSEN, R. H. *India: Population, Economy and Society.* New Delhi: Macmillan Company of India, 1978–79.
CHANDIGARH ADMINISTRATION. *Union Territory of Chandigarh, Annual Plan: 1982–83.* Chandigarh, 1982.
CHANDIGARH ADMINISTRATION, LAW DEPARTMENT. *Chandigarh Code,* vol. 1. Chandigarh, Mar. 31, 1970.
———. *Chandigarh Code,* vol. 2. Chandigarh, Mar. 31, 1970.
———. *Chandigarh Code,* vol. 3. Chandigarh, Mar. 31, 1972.
———. *Chandigarh Code,* vol. 4. Chandigarh, Jan. 31, 1975.
CHIPKIN, C. M. "CHANDIGARH." *South African Architectural Record,* vol. 43, Dec. 1958, pp. 18–27.
CHOWDHURY, J. K. "The New Industrial Township: Nangal." *Urban and Rural Planning Thought,* vol. 1, Jan. 1958, pp. 12–27.
CHOWDHURY, U. E. "Recent Work of Pierre Jeanneret." *Progressive Architecture,* vol. 45, Feb. 1964, pp. 148–53.
———. "Le Corbusier in Chandigarh: Creator and Generator." *Architectural Design,* vol. 135, Oct. 1965, pp. 504–13.
"Construction en pays chauds—Inde: Chandigarh." *Architecture d'aujourd'hui,* no. 67, Oct. 1956, pp. 172–97.
"Corbu in India." *Architectural Forum,* vol. 106, Apr. 1957, pp. 142–47.
CORBUSIER, LE. *Vers une architecture.* Série l'esprit nouveau. Paris: G. Crés

et Cie., 1923; Trans. Frederick Etchells as *Toward a New Architecture*. New York: Brewer and Warren, 1927.

———. *Oeuvre complète 1910–29*. Zurich: Girsberger, 1929.
———. *Oeuvre complète 1921–34*. Zurich: Girsberger, 1935.
———. *Oeuvre complète 1934–38*. Zurich: Girsberger, 1939.
———. *Oeuvre complète 1938–46*. Zurich: Girsberger, 1946.
———. *Oeuvre complète 1946–52*. Zurich: Girsberger, 1953.
———. *Oeuvre complète 1952–57*. Zurich: Girsberger, 1958.
———. *La Ville radieuse*. Boulogne: Editions de l'architecture d'aujourd'hui, 1935. Trans. Pamela Knight, Eleanor Levieux, and Derek Coltman. *The Radiant City: Elements of a Doctrine of Urbanism to Be Used as the Basis of Our Machine-age Civilization*. London: Faber & Faber, 1967.
———. *Les Trois Etablissements humains*. Paris: Denoel, 1944.
———. *When the Cathedrals Were White: A Journey to the Country of Timid People*. New York: Reynal and Hitchcock, 1947.
———. *The Modulor II*. Trans. Peter de Francia & Anna Bostock. Cambridge: Harvard Univ. Press, 1958.
———. *Creation is a Patient Search*. New York: Praeger, 1960.
———. *Le Corbusier 1910–1960*. Zurich: Girsberger, 1960.
———. *Le Corbusier Talks with Students from the School of Architecture*. Trans. Pierre Chase. New York: Orion Press, 1961.
———. *The City of Tomorrow and Its Planning*. Trans. from the 8th French edition of *Urbanisme* by Frederick Etchells. Cambridge, Mass.: The MIT Press, 1971.
———. *Looking at City Planning*. Trans. Eleanor Levieux. New York: Grossman Publishers, 1971.
———. "Architecture: The Expression of the Materials and Methods of Our Times." *Architectural Record*, vol. 66, New York, 1929, pp. 123–28.
———. "The Minimal House: A Solution." *Architectural Record*, vol. 68, Aug. 1930, pp. 133–37.
———. "Twentieth Century Living and Twentieth Century Building." *Decorative Art—The Studio Yearbook*, 1930, pp. 9–20.
———. "The Future of the Architectural Profession." *Plan*, no. 2, 1947, pp. 4–6.
———. "Chandigarh—Ville radieuse des Indes." *L'Architecture d'aujourd'hui*, vol. 22, Feb.–Mar. 1953, pp. 102–3.
———. "Chandigarh—The New Capital of the Punjab." *The Architect and the Building News*, vol. 204, Nov. 26, 1953, pp. 669–71.
———. "Ancora Chandigarh." *L'Architettura: Cronaca e storia*, vol. 2, no. 10, Aug. 1956, pp. 264–65.
———. "Chandigarh: The Secretariat, the Assembly Building, the Civic Centre." *Architectural Design*, vol. 31, Feb. 1961, pp. 60–63.
———. "Chandigarh: The New Assembly Building." *Design Annual*, vol. 6, July 1962, pp. 109–14.

CORREA, CHARLES. "The Assembly, Chandigarh." *Architectural Review*, vol. 135, June 1964, pp. 404–12.

CRANE, DAVID. "Chandigarh Reconsidered." *American Institute of Architects Journal*, vol. 33, May 1960, pp. 32–39.

DAVIES, ROSS, AND PETER HALL, EDS. *Issues in Urban Society*. Middlesex, England: Penguin Books, 1978.

DE SOUZA, ALFRED, ED. *The Indian City: Poverty, Ecology and Urban Development*. New Delhi: South Asia Books, 1978.

DHAR, D. N. "Current Trends in Indian Architecture Today." *Journal of the Indian Institute of Architects*, vol. 20, no. 3, July-Sept. 1954, pp. 9–10.

DOABIA, T. S. *The Capital of Punjab (Development and Regulation) Act, 1952*. Chandigarh: Jain General House, n.d.

DREW, JANE. "Chandigarh Capital City Project." *Architects' Year Book*, no. 4, London, 1953, pp. 56–66.

———. "On the Chandigarh Scheme." *Marg*, vol. 6, no. 4, Bombay, 1953, pp. 19–25.

DREW, JANE, WITH EDWIN MAXWELL FRY. *Village Housing in the Tropics*. London: Lund Humphries, 1947.

———. "4-D Designing as Opposed to Town Planning." *Journal of the Institute of Town Planners* (India), vol. 2, Apr. 1955, pp. 8–10.

D'SOUZA, VICTOR S. *Social Structure of a Planned City: Chandigarh*. Bombay: Orient Longmans, 1968.

EVANS, HAZEL, ED. *New Towns: The British Experience*. London: C. Knight, for the Town and Country Planning Association, 1972.

EVENSON, NORMA. *Chandigarh*. Berkeley: Univ. of California Press, 1966.

FISHMAN, ROBERT. *Urban Utopias in the Twentieth Century*. New York: Basic Books, 1977.

FOX, RICHARD G., ED. *Urban India: Society, Space and Image*. Durham: Duke Univ. Press, 1970.

FRY, EDWIN MAXWELL. *Fine Buildings*, London: Faber & Faber, 1944.

———. *Art in a Machine Age: A Critique of Contemporary Life Through the Medium of Architecture*. London: Methuen, 1969.

———. *Autobiographical Sketches*. London: Elek, 1975.

———. "The Bauhaus spirit." *Royal Institute of British Architects Journal (RIBA)*, 3rd ser., vol. 46, June 26, 1939, pp. 835–36.

———. "Architecture and Its Problems." *Architectural Association, Journal*, vol. 60, Apr., 1945, pp. 141–46.

———. "The Future of Architecture." *Architects' Year Book*, vol. 1, 1945, pp. 7–10.

———. "Colonial Planning and Housing." *Architectural Association, Journal*, vol. 62, Nov., 1946, pp. 53–60.

———. " . . . A Letter about Architecture." *British Thought* (New York), 1947, pp. 38–46.

———. "The Architect and His Time." *Architects' Year Book*, vol. 3, 1949, pp. 9–12.

———. "Town Planning in West Africa." *South African Architectural Record*, vol. 34, Sept., 1949, pp. 196–98.

———. "Chandigarh: Birth of a Capital." *Sunday Statesman*, New Delhi, May 6, 1951.
———. "Chandigarh: A New Town for India." *Town and Country Planning*, vol. 21, May 1953, pp. 217–21.
———. "African Experiment." *Journal of the Indian Institute of Architects*, vol. 19, no. 3, July-Sept. 1953, pp. 11–12.
———. "Houses at Chandigarh, India." *Architects' Journal*, vol. 119, Feb. 4, 1954, pp. 159–68.
———. "The Interpretation of Environment." *Arts and Architecture*, vol. 71, Apr. 1954, p. 21.
———. "Chandigarh: The Capital of East Punjab." *RIBA*, 3rd ser., vol. 62, no. 3, Jan. 1955, pp. 87–97.
———. "Chandigarh: The Capital of the Punjab." *Builder*, vol. 188, Jan. 7, 1955, pp. 7–9.
———. "Chandigarh—New Capital City." *Architectural Record*, vol. 117, June 1955, pp. 139–48.
———. "A Discursive Commentary." *Architects' Year Book*, vol. 6, London, 1955, pp. 7–10.
———. "A College in the Tropics: Ibadan" (English translation). *Zodiac*, no. 2, 1958, pp. 127–36.
———. "Architects to the Rescue!" *RIBA*, 3rd ser., vol. 66, no. 8, June 1959, pp. 285–87.
———. "Chandigarh: the Punjab Scene." *Architects' Year Book*, vol. 11, 1965, pp. 266–68.
———. "Le Corbusier—His Impact on Four Generations." *RIBA*, vol. 72, Oct. 1965, pp. 497–500.
———. "The Legacy of Bauhaus: Language of 'Extraordinary Dialogue' with Industry." *Building*, vol. 215, no. 44, Nov. 1, 1968, pp. 85–86.
FRY, EDWIN MAXWELL, AND JANE DREW. *Tropical Architecture in the Dry and Humid Zones*. 2nd ed. Melbourne, Fla.: R. E. Krieger Pub. Co., 1982. First ed. pub. London: B. T. Batsford, 1964.
———. "Chandigarh and Planning Development in India." *Asian Review*, vol. 51, Apr. 1955, pp. 110–23.
FRY, EDWIN MAXWELL, WITH ARTHUR KORN. "The M.A.R.S. Plan for London." *Perspecta*, vol. 13/14, 1971, pp. 163–73.
GAGNON, GILES. "Chandigarh." *Royal Architectural Institute of Canada Journal*, vol. 34, June 1957, pp. 193–200.
GALANTAY, ERVIN Y. *New Towns: Antiquity to the Present*. New York: George Braziller, 1975.
GILLIE, F. B. *An Approach to Town Planning*. The Hague/Paris: Mouton, 1971.
GLASS, R. *Social Background of a Plan or Study of Middlesborough*. London, 1948.
GOKHALE, BALKRISHNA GOVIND. *Surat in the Seventeenth Century: A Study in Urban History of Pre-Modern India*. Scandinavian Institute of Asian Studies No. 28. London: Curzon Press, 1978.

GOLANY, GIDEON, ED. *International Urban Growth Policies*. New-Town Contributions. New York: John Wiley & Sons, 1976.
GOVERNMENT OF INDIA. *Report of the State Reorganization Commission*. New Delhi, 1955.
———. *The Shah Commission Report*. New Delhi, 1966.
GOVERNMENT OF INDIA; MINISTRY OF HEALTH. *Report of the Committee on Urban Land Policy*. N.p.: N.p., n.d.
GOVERNMENT OF INDIA, MINISTRY OF INFORMATION & BROADCASTING. *Jawaharlal Nehru's Speeches: September 1946–May 1949*. Vol. 1. 2nd ed. New Delhi, 1958.
———. *Jawaharlal Nehru's Speeches: 1949–53*. 2nd ed. New Delhi, 1957.
———. *Jawaharlal Nehru's Speeches: September 1957–April 1963*. Vol. 4. New Delhi, Aug. 1964.
———. *Jawaharlal Nehru's Speeches: 1963–64*. Vol. 5. New Delhi, Nov. 1968.
GOVERNMENT OF INDIA, MINISTRY OF LAW. *The Punjab Reorganization Act, 1966*. New Delhi, 1967.
GOVERNMENT OF INDIA, PLANNING COMMISSION. *First Five Year Plan: A Summary*. New Delhi, Dec. 12, 1952.
———. *Economic Survey: 1981–82*. New Delhi, 1982.
GOVERNMENT OF PUNJAB. *Demands for Grants of the Punjab Government: 1982–83*. Chandigarh, 1982.
GOVERNMENT OF PUNJAB, DIRECTOR OF PUBLIC RELATIONS. *Punjab: The Possible Dream*. Chandigarh, 1975.
GOVERNMENT OF PUNJAB, ECONOMIC AND STATISTICAL ORGANIZATION. *Chandigarh: Socio-Economic Survey in May, 1957*. Publication no. 13. Simla: The Civil & Military Press, 1958.
GOVERNMENT OF PUNJAB, LEGISLATIVE DEPARTMENT. *The Punjab Urban Estates (Development and Regulation) Act, 1964*. Punjab Act. no. 22 of 1964. Chandigarh, 1964.
———. *The Punjab Urban Estates (Development and Regulation) Rules, 1974*. Chandigarh, 1974.
GUPTA, NARAYANI, *Delhi Between Two Empires 1803–1931: Society, Government and Urban Growth*. Delhi: Oxford Univ. Press, 1981.
HAJRA, S. *Bihar and Punjab: A Study in Regional Economic Disparity*. New Delhi: Economic and Scientific Research Foundation, 1973.
HAMBLY, GAVIN. *Cities of Mughal India*. London: Elek, 1968.
HAVELL, E. B. *Indian Architecture*. London: J. Murray, 1918.
HELLMAN, HAL. *The City in the World of the Future*. New York: M. Evans and Co., 1970.
HERBERT, JOHN D. *Urban Development in the Third World: Policy Guidelines*. New York: Praeger Publishers, 1979.
HERSHMAN, PAUL. *Punjabi Kinship and Marriage*. Ed. Hilary Standing. New Delhi: Hindustan Pub. Corp. 1981.
HINES, THOMAS S. *Richard Neutra and the Search for Modern Architecture*. New York: Oxford Univ. Press, 1982.

HITCHCOCK, HENRY RUSSELL. "The Evolution of Wright, Mies, and Le Corbusier." *Perspecta*, no. 1, Summer 1952, pp. 8–15.

HOWARD, EBENEZER, *To-morrow: A Peaceful Path to Real Reform* (1898). Revised and reissued in 1902 as *Garden Cities of To-morrow*. Edited, with a preface by F. J. Osborn, and an introductory essay by Lewis Mumford. London: Faber & Faber, 1946.

HOWARD, SEYMOUR. "Living with Corbu." *Progressive Architecture*, vol. 51, Nov. 1970, pp. 90–97.

IBBETSON, DENZIL. *Punjab Castes: Races, Castes and Tribes of the People of Punjab*. New Delhi: Cosmo Pub., 1981.

IMRIE, MARY. "Hong Kong to Chandigarh." *Royal Architectural Institute of Canada Journal*, vol. 35, May 1958, pp. 160–63.

"Industry Builds Kitimat—The First Complete New Town in America." *Architectural Forum*, vol. 101, July 1954, pp. 128–47; Aug. 1954, pp. 120–27; Oct. 1954, pp. 158–61.

JACKOBSON, LEO, AND VED PRAKASH, EDS. *Urbanization and National Development*. Beverly Hills, Calif.: Sage Publications, 1971.

JEANNERET, PIERRE. "Houses at Chandigarh, India." *Architects' Journal*, vol. 119, Feb. 4, 1954, pp. 159–68.

———. "The Changing Face of Chandigarh." *Design Annual*, vol. 7, July 1963, pp. 81–100.

———. "Four Recent Projects from Chandigarh." *Design* (Bombay), vol. 3, Mar. 1967, pp. 11–20.

JEANNERET, PIERRE, WITH B. P. MATHUR. "University Library Building." *Indian Architect*, vol. 5, Mar. 1963, pp. 15–18.

JENCKS, CHARLES. *Le Corbusier and the Tragic View of Architecture*. London: Allen Lane, a division of Penguin Books, 1973.

———. *Modern Movements in Architecture*. Garden City, N.Y.: Doubleday/Anchor, 1973.

JONES, KENNETH W. "Communalism in the Punjab: The Arya Samaj Contribution." *Journal of Asian Studies*, vol. 27, no. 1, Nov. 1968, pp. 39–54.

JUPPENLATZ, MORRIS. *Cities in Transformation: The Urban Squatter Problem of the Developing World*. St. Lucia, Queensland, Australia: Univ. of Queensland Press, 1970.

KING, ANTHONY. *Colonial Urban Development*. London and Boston: Routledge & Kegan Paul, 1976.

KOENIGBERGER, OTTO H. "Housing and Town Planning Problems of Burma." *Journal of the American Institute of Planners*, vol. 18, no. 1, Winter 1952, pp. 14–20.

———. "New Towns in India." *Town Planning Review*, vol. 23, no. 2, July 1952, pp. 92–132.

KUMAR, SANTOSH, ED. *Le Corbusier: 80th Birthday Anniversary Issue*. Bombay: International Cultural Organization, 1967.

LAMBA, N. S. "Emerging Capitals and New Towns." *Journal of the Institute of Town Planners*, no. 63, June 1971.

LEBOWITZ, MILTON. "The Process of Planned Community Change: A Comparative Analysis of Five Community Welfare Council Change Projects." Ph.D. diss., Columbia Univ. 1961. Ann Arbor, Mich.: Xerox University Microfilms 1975.

"Le Corbusier in the U.S.A." *Progressive Architecture*, vol. 42, June 1961, p. 71.

MALHOTRA, S. L. *Gandhi and the Punjab.* Ed. I. D. Sharma. Chandigarh: Punjab Univ. Publication Bureau, 1970.

MALHOTRA, V. P. "A Note on Chandigarh Capital Giving Its History and Administrative Set Up." Chandigarh, n.d.

MALIK, YOGENDRA, "Conflict over Chandigarh: A Case Study of an Interstate Dispute in India." *Contributions to Asian Studies*, vol. 3, 1973, pp. 51–63.

Marg (Bombay), vol. 14, no. 1, Dec. 1961. Devoted to Chandigarh, the issue contains articles by Le Corbusier, Maxwell Fry, Jane Drew, Pierre Jeanneret, M. S. Randhawa, U. E. Chowdhury, and others.

MAYER, ALBERT. *The Urgent Future.* New York: McGraw-Hill Book Co., 1967.

MAYER, ALBERT, ET AL. *Pilot Project, India: The story of Rural Development at Etawah, Uttar Pradesh.* Berkeley: Univ. of California Press, 1958.

MAYER, ALBERT. "The Architect and the World." *Royal Architectural Institute of Canada Journal*, vol. 13, June 1936, pp. 117–19.

———. "A Technique for Planning Complete Communities." *Architectural Forum*, vol. 66, nos. 1 and 2, Jan. and Feb. 1937, pp. 19–36, and pp. 126–46.

———. "What's the Matter with Our Site Plans?" *Pencil Points (Progressive Architecture)*, vol. 23, no. 5, May 1942.

———. "Horse Sense Planning." *Architectural Forum*, vol. 79, Nov. 1943, pp. 59–63.

———. "A Note on Post-War Planning in India." *Calcutta Review*, Aug. 1944, pp. 111–18.

———. "Americans in India." *Survey Graphic*, Mar. 1947.

———. "The Greater Bombay Master Plan." *Eastern Rotary Wheel*, Sept. 1948, pp. 12, 13, 21.

———. "Nehru, the Man—and India's Travail." *Survey*, Dec. 1949, pp. 658–61.

———. "Planning a New Capital." *National Herald* (Lucknow), June 15, 1950.

———. "The New Capital of the Punjab." *Journal of the American Institute of Architects*, vol. 14, Oct. 1950, pp. 166–75.

———. "A New-Town Program." *Journal of the American Institute of Architects*, vol. 15, Jan. 1951, pp. 5–10.

———. "Planning in India: Steps in Village Development." *Manchester Guardian*, Nov. 10, 1951.

———. "Creating a Community." *Journal of the American Institute of Architects*, vol. 24, Aug. 1955, pp. 62–69; Sept. 1955, pp. 103–10.

———. "New Way of Life in Britain's New Towns." *Town and Country Planning*, vol. 24, May 1956, pp. 238–42.
———. "Architecture and Life." *Shelter*, vol. 5, Oct. 1958, pp. 4–5.
———. "Social Analysis and National Economic Development in India." *Pacific Affairs*, vol. 35, no. 2, Summer 1962, pp. 128–40.
———. "Architecture as Total Community: The Challenge Ahead." *Architectural Record*, vol. 135, Mar. 1964, pp. 137–44.
———. "Architecture as Total Community: The Challenge Ahead." *Architectural Record*, Apr. 1964, pp. 169–78.
———. "Architecture as Total Community: The Challenge Ahead." *Architectural Record*, May 1964, pp. 145–52.
———. "Architecture as Total Community: The Challenge Ahead." *Architectural Record*, vol. 136, July 1964, pp. 157–62.
———. "Architecture as Total Community: The Challenge Ahead." *Architectural Record*, Aug. 1964, pp. 129–38.
———. "Architecture as Total Community: The Challenge Ahead." *Architectural Record*, Sept. 1964, pp. 197–206.
———. "Architecture as Total Community: The Challenge Ahead." *Architectural Record*, Oct. 1964, pp. 139–48.
———. "Greenbelt Towns Revisited: In Search of New Directions for New Towns for America." *Journal of Housing*, vol. 24, no. 1, Jan. 1967, pp. 12–26.
———. "Greenbelt Towns Revisited: In Search of New Directions for New Towns for America." *Journal of Housing*, vol. 24, no. 2, Feb./Mar. 1967, pp. 80–85.
———. "Greenbelt Towns Revisited: In Search of New Directions for New Towns for America." *Journal of Housing*, vol. 24, no. 3, Apr. 1967, pp. 151–60.
———. "Architecture with Inner Meaning: Notes Toward a Definition of Urban Design." *Architectural Forum*, vol. 135, no. 4, Nov. 1971, pp. 60–63.
McGree, T. G. *The Urbanization Process in the Third World*. London: G. Bell & Sons, 1971.
Merlin, Pierre. *New Towns Regional Planning and Development*. Trans. Margaret Sparks. London: Methuen & Co., 1971.
Misra, R. P., ed. *Million Cities of India*. New Delhi: Vikas Publishing House, 1978.
Mitra, Asok, and Ram Prakash Sachdev. *Population and Area of Cities, Towns, and Urban Agglomeration: 1872–1971*. An ICSSR/JNU Study, 1980. New Delhi: Allied Publications, 1980.
Mohan, Rakesh. *Urban Economic and Planning Models*. World Bank Staff Occasional Papers, no. 25. Baltimore: Johns Hopkins Univ. Press, 1979.
Mumford, Lewis. *The City in History*. London and New York: Penguin Books, 1966.
———. "Matthew Nowicki." *Architectural Record*, vol. 115, June 1954, pp. 139–49.

———. "Matthew Nowicki as an Educator." *Architectural Record*, vol. 116, July 1954, pp. 128–35.
———. "Nowicki: His Architectural Achievement." *Architectural Record*, vol. 116, Aug. 1954, pp. 169–75.
———. "Nowicki's Work in India." *Architectural Record*, vol. 116, Sept. 1954, pp. 153–59.
———. "Opinions on the New Towns." *Town and Country Planning*, Mar. 1956, pp. 161–64.
———. "Trend is not Destiny." *Architectural Record*, vol. 142, no. 6, Dec. 1967, pp. 131–34.
NAIR, L. R., ED. *Why Chandigarh?* Simla: Publicity Department, Punjab Government, 1950.
NAIR, L. R. "Chandigarh: India's City of Tomorrow." *New Commonwealth*, vol. 24, Oct. 13, 1952, pp. 366–69.
NAYAR, BALDEV RAJ. *Minority Politics in the Punjab*. Princeton, N.J.: Princeton Univ. Press, 1966.
New Concepts and Technologies in Third World Urbanization. Proceedings of the Second Annual Spring Colloquium sponsored by the Subcommittee on Comparative Urbanization of the Committee on International and Comparative Studies, May 17–18, 1974, Univ. of California, Los Angeles.
NILSSON, STEN A. *European Architecture in India, 1750–1850*. Trans. Agnes George and Eleonore Zettersten, London: Faber & Faber, 1968.
———. *The New Capitals of India, Pakistan and Bangladesh*. Trans. Elisabeth Andreasson. Lund, Sweden: Studentlitteratur, 1973.
NOWICKI, MATTHEW. "Origins and Trends in Modern Architecture." *Magazine of Art*, vol. 44, Nov. 1951, pp. 273–79.
———. "A Letter to Albert Mayer." *Perspecta*, vol. 5, 1959, pp. 23–25.
OSBORN, FREDERIC J. *Green Belt Cities*. London: Evelyn, Adams & Mackay, 1969.
OSBORN, FREDERIC J., AND ARNOLD WHITTICK. *The New Towns: The Answer to Megalopolis*. London: Leonard Hill, 1969.
PAPADAKI, STAMO, ED. *Le Corbusier: Architect, Painter, Writer*. New York: Macmillan Co., 1948.
PAPOLA, T. S. *Urban Informal Sector in a Developing Economy*. New Delhi: Vikas Publishing House, 1981.
PARKER, R. S., AND P. N. TROY, EDS. *The Politics of Urban Growth*. Canberra: Australian National Univ. Press, 1972.
PARKS, JOHN A. "Review of Town Planning in Britain and How India Can Benefit from It." *Journal of the Indian Institute of Architects*, vol. 18, no. 3, July–Sept. 1952, pp. 11–18.
PERRY, CLARENCE. "The Neighborhood Unit." *Neighborhood and Community Planning*, vol. 7, 1929.
Post-War Development Plan Punjab. N.p.: N.p., n.d.
PRAKASH, VED. *New Towns in India*. Monograph and Occasional Paper Series, Monograph no. 8. Durham, N.C.: Duke Univ., 1969.

QUADEER, M. A. "Do Cities 'Modernize' the Developing Countries? An Examination of the South Asian Experience." *Comparative Studies,* vol. 16, June 1974, pp. 266–83.
RAI, MANGAT E. N. *Civil Administration of the State Government in India.* Cambridge: Harvard Univ. Press, Center for International Affairs, Oct. 1983.
RAND, CHRISTOPHER. "City on a Tilting Plain." *New Yorker,* vol. 31, Apr. 30, 1955.
RANDHAWA, M. S. *Chandigarh.* Chandigarh: N.p., n.d.
RAO, P. RAM MOHAN. *Growth of Cities: A Case Study of Warangal.* Delhi: Inter-India Publications, 1981.
RATCLIFF, JOHN. "Impressions of l'Unité D'Habitation." *Journal of the American Institute of Architects,* vol. 24, no. 5, Nov. 1955, pp. 205–7.
RENAUD, BERTRAND. *National Urbanization Policy in Developing Countries.* New York and London: Oxford Univ. Press, 1981.
ROBERTS, BRYAN. *Cities of Peasants: The Political Economy of Urbanization in the Third World.* London: Arnold-Heinemann, 1978.
ROSENTHAL, DONALD B., ED. *The City in Indian Politics.* Faridabad: Thomson Press (India), 1976.
SABERWAL, SATISH. *Mobile Men: Limits to Social Change in Urban Punjab.* New Delhi: Vikas Publishing House, 1976.
SAINI, B. S. *The Social and Economic History of the Punjab, 1901–1939 (Including Haryana and Himachal Pradesh).* Delhi: ESS Publications, 1975.
SANDERSON, GORDON. *Types of Modern Indian Buildings.* Allahabad: Government Press, 1913.
SANTHANAM, S. *Union-State Relations in India.* New Delhi: Indian Institute of Public Administration, 1960.
SARHADI, AJIT SINGH. *Punjabi Suba: The Story of the Struggle.* Delhi: Gurdaskapur Pub. 1970.
SARIN, MADHU. *Planning and the Urban Poor: The Chandigarh Experience, 1951–75.* 2 vols. A Research Report Sponsored by the Ministry of Overseas Development, London, at the School of Environmental Studies, University College, London, Dec. 1975.
SENIOR, DEREK, ED. *The Regional City: An Anglo-American Discussion of Metropolitan Planning.* London: Longmans, Green and Co., 1966.
SERENYI, PETER, ED. *Le Corbusier in Perspective.* Englewood Cliffs, N.J.: Prentice-Hall, 1975.
SHARMA, SRI RAM. *Administrative Set-up at Chandigarh.* Institute of Public Administration, Punjab, undated.
SHARP, THOMAS. *Town Planning.* London, 1945.
SINGH, ANDREA MENEFEE, AND ALFRED DE SOUZA, *The Urban Poor: Slum and Pavement Dwellers in the Major Cities of India.* New Delhi: Manohar Pub., 1980.
SINGH, GANDA. "The Origins of the Hindu-Sikh Tension in the Punjab." *Journal of Indian History,* vol. 39, Apr. 1961, pp. 120–23.

SINGH, HARBANS, AND N. GERALD BARRIER, EDS. *Punjab Past and Present: Essays in Honour of Dr. Ganda Singh.* Patiala: Punjabi University, 1976.
SINGH, KHUSHWANT. *The Fall of the Kingdom of the Punjab.* Bombay: Orient Longmans, 1962.
———. *A History of the Sikhs.* 2 vols. Princeton, N.J.: Princeton Univ. Press, 1963–66.
SINGH, MOHINDER. *The Akali Movement.* Delhi: Macmillan Company of India, 1978.
SINGH, PRITAM. *Emerging Pattern of Economic Life in Punjab.* Bombay: Thacker & Co., 1975.
SINGH, SATINDER. *Khalistan: An Academic Analysis.* New Delhi: Amar Prakasham, 1982.
SINGH, SUNDRA RANI. *Urban Planning in India: A Case Study of Urban Improvement Trusts.* New Delhi: Ashish Publishing House, 1979.
SINHA, M. M. P. *The Impact of Urbanization on Land Use in the Rural-Urban Fringe.* New Delhi: Concept Pub., 1980.
SIVARAMAKRISHNAN, K. C. *Indian Urban Scene.* Simla: Indian Institute of Advanced Study, 1978.
SMITH, W. M., ED. *Behavior, Design, and Policy Aspects of Human Habitats.* Green Bay: Univ. of Wisconsin, 1972.
SOVANI, N. Y. *Urbanization and Urban India.* New York: Asia Publishing House, 1966.
SRINIVAS, M. N. *Social Change in Modern India.* Berkeley: Univ. of California Press, 1969.
STALLEY, MARSHALL, ED. *Patrick Geddes: Spokesman for Man and the Environment.* New Brunswick, N.J.: Rutgers Univ. Press, 1972.
STEIN, CLARENCE. "Towards New Towns for America." *Town Planning Review*, Liverpool, Jan. 1950.
STEINBACH, HENRY. *The Punjab: Being a Brief Account of the Country of the Sikhs.* Reprint. Karachi: Oxford Univ. Press, 1976.
STRETTON, HUGH. "Urban Planning in Rich and Poor Countries." *Journal of Developing Areas,* vol. 16, no. 1, Oct. 1981.
SUNDARAM, K. V. *Urban and Regional Planning in India.* New Delhi: Vikas Publishing House, 1977.
TANDON, PRAKASH. *Punjabi Century 1857–1947.* Berkeley: Univ. of California Press, 1968.
TEWARI, V. N. *The Language of Chandigarh.* Chandigarh: Sahitya Sangam, 1967.
THACKER, M. S. *India's Urban Problem.* Mysore: Univ. of Mysore, 1965.
TINKER, HUGH. *Race and the Third World City.* An International Urbanization Survey Report to the Ford Foundation, Apr. 26, 1971.
"Tropical Architecture." *Journal of the Indian Institute of Architects,* vol. 19, no. 3, July–Sept. 1953, pp. 6–8.
TUNNARD, CHRISTOPHER. "Cities by Design." *Journal of the American Institute of Planners,* vol. 17, Summer 1951, pp. 142–50.

TURNER, ROY, ED. *India's Urban Future.* Berkeley: Univ. of California Press, 1962.
TYRWHITT, JAQUELINE. "Chandigarh." *Royal Architectural Institute of Canada Journal,* vol. 32, Jan. 1955, pp. 11–20.
VAGALE, L. R. *A Case Study of Chandigarh and Environs in the Regional Setting.* United Nations Economic Commission for Asia and the Far East, sponsored by the United Nations and the Government of Japan, at Nagoya, Japan, Oct. 10–20, 1966.
———. "Population Trends in India and Their Implications in Town Planning, Housing and Urban Development." New Delhi: School of Planning and Architecture, 1967.
VARMA, P. L. "Chandigarh—The City of Tomorrow." *Nirman,* Apr.–June 1954, pp. 10–11.
VAZ, J. L. "Architecture of Bhubaneshwar: New Capital, Orissa." *Journal of the Indian Institute of Architects,* vol. 20, no. 2, Apr.–June 1954, pp. 3–4.
VON LAUE, THEODORE H. *The Global City.* Philadelphia: Lippincott, 1969.
VON MOOS, STANISLAUS. *Le Corbusier: Elements of a Synthesis.* Cambridge, Mass.: The MIT Press, 1979.
WALDEN, RUSSELL, ED. *The Open Hand: Essays on Le Corbusier.* Cambridge: Mass.: The MIT Press, 1977.
WALTON, JOHN, AND LOUIS MASOTTI, EDS. *The City in Comparative Perspective: Cross-National Research and New Directions in Theory.* Beverly Hills, Calif.: Sage Publications. Distributed by Halsted Press, New York, 1976.
WEITZ, RAANAN, ED. "Rehovot Conference on Urbanization and Development in Developing Countries." Jerusalem and Rehovot, Israel, 1971. *Urbanization and the Developing Countries: Report on the Sixth Rehovot Conference.* New York: Praeger Publishers, 1973.
"What Corbu Has Been Up To?" *Architectural Forum,* vol. 99, Sept. 1953, pp. 142–49.
YATES, PETER. "Le Corbusier: A Personal Appreciation." *Builder,* vol. 209, Oct. 22, 1965, p. 65.
ZINKIN, TAYA. "India's Most Modern City: Chandigarh." *Journal of the American Institute of Architects,* vol. 62, Nov. 1954, pp. 87–94.
———. "No Compromise with Corbusier." *Guardian,* Sept. 11, 1965.

INDEX

Abercrombie, Sir Patrick, 34
Abohar, 137
Ackerman, Frederick, 31
Adams, Frederick, 25
Adams, John Quincy, 46
Agricultural city, 119
Akali Dal party, 15–16, 20, 127, 133, 134, 136, 138, 146, 161n.54
Allahabad Municipality, 24
Ambala
—city, 3, 4, 6, 7, 10–11, 14, 138, 145
—district, 12, 135
Ambala District Congress Committee, 15
Ambegaokar, K. G., 39
American City, 50
Amritsar, 6, 7, 16, 135, 145
Anand Bhavan (Allahabad), 46, 47
Anandpur Sahib Resolution, 138
Anti-Capital Committee. *See* Anti-Rajdhani Committee
Anti-Rajdhani Committee, 15, 19–20
Antwerp, 87
Architects
—foreign: on Chandigarh project, 25, 26, 31–36, 37–39, 42–44. *See also names of individual architects*
—Indian: on Chandigarh project, 106, 127; inadequacy of, 23, 24, 25, 26, 31, 36, 37, 48, 146
Architectural Forum, 50
Architecture
—"Anglo-Indian," 24
—Indian: blended with modern architecture, 68, 88; lapsed tradition for, 24, 28–29; Nehru's views on, 28–29
Arcosanti (Arizona), 43–44
Aristotle, 21, 63
Art Nouveau, 81, 82, 83
Arts and Crafts Movement, 76, 80
Arunachal state, 1
ASCORAL (Assemblée de Constructeurs pour une Révolution Architecturale), 119
Assam state, 1, 19
Assemblée de Constructeurs pour une Révolution Architecturale. *See* ASCORAL
Assembly building, Chandigarh. *See* Capitol Complex (Chandigarh)
Autobiographical Sketches (Fry), 74

Bachiocci, Mario, 26
Bahawalpur, refugees from, 3

Baker, Herbert, 25
Bakunin, Mikhail, 74
Baldwin Hills (Los Angeles), 57
Banaur, 123, 139, 142
Bangladesh, 1
Banneker, Benjamin, 88
Barcelona, 87
Bauer, Catherine, 31
Bauhaus School, 77, 78, 82
Behrens, Peter, 82–83
Bellmawr Housing for Mutual Defense Homes Division, 50
Betjeman, John, 76
Bhaisa Tibbi, 124
Bhakra-Nangal, 137
Bhakra-Nangal project, 22
Bhandari, P. L., 40
Bhargava, Gopichand, 15, 21, 35
Bhatinda, 135
Bhubaneshwar (Orissa), 1, 25, 31
Bilaspur, 124
Bogotá (Colombia), 86, 107, 113
Bombay, 1, 32, 53, 137
Bose, Ashish, 160n.31
Brasília (Brazil), 124, 129
Brise-soleils, 114, 115
British Housing and Town Planning Act (1909), 24
Brown, Percy, 24
Brutalism, 85
Buenos Aires, 87, 107
Buckley, James, 33, 55, 59, 61
Building Rules and Chandigarh (Sale and Site) Rules (1952), 13, 127

Cabinet Sub-Committee (New Capital), 17
Calcutta, 3
Canberra (Australia), 45
Capital Administration Punjab Municipal Act (Number 27, 1952), 123–24
Capital of Punjab (Development and Regulation) Act (1952), 13, 111, 122, 127, 145

Capital Project of East Punjab: administration of, 131; central government's role in, 10, 13, 122, 135, 145; financial constraints on, 9; infrastructure considerations for, 7; land allocation by, 16–17, 19; land requisitioned by, 15, 17, 145; opposition to site selected for, 14–17, 19, 21; security considerations for, 6–7; site selection by, 3–4, 6–13, 17, 19, 20
Capitol Complex (Chandigarh): Assembly at, 115–16, 126; changes needed in plan for, 126; Le Corbusier plan for, 90, 105, 109, 110, 111, 112–18, 152; governor's residence at, 116, 126; High Court in, 114, 126; Martyr's Memorial in, 118; Mayer plan for, 43, 59–60; Monument of the Open Hand at, 116, 117–18; Museum of Knowledge at, 116–17; Nowicki plan for, 65, 66–67, 69; problems in construction of, 126; Secretariat at, 114–15, 126
Carpenter Center, Harvard (Le Corbusier), 85
Carr-Saunders, Sir Alexander, 42
Carrère and Hastings (architects), 75
Census
—1941, 19
—1949 (of displaced persons), 19
—1971, 139, 140
—1981, 140
Chandi (goddess of Power), 13
Chandigarh: airport, 125; architects for, 25, 26, 31–36, 37–39, 42–44, 105–6; business/industrial district in, 56, 61, 67, 90, 109, 110, 111, 118, 119, 125, 142–43; chowk in, 111–12; City Center for, 109, 110, 111–12; climate of, 13, 55, 57; Le Corbusier plan for, xi, 23, 29, 40–41, 42, 44, 64, 70, 72–74, 87, 88–120, 121, 124–25, 147;

cultural center in, 118; greenbelts in, 61, 63–64, 109, 119–20, 123; landscaping of, 119–20; leisure valley in, 109, 118; maintenance of plan for, 122–25, 149; Mayer plan for, xi, 17–18, 19, 20, 21, 23, 26, 29, 31, 33–35, 36, 37, 50, 53–65, 72, 89–104, 110; Mayer visit to, 33; military cantonment in, 125; Nehru's influence on, 25–31, 35, 87–88, 104–5, 121, 145; Nowicki plan for, 64–69; openness in plan for, 55; opposition to, 14–17, 19, 144; population of, 153; problems in development of, 125–36, 141–42, 147, 154–55; purpose of development in, xi, xii, 1, 2–3, 43, 52; railway service to, 18, 61, 90, 110, 127; regional impact of, 140, 141–43; sale of land in, 19, 129; selected as site of new East Punjab capital, 10–13, 17, 19, 20, 145; shortcomings of, 152–55; traffic in, 58, 103, 106, 108–9; topography of, 13, 56; as union territory, 137–38, 139–40; unplanned growth in, 125–26, 130, 139, 140, 141, 151, 153–54; water supply for, 18–19, 142. *See also* Capitol Complex (Chandigarh); Punjab University
Chandigarh (Sale and Site) Rules (1952), 13, 127
Chandigarh (Tree Preservation) Order (1952), 13
Chandi Mandir, 124
Chandimandir Cantonment, 139, 142
Chapel of Notre Dame, Ronchamp, Haute-Saône (Le Corbusier, 1950–55), 74, 85
Chapman, Ralph, 49
Charter of Athens (1933), 41, 111
Chen Yi, 27
Chesneaux, Jean, 160n.31

Chicago Civic Center, 54
Chitale, Mr., 34
Chowdhury, J. K., 106, 118
Chowdhury, U. E., 106, 125, 141
Churchill, Henry, 50
Churchill, Winston, 27
CIAM (Congrès Internationaux d'Architecture Moderne), 41, 72, 76, 111. *See also* MARS
CIAM Town-Planning Grid, 104–5
Circut House, Chandigarh (Jeanneret), 116
Citrohan House (Le Corbusier, 1922), 83
City Beautiful concept, 54
Climate, as consideration in architecture, 13, 55, 57, 78, 111
Coates, Wells, 76
Coffey, Clara, 33, 55
Colonialism: architecture of, 23–24; effect on Indian government, 10, 23, 132; slow recovery from, 36–37
Committee on Post-War Housing (American), 50
Communists, 146
Concorde, Place de la (Paris), 54
Congrès Internationaux d'Architecture Moderne. *See* CIAM
Congress party, 16, 32, 134, 138
Connell, Amyas, 76
Le Corbusier (Charles-Edouard Jeanneret): as architect of Chandigarh, xi, 23, 29, 40–41, 42, 44, 64, 70, 72–74, 87, 88–120, 121, 124–25, 147; background of, 73, 74, 79–87; Capitol Complex plan by, 90, 105, 112–18, 152; City Center plan by, 109, 110, 111–12; death of, 151; Fry's opinion of, 73–74; ideals of, xi, 41, 73, 81–82, 152; Nowicki's apprenticeship with, 65; as "Spiritual Director" of Chandigarh project, 106; visits to Chandigarh by, 71
Costa, Lucio, 124

Cox, W. J., 53
Cubism, 83

Dacca (Bangladesh), 3
Dadu Majra, 130
Dagshai, 3
Dar Commission, 132
Denby, Elizabeth, 76
Dera Basi, 139, 142, 143
Dermée, Paul, 84
Design and Industries Association, 76
Dethe, J. S., 106
Devagiri, 7
Devonshire House (Piccadilly, London), 75
Dhara Karori, 124
Dietrick, William H., 64
District, of superblocks, 52–53
Doaba, 4
Dogra, R. N., 6
Domino Houses (Le Corbusier, 1914), 83
Drake, Lindsay, 42
Drew, Jane Beverly: as architect of Chandigarh, xi, 23, 41–43, 71, 87, 105, 107, 129; background of, 41–42, 71, 76, 78; description of Le Corbusier's plan for Chandigarh, 109; influence on Le Corbusier, 85; opinion of Monument of the Open Hand, 117–18
Duni Chand, Lala, 15, 16

East Bengal, 1
East Pakistan, 1, 3
East Punjab state: displaced persons in, 19; economic development of, 4–5, 9–10; new capital selected for, 2–13; partition of (1966), 2, 121, 132–33, 141, 145, 151; population of, 4, 5. *See also* Capital Project of East Punjab
Eberlin, Ralph, 33, 55
L'Enfant, Pierre Charles, 55, 88
England, new towns movement in, 21–22

Entwistle, Clive, 43
L'Eplattenier, Charles, 79–81
L'*Esprit nouveau*, 84
Etawah district, rural development program in, 25, 32
Etchells, Fredrick, 78

Fallet villa (Le Corbusier, 1906), 80, 83
Faridabad, 25, 31, 32
Fatehgarh, 50
Fazilka tehsil, 136–37
Federal Works Agency (FWA), 50
Ferozpur, 135
Festival of Britain program, 41, 42
Fletcher, A. L., 5, 26, 61, 144
Foley Square (New York), 54
Fort Greene Houses, 50
Forty-Second Street Library (New York), 75
Fry, Edwin Maxwell: as architect of Chandigarh, xi, 23, 41–44, 70, 71, 87, 105, 110, 130; autobiography of, 74; background of, 41, 72, 73, 74–79; on climate of Chandigarh, 13, 57, 75, 111; correspondence with Mayer, 90; ideals of, 73–74; influence on Le Corbusier, 85; on lack of administrative control for Chandigarh project, 122; opinion of Le Corbusier, 73–74; relationship to Thapar and Varma, 72–73
FWA. *See* Federal Works Agency

Gadgil, N. V., 33–34
Gandhi, Indira, 46, 136, 138
Gandhi, Mahatma: ideals of, 22–23, 27, 49; Mayer meeting with, 49
Gandhi, Rajiv, 138
Gandhi-Longowal accord, 138
Gandhidham, 25
Gandhinagar, as new capital, 1
Gandhipura, proposed, 6
Garden City Movement (English), 57, 85, 88
Geddes, Patrick, 24, 51, 105
Geneva (Switzerland), 87

Germany, 76–77
Ghaggar River, 18, 142
Glass, Milton, 31, 33, 55
Golden Temple, army attack on, 138
Governor's House, Chandigarh. *See* Capitol Complex (Chandigarh)
Les Grands Initiés (Schure), 81
Greeley, Roland, 25
Greenbelt communities, 50, 57
Greenbelts, use of, 51, 61, 63–64, 109, 119–20, 123
Greenbrook, 50, 53, 58
Green party, 117
Greenways, for vehicular traffic, 53
Griffin, Walter Burley, 45
Gropius, Walter, 74, 77–78, 82
Gujarat state, 25, 137
Gurdaspur, 135
Gurgaon, 135

Hanumanthaiya, K., 6
Haryana state: discord with Punjab, 8, 11, 18, 134–37, 138–39, 151; joint management of Bhakra-Nangal, 137; new capital for, 1
Hastings, H., 76
Havell, E. B., 24
High Court, Chandigarh. *See* Capitol Complex (Chandigarh)
Himachal Pradesh state, 1, 135, 137
Hind Kisan Panchayat, 15
Hindus: as dominant culture, xii; movement of into India, 1; relations with Sikhs, xii, 8, 133, 134
Hindustan Machine Tools (H.M.T.) Township, 139, 142
Hissar, 135
Hitler, Adolf, 86
Hoare, Sir Samuel, 77
Hoffmann, Joseph, 81
Hoshiarpur, 135
Howard, Sir Ebenezer, 21–22
Human Establishments, Three, 119
Husain, Tajamul, 6

Ibadan University project (Nigeria), 41, 42

Ideal cities: of Aristotle, 63; of Fry, 73; of Le Corbusier, 73, 86; of Plato, 63
Impington College, Cambridgeshire (Gropius and Fry, 1936), 77
India: American indifference toward, 49; dependence on foreign expertise, 36–37, 48; independence of, (1947), 1; missionary work in, 49–50; partition of (1947), 1, 19; proposal to move capital of, 6–7; reorganization of states in, 132; urban growth in, 1–2; urban planning in, 22, 24, 25, 48, 147
Indian Board of Town Planners, 25
Indian Ministry of Defense, 124
Indian Ministry of Works and Housing, 140
Industrial Age, 82, 86
Industrial city, linear, 119, 125
Industrialization, 73, 75, 76, 77
Infrastructure, as consideration for new capital, 7, 145
Inter State Chandigarh Region, 140, 141–43. *See also* Chandigarh
Italy, 76
Iyengar, B. R. C., 17

Jagadhri tehsil, 135
Jagat Narain, Lala, 16, 17, 146
Jamshedpur, 24
Jan Marg (the People's Avenue), Chandigarh, 109, 110
Jeanneret, Charles-Edouard. *See* Le Corbusier
Jeanneret, Pierre: as architect of Chandigarh, xi, 23, 40, 42, 43, 70, 71, 105, 119, 124, 125, 129, 131, 151; background of, 71–72; Circut House by, 116
Joglekar, Mr., 34
Jones, Owen, 81
Jullundar, 3, 6, 7, 16, 135, 145
Jyanti-Devi-Ki-Rao River, 142

Kabir, Humayan, 46

Kairon, Pratap Singh, 125, 131
Kalka, 3, 123, 139, 142
Kalka-Ambala railway line, 56
Kalyani, 26
Kamala Nehru Hospital, 46
Kamstra, Allen, 50
Kanpur (Uttar Pradesh), 32, 49, 53
Kapurthala, 135
Karnal, 7, 135
Karsan, 130
Kasauli, 3
Kashmir, hostilities in, 6
Katial, C. L., Dr., 39
Kaur, Rajkumari Amrit, 16, 21, 146
Khalistan ("Land of the Pure"), 133, 134
Khanna, D. C., 6
Kharar, 12, 123, 125, 135, 139, 142, 143
Khudda Jassu, 130
Khudda Lahora, 130
Kitimat (British Columbia), 51
Koenigsberger, Otto, 25, 31, 32, 78
Kohn, Robert, 31
Korn, Arthur, 76
Kurali, 139, 142, 143

Lacoste, M., 43
Lahore: loss of, xi, 2, 3, 8; need to replace, 2–5, 23, 144
Lalru, 143
Lamba, N. S., 106
Land Acquisition Act (1894), 12
Landsberg, H. E., 33, 55
Lasdun, Denys, 42
Laval, Pierre, 77
Lawn Road Flats, London (Coates, 1934), 76
Leisure valley, Chandigarh, 109, 118
Liverpool School of Architecture, 75
Livestock Pavilion (Raleigh, N. C.), 64
London, urban planning in, 22, 25, 34, 76
Longowal, Harchand Singh, 138

Lubetkin, B., 39, 76
Lucas, Colin, 76
Ludhiana, 4, 6, 7, 10–11, 135, 145
Lutyens, Sir Edwin, 25, 72

McDonald, Thomas, 90
"Machine aesthetics," 84
Machine Age, Second, 73, 117, 118, 119
Machine Art, 82
Madhya Marg (the Middle Avenue), Chandigarh, 109
Maharashtra state, 137
Mahendragarh, 135
Main rouge (Le Corbusier, 1930), 117
Malhotra, Jeet, 106
Manauli kanungo circle, 135
Manikam, Mr., 34
Mani Majra, 124, 135, 142
MARS (Modern Architectural Research), 76, 77. *See also* CIAM
Marseilles, Le Corbusier apartment block in, 86, 114
Martyr's Memorial, Chandigarh. *See* Capitol Complex (Chandigarh)
"Mass-building," 43
Materials, building: preferred by Le Corbusier, 85; used in Chandigarh buildings, 68–69, 113, 127
Mathai, M. O., 34
Mathur, B. P., 106, 119
Maumelle (Arkansas), 51
Mayer, Albert: background of, 25, 31–32, 45–51; correspondence with Fry, 89–90; dropped from Chandigarh project, 38, 44, 70–71; ideals of, 45–46; meeting with Nehru, 46, 48; plan of Chandigarh by, xi, 19, 23, 25, 31, 32, 34–35, 50, 53–65, 72, 89–104, 110, 146; on problems of American cities, 51–52; unwillingness to live in India, 71; visit to Chandigarh (1950), 33; writings of, 50, 51

Mayer and Whittlesey (architects), 31, 70
Mayer, Whittlesey, and Glass (architects), 31
Mehta, Mr., 34
Menon, Krishna, 34
Mies van der Rohe, Ludwig, 74, 78, 82
Missionaries, in India, 49–50
Modak, N. V., 32, 33, 34, 53
Modern Architectural Re-Search. *See* MARS
Modernization, of India, xi, 1; conflict with Gandhian ideals, 22–23, 49; expressed in architecture, 29, 48, 52, 148–49; Nehru's view of, 27–28, 29–31, 47, 87–88, 148
Modular system (Le Corbusier), 74, 85, 111
Mody, Piloo, 106
Moga (Punjab), 50
Montevideo, 107
Monumentalism: desired by Punjabis, 63; discredited, 60
Monument of the Open Hand, Chandigarh. *See* Capitol Complex (Chandigarh)
Morinda, 139, 142, 143
Moser, Werner, 26
Mumford, Lewis, 31, 51
Museum of Knowledge, Chandigarh. *See* Capitol Complex (Chandigarh)
Muslims: land left by evacuees, 12; in Ludhiana, 7; movement of into Pakistan, 1
Mussolini, Benito, 77, 87

Nagaland state, 1
Naraingarh tehsil, 135, 139, 142
Narang, K. S., 131
Narkanda River, 142
National Association of Housing Officials (American), 50
National Public Housing Conference (American), 50

Nayar, D. P., 126
Nehru, Jawaharlal: on Capital Project of East Punjab, 9, 10; death of, 151; ideals of, xi, 27–28, 30; ignoring proposal to move Indian capital, 7; influence on master plan for Chandigarh, 25–31, 35, 87–88, 104–5, 121, 124–25; meeting with Mayer, 46, 48; on modernization, 2–28, 29–31, 47, 87–88, 148; on refugee problem, 2, 35; support for Chandigarh site, 12, 16, 21, 145; support for Le Corbusier, 87–88
Nehru, Kamala, 46
Neighborhood, as basic unit of Chandigarh, 55, 61–63, 103, 110
"Neighborhood Unit" (Perry, 1929), 62
New Deal (American): Le Corbusier's view of, 87; housing policies of, 31, 32
New Delhi, construction in, 1, 24–25, 26–27, 55, 60, 112
New Haven Housing Authority, 50
New Rochelle, public housing in, 50
New York State Housing Division, 50
New York Times, 50
Niemeyer, Oscar, 124
Nietzsche, Friedrich, 81, 86
Nilokheri, 25
Northern railroad, diverted to Chandigarh, 18
Northwest Frontier Province, refugees from, 3
North-Zonal Council, 141
Notre Dame, Chapel of, at Ronchamp, Haute-Saône (Le Corbusier, 1950–55), 74, 85
Nowicki, Jacek, 69, 167n.55
Nowicki, Matthew: as architect of Chandigarh, 33, 38, 50, 55, 64–69, 72, 103; death of, 69, 70, 71

Orissa state, 25, 31
Ozenfant, Amédée, 83, 84

Pakistan, divided from India, 1
Parwanoo, 139
Patel, Sardar, 7
Patiala and East Punjab State Union. *See* PEPSU
Patiala Rao River, 13, 15
Patiala state, 11, 135
Pedestrians: Le Corbusier's considerations for, 84, 106; Mayer's considerations for, 52
PEP (Political and Economic Planning Group), 77
PEPSU (Patiala and East Punjab State Union), 2, 14, 126, 133
Periphery Control Act (1952). *See* Punjab New Capital (Periphery Control) Act
Perret, Auguste, 40, 71, 81, 83, 113
Perry, Clarence Arthur, 62
Petit, M. Claudius, 40, 42
Petsamo (Finland), 76
Phillaur, 7
Piazza San Marco (Venice), 54
Pilotis (stilts), 84, 115
Pinjore, 125, 139, 142
Plan Obus, Algiers (Le Corbusier), 87
Plan Voisin (Le Corbusier, 1925), 73–74, 85
Plato, 63
Pleydell-Bouverie, D., 76
Political and Economic Planning Group. *See* PEP
Post and Telegraph Building (Le Corbusier), 112
Prabhawalker, A. R., 106
Pritchard, Jack, 77
Provensal, Henri, 81
Public Works Department. *See* PWD
Punchkula, 139, 140, 142
Punjab Municipal Act (1911), 122
Punjab New Capital (Periphery Control) Act (1952), 13, 120, 122–23, 124, 141
Punjab state: bifurcation of (1966), 2, 121, 132–33, 141, 145, 151; discord with Haryana, 8, 11, 18, 134–37, 138–39, 151; influx of refugees to, 2; joint management of Bhakra Nangal, 137
Punjab *Tribune*, 124, 133
Punjab University: design of, 106, 118–19; location of, 56, 61, 65, 109, 111, 118
Purusha (the Cosmic Man), 59
PWD (Public Works Department), 72–73

Radburn (New Jersey), 50, 52, 57, 63, 72
Radcliff Award, 2
Radiant City. *See* La Ville Radieuse
Radio concentric city, 119
Railroad: effect of on urban growth, 61; service to Chandigarh, 18, 61
Rajasthan state, 137
Rajendra Park, Chandigarh, 109
Randhawa, M. S., 120, 123, 124, 125, 130, 131
Refugees: census of, 19; due to partition of India, 1–2, 3; rehabilitation of, 22; taken into consideration in Chandigarh master plan, 35
La Rochelle-Pallice, 86
Rohtak, 135
Ronchamp, Chapel of Notre Dame at (Le Corbusier, 1950–55), 74, 85
Roosevelt, Franklin D., 31
"Round Books," 116–17
Rousseau, Jean Jacques, 124
Ruskin, John, 81
Russia: dependence on foreign expertise, 48; utopian communities in, 63

Saarinen, Eero, 64
Saarinen, Eliel, 38

Sachar, Bhim Sain, 16, 146
Sahibzada Ajit Singh (S.A.S.) Nagar, 139, 140, 141–42
Sahni, M. R., 17
Sainte-Dié, 86, 113
St. Peter's (Rome), 54
Samsara, 89
Samuel, Godfrey, 76
Sanchi, Buddhist stupa at, 60, 67
Sanderson, Gordon, 24
Sangrur, 135
São Paulo, 107
Sarvodaya, 22
Sassoon House, Peckham (Fry), 77
Satyagraha, 14, 15
School of Tropical Architecture, 78
Schure, Edouard, 81
Second Industrial Age, 87
Second Machine Age, 73, 117, 118, 119
Secretariat building, Chandigarh. *See* Capitol Complex (Chandigarh)
Sectors, in Le Corbusier plan for Chandigarh, 107–8, 110, 152
Security, as consideration for new capital, 6–7, 145
Seminar and Exhibition of Architecture (1959), 28
Sert, José Luis, 86
Seven-V rule, 107–8
Shah, K. K., 136
Shah Commission, 134, 135
Shand, P. M., 76, 77
Sharma, M. N., 106
Shastri, Lal Bahadur, 127
Shivalik Range, Himalayas, 13, 116, 118
Sikhs: militancy of, 133–35, 138; movement of into India, 1; political status of, xii, 16, 133–34; relations with Hindus, xii, 8, 133
Simla (Himachal Pradesh): British use of, 2, 3; considered as site for new East Punjab capital, 3, 6, 145; plans for new East Punjab capital made at, 2, 144; redevelopment of, 1
Sind, refugees from, 3
Singh, Baldev, 6, 16, 146
Singh, Rao Birinder, 136
Singh, Sardar Hukum, 16
Siswan River, 142
Sitte, Camillo, 57, 88
Sittingbourne (England), model village near, 75
Skinner, R. T. F., 76
Socialist party, 15, 20
Soleri, Paolo, 44
Staatliches Bauhaus, 77, 78, 82
Stalin, Joseph, 27, 86
Standard Oil Building (New York), 75
States Reorganization Act (1956), 133
States Reorganization Commission, 132
"Statute of Land," 124
Stein, Clarence, 31, 33, 50, 55, 59, 62, 63
Stockholm, 87
Suketra, 124
Sukhna Cho River, 13, 15, 59, 61
Sukhna Lake, Chandigarh, 109, 124, 137
Sunhouse, Hampstead (Fry, 1935), 77
Sunnyside (New York), 63
Superblock L-37, 67, 68
Superblocks: in Baldwin Hills (Los Angeles), 57; as centerpiece of Mayer's plan for Chandigarh, 35, 52–53, 60, 89, 110; for Chandigarh housing, 56, 67–68; neighborhood units of, 62, 110; plan for construction of, 37. *See also* Sectors
"Supplementary Notes to the Architectural Study of Superblock L-37" (Nowicki), 68
Surajpur, 124
Survey Graphic (special housing issue), 50

Sutlej River, 7
Sweet, C., 76

Tangri River, 142
Temple, Fred, 24
Thapar, P. N.: as administrative head of Capital Project, 13–14, 31, 90, 122; Fry's opinion of, 72; in selection of Chandigarh planners, 31, 32, 36, 38–42, 71, 86; temporarily removed from Chandigarh project, 122
To kinon asti (glorious city), 45
To-morrow: A Peaceful Path to Real Reform (Howard, 1898), 21
Towards a New Architecture (Le Corbusier, 1923), 78
Town planning. *See* Urban planning
Town Planning According to Artistic Principles (Sitte), 57
Town Planning Institute, New Delhi, 1
Transportation system, planning for, 58, 103, 106, 108–9
Trivedi, Governor, 36
Trudgett, Dudley, 49
Truman, Harry S., 25, 55
Tughluk, Muhammad, 7
Types of Modern Indian Buildings (Sanderson, 1913), 24

Unité d'habitation, of Le Corbusier, 41, 74
United Nations: architecture of, 60; Economic Commission, 140
United States Housing Authority (USHA), 31, 50
Uppal, Sardar Jaswant Singh, 16
Urban growth, Indian, 1–2
Urban planning: applied to Chandigarh development, 21, 22; Le Corbusier's views on, 83–84; failure of, 51; in India, 22, 24, 25, 48, 147; and maintenance, 121–22; Mayer's views on, 31; and social engineering, 148–50; success of, xii, 122
"Urban village," 52
Urgent Future (Mayer, 1967), 51
USHA. *See* United States Housing Authority
Uttar Marg (the Northern Avenue), Chandigarh, 109
Uttar Pradesh, urban planning in, 49, 50, 146

Vagale, L. R., 140
Varma, P. L.: on Advisory Committee of the Chandigarh Capital Project Control Board, 124; as chief engineer of Punjab, 14, 109; Fry's opinion of, 72; population estimate for new capital, 5, 144; in selection of Chandigarh planners, 26, 33, 36, 38–42, 86
Vellore, 50
Vers une architecture (Le Corbusier, 1923), 78
Viceregal Palace, New Delhi, 72
Villas superposées (Le Corbusier), 84
La Ville contemporaine (Le Corbusier), 72, 84, 85
La Ville Radieuse (Le Corbusier, 1935), 59, 73, 85
La Ville radieuse (Le Corbusier, 1935), 86
Villes noires, 23
Vira, Dharam, 33
Voisin. *See* Plan Voisin

Ward, Basil, 76
Washington, D.C., plan of, 55, 88
Weber, Max, 86
West Africa, Drew and Fry in, 41, 75, 76, 78
West Bengal, 3, 19, 26
Western United Provinces, 25
West Pakistan, 1, 2, 133
West Punjab, 1, 3

When the Cathedrals Were White: A Journey to the Country of Timid People (Le Corbusier, 1935), 87
Whittlesey, Julian, 31, 33, 55
Wiener, Paul Lester, 86

Wright, Frank Lloyd, 38
Wright, Henry, 31, 50, 63

Yorke, F. R. S., 76

Zinkin, Taya, 85

Ravi Kalia is a member of the History Department, Occidental College, Los Angeles, California. He received his B.A. (Honors) and M.A. degrees from Delhi University, India, and his Ph.D. and M.B.A. degrees from the University of California, Los Angeles. His articles have appeared in *Habitat International* and *India Quarterly*, as well as in the *Oregonian, Los Angeles Herald Examiner, Hindustan Times* (New Delhi), and *Statesman* (New Delhi); and currently he is working on a study of the ancient sacred city of Bhubaneswar and its planned township, the latter constructed after 1948 as the capital of Orissa state.